T0330309

A Research Agenda for Transport Policy

**Elgar Research Agendas** outline the future of research in a given area. Leading scholars are given the space to explore their subject in provocative ways and map out the potential directions of travel. They are relevant but also visionary.

Forward-looking and innovative, Elgar Research Agendas are an essential resource for PhD students, scholars and anybody who wants to be at the forefront of research.

Titles in the series include:

A Research Agenda for Entrepreneurship Education
*Edited by Alain Fayolle*

A Research Agenda for Service Innovation
*Edited by Faïz Gallouj and Faridah Djellal*

A Research Agenda for Global Environmental Politics
*Edited by Peter Dauvergne and Justin Alger*

A Research Agenda for New Institutional Economics
*Edited by Claude Ménard and Mary M. Shirley*

A Research Agenda for Regeneration Economies
Reading City-Regions
*Edited by John R. Bryson, Lauren Andres and Rachel Mulhall*

A Research Agenda for Cultural Economics
*Edited by Samuel Cameron*

A Research Agenda for Environmental Management
*Edited by Kathleen E. Halvorsen, Chelsea Schelly, Robert M. Handler, Erin C. Pischke and Jessie L. Knowlton*

A Research Agenda for Creative Tourism
*Edited by Nancy Duxbury and Greg Richards*

A Research Agenda for Public Administration
*Edited by Andrew Massey*

A Research Agenda for Tourism Geographies
*Edited by Dieter K. Müller*

A Research Agenda for Economic Psychology
*Edited by Katharina Gangl and Erich Kirchler*

A Research Agenda for Entrepreneurship and Innovation
*Edited by David B. Audretsch, Erik E. Lehmann and Albert N. Link*

A Research Agenda for Financial Inclusion and Microfinance
*Edited by Marek Hudon, Marc Labie and Ariane Szafarz*

A Research Agenda for Global Crime
*Edited by Tim Hall and Vincenzo Scalia*

A Research Agenda for Transport Policy
*Edited by John Stanley and David A. Hensher*

# A Research Agenda for Transport Policy

*Edited by*

JOHN STANLEY

*Adjunct Professor, Institute of Transport and Logistics Studies, The University of Sydney Business School, The University of Sydney, Australia*

DAVID A. HENSHER

*Professor of Management and Founding Director, Institute of Transport and Logistics Studies, The University of Sydney Business School, The University of Sydney, Australia*

Elgar Research Agendas

Edward Elgar
PUBLISHING

Cheltenham, UK • Northampton, MA, USA

Published by
Edward Elgar Publishing Limited
The Lypiatts
15 Lansdown Road
Cheltenham
Glos GL50 2JA
UK

Edward Elgar Publishing, Inc.
William Pratt House
9 Dewey Court
Northampton
Massachusetts 01060
USA

A catalogue record for this book
is available from the British Library

Library of Congress Control Number: 2019935382

This book is available electronically in the **Elgar**online
Social and Political Science subject collection
DOI 10.4337/9781788970204

ISBN 978 1 78897 019 8 (cased)
ISBN 978 1 78897 020 4 (eBook)

Typeset by Servis Filmsetting Ltd, Stockport, Cheshire

Printed and bound in Great Britain by TJ International Ltd, Padstow, Cornwall

# Contents

# Figures

# Contributors

**David Banister**, Emeritus Professor of Transport Studies, School of Geography and the Environment and Transport Studies Unit, University of Oxford.

**Michael Bell**, Professor and Chair in Ports and Maritime Logistics, Institute of Transport and Logistics Studies, The University of Sydney Business School.

**James Bushell**, PhD candidate, Institute of Transport and Logistics Studies, The University of Sydney Business School.

**Richard de Cani**, Director of Planning, Arup.

**Brian Collins**, Professor of Engineering Policy and Director of the International Centre for Infrastructure Futures, University College London.

**Ritu Garg**, Transport Consultant, Arup London.

**Stephen Greaves**, Professor and Chair in Transport Management, Institute of Transport and Logistics Studies, The University of Sydney Business School.

**David A. Hensher**, Professor of Management and Founding Director, Institute of Transport and Logistics Studies, The University of Sydney Business School.

**Robin Hickman**, Reader (Associate Professor) in Transport and City Planning, The Bartlett School of Planning, Faculty of the Built Environment, University College London.

**Daniel Johnson**, Senior Research Fellow, Institute for Transport Studies, University of Leeds.

**Martin Locke**, Adjunct Professor, Institute of Transport and Logistics Studies, The University of Sydney Business School.

**Rosário Macário**, Professor, CERIS Civil Engineering Research for Innovation and Sustainability, Instituto Superior Técnico, Universidade de Lisboa and C-MAT, Transport and Regional Economics, Faculty of Applied Economics, University of Antwerp.

**Greg Marsden**, Professor of Transport Governance, Institute for Transport Studies, University of Leeds.

**Alan McKinnon**, Professor of Logistics, Kuehne Logistics University, Hamburg.

**Hilde Meersman**, Professor, Department of Transport and Regional Economics, Faculty of Applied Economics, University of Antwerp.

**Rico Merkert**, Professor and Chair in Transport and Supply Chain Management, Institute of Transport and Logistics Studies, The University of Sydney Business School.

**Corinne Mulley**, Professor Emerita, Institute of Transport and Logistics Studies, The University of Sydney Business School.

**Marcela A. Munizaga**, Professor, Faculty of Physical and Mathematical Sciences, Universidad de Chile.

**Chris Nash**, Research Professor, Institute for Transport Studies, University of Leeds.

**John Nelson**, Professor and Chair of Public Transport, Institute of Transport and Logistics Studies, The University of Sydney Business School.

**Harrison Peck**, Transport Consultant, Arup New York.

**Josipa Petrunic**, PhD, Executive Director and CEO, Canadian Urban Transit Research & Innovation Consortium (CUTRIC).

**Michael Roschlau**, PhD, Strategic Adviser, Public Transit and Urban Mobility; retired CEO, Canadian Urban Transit Association (CUTA).

**Georgina Santos**, PhD, Senior Lecturer, School of Geography and Planning, Cardiff University.

**Christopher Standen**, PhD, Research Analyst, Institute of Transport and Logistics Studies, The University of Sydney Business School.

**Janet Stanley**, Associate Professor, Melbourne Sustainable Society Institute, Melbourne School of Design, The University of Melbourne.

**John Stanley**, Adjunct Professor, Institute of Transport and Logistics Studies, The University of Sydney Business School.

**Alejandro Tirachini**, Associate Professor, Department of Civil Engineering, Universidad de Chile.

**Eddy van de Voorde**, Professor, Department of Transport and Regional Economics, Faculty of Applied Economics, University of Antwerp.

**Jackie Walters**, Professor and Director of the Institute of Transport and Logistics Studies (ITLS (Africa)), University of Johannesburg.

**Fuyo (Jenny) Yamamoto**, PhD student, Mobilities and Urban Policy Lab, Graduate School for International Cooperation and Development, Hiroshima University.

**Junyi Zhang**, Professor, Mobilities and Urban Policy Lab, Graduate School for International Cooperation and Development, Hiroshima University.

# PART I

Introduction

# 1   Setting the context

*John Stanley and David A. Hensher*

> *9.50 am Sunday morning 16<sup>th</sup> September 2018. This introductory chapter is being written while the first author is sitting in a Hong Kong hotel lobby, Super Typhoon Mangkhut raging outside. This has just been upgraded to Category 10 level, which shuts the city down; the most powerful storm in the world in 2018, thus far. All flights are cancelled but, hopefully, the flight back home in 34 hours' time will be OK. No-one is using the swimming pool! There was the odd taxi on the road but not any longer, as the storm peak approaches.*

In September 2018 the first author appeared as an expert witness for the Independent Review Committee on Hong Kong Franchised Bus Services. The Committee, set up by the Chief Executive of the Hong Kong Special Administrative Region of the People's Republic of China, is undertaking a safety inquiry, following a bus accident earlier in 2018, which resulted in multiple fatalities. The major focus of evidence presented by the first author was about establishing a robust governance framework focussed on safety risk management, working from legislation through to franchise arrangements and encompassing the environment within which this is located.

Within 24 hours, the lived experience of the first author had thus encountered major transport policy issues of (1) transport network resilience and disruption to human mobility/activities in the face of a major natural disaster (helped along by human activity with respect to climate change) and (2) public transport safety, both of which form part, but only a small part, of this volume. These are not the kinds of transport policy issues most of us would encounter very often. However, in Chapter 3, for example, Janet Stanley argues that we need to plan and shape our future transport policies taking greater account of more frequent and intense occurrences of transport network disruptions, the costs of which will be immense – perhaps easy to forget, unless you are close to the eye of the storm. Then in Chapter 16 Zhang and Yamamoto remind us of some of the safety challenges confronting Asian transport, Jackie Walters discusses safety in relation to informal transport in Africa in Chapter 17 and Brian Collins outlines how technology can help to ease safety concerns, in Chapter 20.

We note these two examples to illustrate the difficulty that we confronted in putting this book together. How do you prioritize such a vast agenda as transport policy? Because the demand for transport is a derived demand, it forms part of most aspects of people's daily lives, as was experienced in Hong Kong. You can look at transport in a narrow sense, largely as just transport, or you can take a *derived demand* approach and seek to understand its importance in helping people, businesses and even our planet to flourish or flounder. We have taken the latter approach, since it is only at this high level, in our view, that you can confidently shape transport policy to make a positive societal difference.

Recognizing the diversity that this approach requires, the book includes chapters that approach research opportunities in transport policy in terms of

- the outcomes that society might want to support, encompassing economic, social and environmental goals and supportive processes. The societal goals perspectives form the focus of chapters 2, 3 and 4 and provide recurring lenses through which to consider transport policy throughout the book;
- governance arrangements, to increase the prospects of desired societal outcomes being achieved (Chapter 5 but also a matter raised by several other chapters, indicating its importance as a research area);
- how desired policy directions might be funded, with a particular focus on roads (Chapter 6);
- the roles that various modes of transport play or might play, encompassing both person and goods movement (chapters 7 to 12);
- challenges and opportunities across different continents (chapters 13 to 18); and
- new delivery models, technologies and data availabilities, and how these might disrupt current paradigms (chapters 19 to 22, but with some other chapters also venturing into these areas).

Each chapter seeks to both frame the current and emerging state of play in its field and then suggest research topics that will help further the development of more effective transport policies.

By seeking a broad approach and examining research opportunities through various lenses, length constraints inevitably mean that chapters must be rather selective in terms of what they cover in depth. Do not be surprised, then, if occasionally something you expected to see covered in some detail falls short of your expectations.

*(Storm update: A hotel room 44 floors up is not much fun in a typhoon. The noise outside is pretty intense. Hope the windows are secure. Several trees have been uprooted and the odd metal sign is flying past. It is time to go downstairs to the bar!)*

The land passenger transport sector lies on the cusp of a major transformation, guided by collaborative consumption, next generation vehicles, demographic change and digital technologies. Whilst there is widespread enthusiasm across the community for this nexus of disruptors, the implications on road capacity, traffic congestion, land use and urban form remain unclear and, by extension, so too whether this emerging transport paradigm will bring a net benefit to the transport system, communities and the planet. Some important issues include the potential proliferation of point-to-point transportation, a continuation of universal vehicle ownership and the demise of fixed route public transport, all of which are matters raised by various industry leaders in technology and transportation.

Mobility as a Service (MaaS), based on shared mobility and modal integration, is promoted as a sustainable alternative, which accounts for the realities of spatial and temporal efficiency. Various models for implementing MaaS are being considered, including the distinction between commercially motivated models (presently well advanced in research and development) and systems which incorporate an institutional overlay. These futures have benefitted significantly by digital disruption. A number of chapters focus on this side of the transport policy research agenda, which will be a very significant factor influencing whether cities and regions are to become more productive, more socially inclusive and with a smaller environmental impact, or whether the changes in question will mainly benefit the few.

Disruptive change is one of the reasons why it is vital to take a broad integrated approach to transport policy, recognizing connections across the various realms of transport (e.g., public transport, roads, ports and air) and extending (for example) to land use policy and planning, housing futures and place making. Integrated governance models are central to progress in this regard and many chapters emphasize the importance of integrated governance, some approaching this from a modal perspective, others from an outcomes perspective and some from a regional setting.

Disruptive change and integrated policy/planning and governance illustrate the universality of the key issues that are covered in this book. They emerge from several different ways of looking at transport policy, emphasizing the importance of the *derived demand* approach. While cities are where these matters increasingly play out, as reflected in most chapters, regional perspectives also have much in common.

The fact that safety has not been a bigger focus of this report probably reflects the reality that the land transport systems in most of our authors' home settings are pretty good. For example, road accident fatality rates in developed countries are typically low and declining, relative to the transport task, with Scandinavian countries typically showing the way. For those interested in transport policy oriented research with a safety focus, however, you will still find plenty of opportunities to undertake useful work. For example, in developed countries, road accident injury rates are commonly on the rise, as are slips, trips and falls on buses (e.g., linked to an ageing user cohort and increasing traffic congestion), while in developing country settings, road accident fatality rates are commonly increasing, as motorization levels increase. Ways to tackle such challenges will include autonomous vehicles, as discussed in several chapters, but a wider range of tools will also be needed.

We thank all contributors for their work on this volume and their preparedness to suffer the demands that we have placed upon them, from word limits to deadlines. All are leaders in their fields and the time they have devoted to this task continues their contribution to improved transport policy outcomes.

To those who are contemplating research in transport policy, we trust that the book sparks your enthusiasm to go on the journey. We can assure you of considerable personal satisfaction and growth along the way and, most importantly, the opportunity to make a difference in enhancing desirable societal outcomes, through your evidence-based transport policy research. The time has never been better in this regard.

Royalties from the book are all being donated to the Institute of Transport Studies at University of Johannesburg, to acquire learning materials for their students. We thank those who have bought the book for their contribution to this purpose.

# PART II

Societal goals-based perspectives

# 2 Transport economics

*David A. Hensher*

## 2.1 Introduction

Transport policy is in the process of being disrupted by significant digital techno-logical advances together with evolutionary social change that are influenced by the new era of accessible information and automation of future mobility activity (see Chapter 21 by Mulley, Nelson and Hensher on MaaS). New opportunities are starting to open up to provide ways of delivering on aspirations that have always been with us, such as improved accessibility, greater liveability of our environ-ment, reduced costs of mobility, more equity in service provision, and mitigating climate change. Smart cities are touted as the setting within which we can improve the efficiency, equity and environmental sustainability of the way we live our lives. Governments will continue to play a major role in supporting the virtues of the market place (as new entrepreneurs enter the transport market to provide mobility centric mode neutral services, hopefully with a greater support for collaborative and sharing virtues), while also containing the negative features of economically deregulated markets and all unpriced externalities.

Economics remains a crucial cornerstone of transport policy, offering, through an explanation of how society operates and could operate in terms of resource allocation, a commentary and guidelines on ways to deliver efficient, equitable and environmentally sustainable (triple bottom line) outcomes, all of which matter in judging social welfare. An important distinction is made between sectoral and economy-wide influences on good transport policy, where the latter is driven by the economic welfare of people (measured through consumer and producer surpluses), and the former by options and opportunities within the sector to not only 'do the right things' but to 'do things right'. Both matter and must be included in a compre-hensive assessment of transport policy. Within the framework of STO – strategic, tactical and operational foci (van de Velde 1999) – transport policy should be aligned with strategic goals translated at the tactical level into ways to achieve these goals, and which then are implemented at the operational level by actions on the ground. Given the strategic goals, it is at the tactical level that the majority of the focus of economics as an advisory toolkit plays a pivotal role.

In this chapter we focus on some elements of this toolkit that can guide the interpretation of policies and plans to achieve societal goals and which can lead to recommendations of how best to deliver triple bottom line outcomes.

## 2.2    Integrated transport and land use systems

One of the most important features of a comprehensive transport policy platform is an ability to identify candidate initiatives (i.e., projects and policies) that are value-adding to the performance of transport networks and to the economy/society as a whole. Standard methods of identifying a shortlist of projects to assess are often qualitative in nature and/or influenced by prejudices of elected officials or their advisers, without a systematic way of narrowing the many potential options to evaluate, in sufficient detail, a truly value-adding set. There is a case to be made for having a capability to undertake, in a timely manner, a scan of a large number of potentially worthy initiatives that can offer forecasts of passenger and freight demand, benefit-costs ratios and economy-wide outcomes. Such a framework would then be meaningful in the sense of offering outputs that are similar to those that are the focus of assessments typically spread over many months, if not years, on a very few (often arbitrarily or politically motivated) projects which may exclude those which have the greatest merit.

This aspiration has led to the development of MetroScan, a transport planning application system that enables a timely assessment of many potentially valuable initiatives associated with transport networks, projects and policies. We introduce MetroScan as a way of highlighting the broadening set of behavioural models that reflect the many ways in which individuals, households or businesses respond to change in the transport system. The analytical framework of MetroScan highlights many opportunities for ongoing research agendas.

A schematic overview of MetroScan is given in Figure 2.1. This shows the interconnectedness between the transport and land use demand model systems, benefit-cost analysis and economic impact analysis. MetroScan consists of several state-of-the-art components that have been integrated into this quick-scan tool. It also summarises the underlying behavioural suite of travel, location and vehicle choice models that provide the rich evidence on how passengers, freight distributors, service providers, and locators of household and firms respond to transport-related initiatives in a user-specified short to long term.

MetroScan applications to date have highlighted new insights. For example, Stanley et al. (2018) suggest higher long-term response elasticities of VKT to price than would have previously been assumed. Hensher et al. (2018) find that allowing firm location choices to interact with travel choices in contrast to fixing the number of firms at each location, combined with an associated single annual growth rate that is constant across all locations, takes into account inducement effects, which results in a different distribution of firm locations in

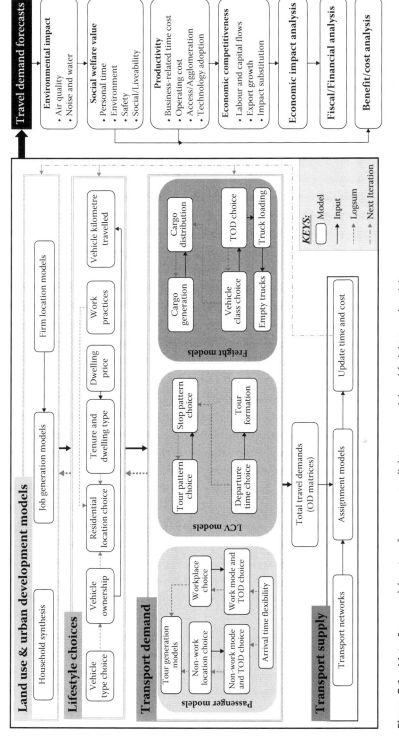

**Figure 2.1** MetroScan model system for passenger, light commercial and freight travel activity

forecast years. This has a notable influence on overall productivity (agglomeration) benefits.

There are a number of innovations that should continue to be reflected in future research platforms, especially the integration of passenger and freight model systems and the feedback loops between location decisions of households and firms and travel demand. Additional features that need to be integrated include mobility as a service (MaaS) subscriptions packages, as multimodal ways of obtaining access to the growing number of mobility services (including autonomous vehicles) within a more collaborative and sharing society. MetroScan reinforces how transportation is critically interconnected with land use and the wider economy, and that the consequences of transport policy must take these relationships into account. Analytical frameworks that fail to do so will increasingly be misleading and of limited value in the policy assessment context.

## 2.3    Agglomeration effects as a wider economic impact

Wider economic impacts (WEIs) are improvements in economic welfare that are acknowledged, but that have not been typically captured in traditional cost-benefit analysis. They arise from market imperfections; that is, prices of goods and services differing from costs to society as a whole. There are three main categories of WEIs that may be relevant for transport initiatives: agglomeration economies, output change in imperfectly competitive markets, and tax revenues from labour markets.

With a growing interest in accommodating WEIs of transport infrastructure investment, policy analysts and researchers need to identify whether transport investment gives rise to agglomeration (economic) benefits (generally seen as a major WEI), and if so, how substantial might these benefits be? These effects are included in MetroScan. Agglomeration economies occur when agents (i.e., firms, workers, individuals, households) benefit from being *near* to other agents (Venables 2007). Nearness can involve physical proximity, but transport plays a crucial role because, in most contexts, speed and low transportation costs provide a direct substitute for physical proximity. We are specifically concerned with production agglomeration economies, which derive from proximity between firms and the sources of these agglomeration economies: workers, other firms and other facilities.

If there is a need or desire to adopt a single, composite agglomeration metric for generic use across all types of policy initiatives, and a travel demand model is available, then the single best candidate is a measure of effective (employment) density based on generalised cost (value of travel time savings and travel expenses) between geographical zones. The reasons are as follows:

- An employment-density-based measure captures the economic structure of an area better than purely population-based measures and hence better reflects the conflicting and competing influences relative to study area size.

- Agglomeration externalities are not felt exclusively in one area, as the gravity model structure of the effective density measure accounts for spatial spillovers between all zones. In other words, the externality benefits are linked with the accessibility of each zone to all jobs, in a way which diminishes as the generalised cost between zones increases.

The employment *effective density* measure for each zone, and for each industry category, can be calculated using a known formula developed by Graham (2006, 2007) and Melo et al. (2009), which requires data on employment in industry $i$ in zone $z$, and the distance (or generalised cost) between pairs of zones conditioned on a distance (or generalised cost) decay parameter. Agglomeration economies are the product of the percentage change of effective employment density, the total number of jobs, GDP per worker, and elasticity of productivity in respect to effective employment density. The total impact of a travel zone is the sum of impacts of all industry sectors. The total impact of the project is the sum of impacts of all affected travel zones. The higher density could be caused by more workers attracted from other areas, new employment and 'effective density' changes due to reduced travel (generalised) cost. The agglomeration economic benefits being estimated refer to the productivity benefits of existing workers and diverted workers as well as new employment in a particular area. With a transport improvement, some localities may gain and others may lose, which is generally referred to as a 'negative' agglomeration impact (as shown in Hensher et al. 2013).

The mark-up of such benefits depends on what might be already captured in the user benefits and clearly if few impacts are accommodated then one might anticipate a relatively high mark-up. It is crucial that this point is recognised as it can influence any meaningful comparison between studies, where we see mark-ups as high as 50 per cent and as low as 2 per cent. Hensher et al. (2012), in a study of a new rail infrastructure project in Sydney, identified a WEI mark up of 17.6 per cent; however, only 2.46 per cent was due to agglomeration effects. The rest was due to the 'general equilibrium' effects or 'wider-economy' linkages and impacts (some of which are broadly related to improved accessibility). It can be said that general equilibrium effects in the case of a spatial economy indicates the transport impacts on the level of spatial or economic geography efficiency, whereas agglomeration effects measure the impacts arising from the utilisation of spatial economies of scale (agglomeration) which are additional to this pure improvement in (spatial) efficiency. The very low contribution of agglomeration effects is in large measure associated with improvements in a public transport mode (i.e., commuter rail) that add in a very marginal way to the rail network which itself in Sydney accounts for less than 12 per cent of all trips. Given a recent focus on finding additional benefits to support public transport, we would suggest that focussing on agglomeration effects may be looking in the wrong place! A focus on positive contributors of public transport such as crowding, urban form and amenity may offer greater returns. When the wider economic benefits were included in the London Crossrail project, the benefit-cost ratio increased by 40 per cent, which is very significant and shows the potential policy relevance of these external benefits to major rail projects.

The ongoing research agenda needs to understand much better the components of WEI and to establish the extent to which these can more easily be incorporated (i.e., internalised) in the standard measures of user benefit, to at least ensure that we are not double counting some of the benefits. Such research also needs to better identify transport settings in which WEI will really make a difference to benefit expectations.

## 2.4    Gaining buy-in to road pricing reform

As the single largest external economic cost of road use in many cities, traffic congestion has continued to ignite the call for road pricing reform. Economists and others see the current charging instruments as inadequate in both delivering efficient outcomes for road use and raising sufficient revenue to fund new infra-structure and much needed maintenance of existing road networks (see Verhoef et al. 2008, Manville and King 2012). The literature is clear about the welfare impacts of road pricing as a first best solution, and the impact of compensatory schemes for drivers with budgetary neutral packages (e.g., De Borger and Proost 2012). However, this literature does not address the greatest challenge in reforming road user charges, which is not about welfare impacts but about devising a scheme which gains public acceptance. The benefits of such a scheme must be convincing to voters, convincing to politicians concerned about their electoral future (see Marcucci et al. 2005, Hensher and Bliemer 2014, Hensher et al. 2013) and satisfy the Treasury.

We have seen congestion charging at a cordon level (e.g., Central London, Stockholm CBD and Milan), and area-wide pricing in Singapore, but governments have struggled to find a way of introducing a scheme for an entire metropolitan area where much of the congestion is spread around. In simple terms, we need to secure buy-in from the population at large and especially car (and truck) users. This means a reform plan that can offer financial benefits as well as travel time savings. Typically, it is assumed that gaining travel time savings means paying more but is this always the case?

With digital technology now widely available (via smart phones) to disrupt the way we deliver improved transport infrastructure and services, we have a real opportunity to offer a trial that is essentially an opt-in (or opt-out) pilot that offers attractive incentives to car (and truck) users to move some amount of travel out of the more severely congested times of the day (including switching some travel to public transport or switching destinations to have shorter and/or less congested trips), so as to relieve the system of congestion, especially severe congestion. It is possible to do this without implementing for the entire travelling population (which has often been a stumbling block), but to give individual travellers a choice such that they can see a benefit to themselves while contributing to improving the performance of the network as a whole. Over time we might expect more travellers to take advantage of the scheme and opt in.

What might we have in mind? Pilot opt-in registrants would need to log existing, and ideally also new, behaviour so that we could check the amount of travel that moved out of the periods which would make travellers eligible for a registration reduction.

1.  We start with a smartphone App to establish, for each person, the typical travel times associated with trips between specific origins (O) and destinations (D) by mode for each time of day. Users can refine starting times to suit their ability to be time-flexible. This will show where travel time gains, in real time, are on offer by specific times of day. This may involve small adjustments in trip commencement times (e.g., 10 mins) or larger adjustments, depending on the specific OD pair. Importantly, travel times are not only based on historical travel times but also on real-time information, and are applicable to each specific traveller, so it is personalised and relevant information. Speed data[1] is also desirable in order to build the App and determine realistic travel times for different departure times. This can be extracted from mobile data that does not require the GPS to be turned on (at least not in urban and suburban areas where mobile coverage is good), provided the mobile operators are willing to provide the data and have the capability of processing the data into trips with mode detection. Clearly this App must be fully functional before we can proceed to the next steps.

2.  Registration reduction is based on trips moving out of peak periods (regardless of whether we have reduced kilometres overall or not). One must obtain trip data for at least three months of a year's travel to be eligible for a discount on registration fees. It should also be monitored every three months to ensure there is no return to periods which are ineligible for registration discount.

3.  The registration fee reduction can be tailored to establish enough incentive to trade a lower registration fee with moving to less congested times of day, which deliver improved travel times. What we have here is a combined benefit of a reduced registration fee and travel time savings.

4.  To compensate for the loss of registration revenue to government, the fee may have to increase if someone stays in the 'peak' period or other periods deemed to be the times of day that we want some trips to be switched out of. This will be reflected in the next period's registration charge, if there is no evidence of switching trips out of the pre-defined peak periods. The adjustment in the registration fee would be on a sliding scale to recognise levels of traffic congestion.[2]

---

1  Michiel Bliemer and Mark Raadsen of ITLS have built such an App in the Netherlands that makes travel time predictions on road networks using loop detectors. TomTom and other equipment have speed data available that they use for their own navigation devices. These so-called 'speed profiles' can be bought. Alternatively, one could use speed data from a model, but that is likely not accurate enough.

2  An alternative approach is an equity-linked argument that government should recognise as part of the sustainable transport for cities *or* that the registration fee for people who do *not* sign up could be increased to provide the incentive to join. For example, people in the UK who do not have water meters have been offered a deal: put in a water meter and if your water bill is higher than you currently pay we will cap it at your current level. This works for the incumbent and of course goes when the property changes hands.

The determination of the adjustment in the registration charge might be based on a level that, together with the available time savings, encourages enough switching to improve traffic flow. If, for example, the average value of travel times savings for car commuters is $16 per person hour (which aligns with practice in urban Australia), then if the time savings on offer in a particular switch is 20 minutes, it is worth paying up to $5.33 per trip (note that it ignores schedule delay penalties, so we think people would be willing to pay less than this). Given an average annual car registration fee of $350, say, if we reduce this by $200 per annum for such a switch, and someone undertakes, say, 10 trips per week over 40 weeks per annum, then the overall benefit is $200 plus $2,133 worth of travel time savings. Since the time benefit does not incur a congestion charge but receives an incentive through discounted registration, this should be attractive to enough motorists to make a difference.

In time, with buy-in, we could start looking towards a distance-based charging scheme (by time of day) with discounted registration fees (as presented in Hensher and Mulley 2014). This is an ongoing approach central to research agendas, as we find mechanisms to garner buy-in for simpler reforms that demonstrate real benefits to users, that can be modified to more sophisticated reforms such as a distance-based system (that is not differentiated by time of day initially) using odometer readings to track registration reduction entitlements. There are significant research opportunities focussed on assessing many possible ways of garnering buy-in and reducing the negative externalities of growing levels of road congestion.

## 2.5    Concluding comments

The selected themes have a strong economic basis and are examples of where current and emerging research agendas can inform better transport policy. A holistic approach to determining which transport-related initiatives will be value-adding under a range of performance criteria is an obvious starting position. It also sets the framework within which some very specific issues need to be articulated and tested, such as wider economic impacts and pricing reform.

## References

De Borger, B. and Proost, S. (2012), 'A political economy model of road pricing', *Journal of Urban Economics*, **71**(1), 79–92.

Graham, D. (2006), 'Wider economic benefits of transport improvements: Link between agglomeration and productivity'. *Stage 2 Report*. Report prepared for Department for Transport, Centre for Transport Studies, Imperial College, London.

Graham, D. (2007), 'Agglomeration, productivity and transport investment', *Journal of Transport Economics and Policy*, **41**(3), 317–343.

Hensher, D.A. and Bliemer, M.C. (2014), 'What type of road pricing reform might appeal to politicians? Viewpoints on the challenge in gaining the citizen and public servant vote by staging reform', *Transportation Research Part A*, **61**, March, 227–237.

Hensher, D.A. and Mulley, C. (2014), 'Complementing distance based charges with discounted regis-tration fees in the reform of road user charges: the impact for motorists and government revenue', *Transportation*, **41**(4), 697–715.

Hensher, D.A., Rose, J.M. and Collins, A. (2013), 'Understanding buy in for risky prospects: Incorporating degree of belief into the *ex ante* assessment of support for alternative road pricing schemes', *Journal of Transport Economics and Policy*, **47**(3), 453–473.

Hensher, D.A., Teye, C., Ellison, R. and Ho, C. (2018), 'Integrating an aggregate model system of intra-metropolitan business location choices into a location-based employment model', ITLS Working Paper, University of Sydney.

Hensher, D.A., Truong, T.P., Mulley, C. and Ellison, R. (2012), 'Assessing the wider economy impacts of transport infrastructure investment with an illustrative application to the North-West Rail Link project in Sydney, Australia', *Journal of Transport Geography*, **24**, 292–305.

Manville, M. and King, D. (2012), 'Credible commitment and congestion pricing', *Transportation*, https://doi.org/10.1007/s11116-012-9430-9.

Marcucci, E., Marini, M. and Ticchi, D. (2005), 'Road pricing as a citizen-candidate game', *European Transport*, **31**, 28–45.

Melo, P., Graham. D.J. and Noland, R.N. (2009), 'A meta-analysis of estimates of urban agglomeration economies', *Regional Science and Urban Economics*, **3**, 332–342.

Stanley, J.K., Ellison, R., Loader, C. and Hensher, D.A. (2018), 'Getting off the greenhouse gas: Public transport's potential contribution in Australian cities', *Transportation Research Part A*, https://doi.org/10.1016/j.tra.2018.01.002.

van de Velde, D.M. (1999), 'Organisational forms and entrepreneurship in public transport (part 1: classifying organisational forms)', *Transport Policy*, **6**, 147–157.

Venables, A. (2007), 'Evaluating urban transport improvements: Cost benefit analysis in the presence of agglomeration and income taxation', *Journal of Transport Economics and Policy*, **41**(2), 173–188.

Verhoef, E., Bliemer, M. Steg, L. and Van Wee, B. (2008), *Pricing in Road Transport: A Multi-Disciplinary Perspective*, Northampton, MA: Edward Elgar Publishing.

# 3 Social perspectives: Transport as if people mattered

*Janet Stanley*

## 3.1 Introduction

How transport impacts people is a relatively new area of research interest, as economic impacts, particularly saving travel time, have traditionally dominated the transport research agenda. This chapter raises some issues around the social aspects of transport, highlighting the importance of mobility for people and how transport may impact personal wellbeing in a positive or negative way. Mobility is vital for people to access services and activities essential for life, whether it is food, education, health services or interpersonal interaction. Thus, there is a need to consider if a person is able to have mobility and how the available transport options impact on a person or a community. While the social impacts of transport need to be considered for all people, equity requires consideration of the impact on those with fewer resources, who can't 'purchase' their way out of an adverse situation, such as moving their living location or buying a car.

Decision-making on transport projects usually and desirably starts from considera-tion about what outcomes are desired from the project, such as improving personal mobility options, encouraging particular land use patterns, reducing greenhouse gas emissions and/or reducing traffic congestion. The various economic, social and environmental outcomes need to be weighed and traded off to get the most favourable outcome. Unfortunately project evaluations don't always adequately consider the full range of social and environmental impacts, information that is needed before a true assessment of costs and benefits can be understood. There is also community concern at present in Australia, for example, that the views of the community are not being adequately sought in relation to new transport proposals (Legacy et al. 2017).

There is increasing research interest that seeks to understand the value of transport for people, and in measurement of the social and environmental externalities in transport evaluations. However, with some important exceptions, such as in some cities in the UK, Europe and Canada, the uptake of this research into transport policy and planning practice has been slow. Other critical issues are increasingly impacting on the provision of transport. These impacts, including climate change, high population growth in some cities, rapid growth in vehicles in industrialising

16

countries and technological change, all need further research if improved transport policy and planning is to result.

While the research agenda on the interface between social issues and transport is very large, this chapter selects some particular issues judged to be important for good social outcomes associated with transport. The chapter discusses the value and impacts of transport on people and communities, and government decision-making. The extensive topic of transport in industrialising countries is raised, as well as the many implications around transport in relation to the growing incidence of natural hazards, as climate change worsens.

## 3.2    The importance of transport for people and society

Too often mobility is considered very narrowly, the trip itself being the object of attention, such as how long the trip takes, traffic congestion and traffic safety. While these are important, so are other issues, such as how accessibility to goods, services, recreation and employment impacts on outcomes for people, and how this varies according to a person's characteristics (e.g., age, financial position and living location). In transport, all people tend to be viewed as 'average' and their need to travel to work and back, generally assumed to be by car in Australia and many other countries, commonly dominates government transport considerations.

In 2003, the Social Exclusion Unit in the UK examined how transport may be linked to social exclusion for particular groups of people: young and elderly, those with poor health and disability, those in poverty, new migrants and those living in isolated regions. Following this report, researchers have shown interest in the association between transport and social inclusion in developed countries, especially in the UK and Australia, and particularly in relation to the elderly (see an important study in the EU by Mollenkopf et al. 2005). Recognising Sen's work (1983) on social inclusion and capability development, a major Australian project attempted to measure social inclusion and understand the drivers that lead to the inclusion/exclusion outcome, transport being a major component in the modelling (Currie 2011). This work has continued, researching social capital further, and how transport is linked to wellbeing, mental health and productivity, rural transport and social exclusion (Kamruzzaman and Hine 2011, Stanley et al. 2018).

However, the research field suffers from a failure to build a connected research output that verifies findings, establishes importance and fills the research gaps, leading to clear guidelines for policy makers and transport planners. In particular, there is an absence of research on social inclusion and transport in industrialising countries, with few studies examining the cultural, transport and infrastructure differences in different countries, an issue discussed further in Section 3.5. Finally, more research is needed on understanding the cost-effectiveness of improving transport to gain social outcomes that lead to the development of personal capabilities, reduction of inequality and the establishment of a well-functioning society.

## 3.3    The impact of transport on people and local communities

As mentioned above, much thinking about transport centres around the commute to and from work, neglecting the critical role played by local transport in meeting a variety of other travel purposes. Good policy for, and planning of, local transport takes account of land use and urban planning, health and personal wellbeing impacts, reducing environmental damage and considering the impact of transport on productivity. A growing body of research is showing the importance of the form of transport associated with personal and societal wellbeing. This work has particularly centred on health and active transport, such as the interface between obesity and mobility in car-dependent countries like Australia, UK and the US, but also the association with other disease states such as cardiovascular problems (Stevenson et al. 2016). There is a small but increasing interest in the impact of land use and transport on personal wellbeing, including the provision of, and access to, public places, open land and natural areas and play areas for children. Access to such areas has been shown to improve a sense of place and belonging, the development of social capital and child development outcomes (Gehl 2010, Lehmann 2015).

However, despite being both a wide-ranging and important area, research on the interface between transport and people is very much in the beginning stages, with large gaps in content, especially around transport and children and youth. Existing research appears to have had only a minor impact on transport planning and even less on urban planning and land use. For example, the many benefits associated with active transport need to be translated into practice and then projects evaluated, including topics such as pedestrian priority at road intersections, wider and improved footpaths and what determines quality in street furniture, public transport stops, safe green pathways and the interface between green and common space and mobility. Research attention is also needed on the social benefits of walking, such as social interaction opportunities, the pleasure of being outdoors and the place of walking in achieving environmental mastery (Gehl 2010).

Other under-researched areas relate to the social impacts on people of environmental degradation and pollution. This includes the profound longer-term impacts of greenhouse gases, where transport is a major contributor. A failure to act on this will have a disproportionate impact on those with poorer health and lower capacities for adaptation. Other forms of adverse impacts associated with transport include air pollution and the impacts of disposal of tyres and car batteries. Traffic noise and traffic volumes impact adversely on health and wellbeing for those who are more highly exposed, with these often being low-income households (Brown 2015, Welch et al. 2013). Possible health effects to transport-associated pollution include cardiovascular diseases, cognitive impairment, sleep disturbance and annoyance, along with adverse impacts on children.

Families experiencing disadvantage and at risk of social exclusion tend to be most adversely impacted by living in close proximity to major roads and highways, as this may be the only location with affordable housing. Further research on these issues is needed, particularly research that links these adverse outcomes on people and communities with land use and urban planning, for example, the location of heavy industry and associated traffic, housing facing bicycle tracks instead of roads.

The impact of the dominance of car use and heavy traffic, as well as its absorption of land space, reaching 50 to 60 per cent of urban land in some contexts, needs further research, both on understanding the impact of this on people, particularly children, whose physical and psychological development increases their vulnerability. Car sharing is often posed as one of the answers, but this again needs considerable research to promote further understanding, as such solutions involve changing many deep-seated behaviours and may place child safety at risk. Outdoor play and independent travel for older children, again developmentally important, should receive much greater research consideration as the options for this are reducing in contemporary cities where density is increasing. This includes evaluation of options such as traffic calming, closing streets, as well as improving the availability and quality of parks and natural environments for children.

Indeed the psychology of car travel, why private vehicles dominate and the role of commercial marketing of vehicles and a car culture, which creates the car as an extended image of the self, especially as connected to the male ego, are all of great importance to understanding how transport must, and will, change in the future. While there is a lot of activity/interest around autonomous and electric vehicles, the conversation largely skirts around how these technological developments are going to impact on people in general and on particular groups of people, such as those with a disability, young, aged and those with few financial resources.

A place-based neighbourhood model for public and active transport promoting the ability to obtain most needs and services locally most of the time, also known as the 20 minute city or neighbourhood, is also gaining interest in some industrialised countries (Stanley et al. 2017). This approach is common by 'default' in many parts of Europe, reflecting the compact historical urban structure, and similarly is (or was) present in much of rural economy-based settings. Detailed requisite components of this model and how to bring about change to facilitate this approach in newly developed and older established areas is a new research opportunity.

## 3.4    Getting the right issues to the table

Research is needed on designing transport for cities, taking an integrated, strategic view in order to achieve the outcomes that a city should achieve, across social, environmental and economic areas (Stanley et al. 2017). While many cities outline their visions and goals, not all have a systematic pathway to achieving these. Vancouver, Canada, however, stands out as a successful approach, where a social goal, 'develop complete communities', is in its shortlist of five targets for the city (Metro Vancouver 2011). London follows a model offering process and governance arrangements of how to achieve good transport options for people. The Greater

London Authority, created in 2000, coordinates economic development, transport, and the police and emergency services in an integrated governance arrangement (Seyers 2018). The model includes an emphasis on transparency and consultation, including with the community.

Although such positive examples can be found, many cities have considerable difficulty achieving a process that adequately considers both the transport needs for people, and the communities' opinions about the transport options they prefer. Melbourne is a case in point. The predicted cost of major transport infrastructure projects in the current pipeline is approaching $100 billion. While the 'impact' on people adjacent to these projects may be considered, little thought is given to the broader implications for people. Such considerations would include: who is going to use these road and rail options and who will miss out; what will be the implications for city sprawl; what are the opportunity costs in relation to local transport, such as more frequent local bus services for those with few other transport options? While there has been some public consultation on some of these projects, there is fairly widespread distrust and apparently little up-take of community views, even where community consultations have taken place (Gleeson and Beza 2014).

Why good transport decision-making for people is failing in some cities needs further interrogation. This will not be easy research, but case-study comparisons between cities, about how and why one city achieved good social outcomes and the other city didn't, would be helpful. Organisational structure, culture and leadership are important to investigate. Comparisons with decision-making in other functional areas may also offer insights as to how processes could be improved and change achieved. The process of community consultation also needs investigation in relation to how consultation is undertaken, who is consulted, about what and when, and how the communities' views are integrated into the decision-making process. Integration of the bottom-up and top-down decision-making has always been a fraught process and needs considerable further research.

## 3.5    A lost opportunity

The United Nation's Millennium Development Goals targeted extreme poverty and promoted education. Seventeen Sustainable Development Goals (SDGs) replaced these goals at the end of 2015, broadening the remit to social and environmental sustainability. These new goals recognised that improvements in outcomes for people involved advances in many dimensions, including transport. Goal 11 relates to the need to make cities and human settlements inclusive, safe, resilient and sustainable, with sub-goal 11.2 referring particularly to transport:

> *By 2030, provide access to safe, affordable, accessible and sustainable transport systems for all, improving road safety, notably by expanding public transport, with special attention to the needs of those in vulnerable situations, women, children, persons with disabilities and older persons.*

While there have been some important successes in achieving a reduction in extreme poverty levels in many countries, particularly in Asia, change has been directed strongly towards the establishment of a market-type economy and a strong reliance on private cars for passenger transport. More than 300,000 kilometres of roads are added every year in the Asian region, construction that has been heavily financed by international development banks to enable freight movement for economic growth (UNESCAP 2013). Allied with this road building has been a rapid growth of private cars. Despite a predicted lowering of demand for cars in the US and Europe, the number of cars worldwide is projected to nearly double the 2016 stock, reaching 2 billion by 2040, with China and India leading much of the growth (Smith 2016).

The rapid change in urban form in industrialising countries has largely not avoided the transport and urban design problems that many Western economies are now trying to correct through the difficult task of retrofitting (Rifkin 2011). This includes issues like urban sprawl, poor public transport services and poor accessibility to services for many of those on a lower income. It is ironic that while industrialising countries are moving strongly to a car-based society, many Western countries are beginning to reduce both car trips and the distance travelled by car (Ellerton and Bray 2018). There is a forgone opportunity in many rapidly changing urban areas to address social transport issues from the start, in order to achieve inclusion, fairness and equality (Stiglitz 2012).

Part of the problem, as noted in Section 3.3, is that local transport is a largely overlooked area in transport policy and planning. Yet, getting local transport right is an important part of responding to the SDG goals and targets. Thus, considerable research is needed on many social aspects of transport in industrialising countries. Understanding local community needs around sense of community, place and belonging, within a cultural context that also incorporates historical design and heritage values, is an important research area that requires work if the SDGs are to be achieved.

The community transport, paratransit and informal transport sector require considerable research, as in smaller and poorer cities up to 90 per cent of trips are non-motorised (Cervero 2013). The neglect of this form of transport, together with the little attention to walking and cycling in many industrialising countries, is in contrast to current trends in most industralised countries, where the infrastructure to improve walking opportunities is increasingly being given high priority in transport planning (Stanley et al. 2017). Consideration of more informal transport should include an exploration of the value of these systems for those at risk of social exclusion, how they can be improved in terms of safety and inclusion and their 'fit' with public transport and other transport systems. Demand-responsive informal transport in industrialising countries is well suited to negotiate high density, poor street layout, while being more affordable for those on a low income, albeit that there are sometimes safety concerns in operation and organisation, which need to be addressed.

Laube (2015) suggests that poor planning from developed countries is behind these problems in Asian cities, where:

> ... we are really exporting our rather toxic traffic planning philosophies designed to road solutions into unprepared vulnerable urban governance situations, so it is a worry what is happening in many countries and cities that are rapidly motorising ...

Research is needed on culturally relevant urban planning.

## 3.6   Transport planning for natural hazards

Climate change is increasing the frequency and severity of natural disasters in the form of sea level rise, floods, storms and cyclones, heatwaves and wildfires. Disasters continue to exact a heavy, and increasing, toll on people, the environment and infrastructure. Overall, more than 1.5 billion people have been affected by disasters in various ways, with women, children and people in vulnerable situations disproportionately affected (United Nations 2015). Thus it is critical to prevent, anticipate and plan for extreme events, as well as plan for recovery and reconstruction, with transport a vitally important part of these responses. Research on best practice preparedness is lagging at present. Research is needed on transport planning that encompasses multiple jurisdictions, agencies, populations, and sectors to prevent loss of life, move people from harm's way, maintain communications and connections, meet basic needs, restore critical infrastructure and services, and help with recovery efforts.

Some critical issues needing further research in relation to the social dimensions of transport include the problem that often roads and urban development hug coastlines, and thus are vulnerable to sea level rises and storm surges. The choices around risk, cost, sense of place and belonging are very complex and need considerably more research. Roads are needed for access and egress in a wildfire emergency to support people and communities at risk or isolated due to the disaster, and where there is a need to evacuate injured people. By way of example, seven people died in a major fire in Victoria at Mount Macedon, in 1983. These people with a disability were waiting on the front verandah of their residence to be picked up and evacuated. Planning for unusual events is needed, such as rail lines buckling under heatwave conditions, thus leaving potentially large numbers of commuters stranded in severe weather conditions. Another area is the provision of transport to move people to safer locations, alternative accommodation, and to food and hospital centres, both during and after the emergency. There are many wide-ranging needs for research in relation to transport around natural hazards, linking this work with urban planning and land use, in both industrialised and industrialising countries.

## 3.7   Conclusions

Given the relatively recent interest in social outcomes and transport, the research field is wide open and the need substantial. This chapter suggests some areas thought to be important by the author, but a researcher can undertake meaningful work in areas much wider than these suggestions. However, it is important to have in mind a number of principles on which this research should be based. These relate to the need to integrate social research with other outcomes in order to consider all impacts and give consideration to the broad choices, costs and benefits to people and society. Most choices will be substantially influenced by value judgements, thus all stakeholders need to have the opportunity to be involved. The assumptions that everyone has the same needs should be questioned, with those commonly less likely to be included in the research given particular attention. Finally, best transport outcomes for people necessitate good environmental outcomes too, as research that explores only short-term impacts may risk neglecting the impact on people of longer-term environmental degradation. The impacts of climate change and transport's role in the production of greenhouse gases is a case in point.

## References

Brown, A. (2015), 'Effects of road traffic noise on health: From burden of disease to effectiveness of interventions', *Procedia Environmental Sciences*, **30**, 3–9.

Cervero, R. (2013), 'Linking urban transport and land use in developing countries', *Journal of Transport and Land Use*, **6** (1), 7–24.

Currie, G. (2011), *New Perspectives and Methods in Transport and Social Exclusion Research*, Bingley: Emerald Books.

Ellerton, T. and Bray, J. (2018), *Number Crunch: Transport Trends in the City Regions*, April, UK: Urban Transport Group.

Gehl, J. (2010), *Cities for People*, Washington, DC: Island Press.

Gleeson, B. and Beza, B. (2014), *The Public City: Essays in Honour of Paul Mees*, Melbourne: Melbourne University Press.

Kamruzzaman, M. and Hine, J. (2011), 'Rural activity spaces and transport disadvantage: Qualitative analysis of quantitative models integrating time and space'. In: *Proceedings of the 43rd Annual Conference of the Universities' Transport Study Group*, Universities' Transport Study Group, Open University, Milton Keynes, pp. 1–12.

Laube, F. (2015), 'Why fund rail when roads are our future?' *Late Night Live, ABC RN*, 3 June.

Legacy, C., Curtis, C. and Scheurer, J. (2017), 'Planning transport infrastructure: Examining the politics of transport planning in Melbourne, Sydney and Perth', *Urban Policy and Research*, **35**(1), 44–60.

Lehmann, S. (2015), 'Low carbon cities: More than just buildings', in S. Lehmann (ed.), *Low Carbon Cities: Transforming Urban Systems*, London: Routledge, pp. 1–56.

Metro Vancouver (2011), *Metro Vancouver 2040: Shaping our Future*, Vancouver: author.

Mollenkopf, H., Marcellini, F., Ruoppila, I., Szeman, Z. and Tacken, M. (2005), *Enhancing Mobility in Later Life*, Amsterdam: IOS Press.

Rifkin, J. (2011), *The Third Industrial Revolution: How Lateral Power is Transforming Energy, The Economy, and the World*, New York: Palgrave Macmillan.

Sen, A. (1983), 'Capability and well-being', in M. Nussbaum and A. Sen (eds.), *The Quality of Life*, Oxford: Clarendon Press, pp. 30–53.

Seyers, L. (2018), *Theories and Practice of Urban Transition: Melbourne's Wicked Transport Planning Environment*, M.Phil. thesis, University of Melbourne.

Smith, M. (2016), 'The number of cars worldwide is set to double by 2040', *Business Insider, World Economic Forum*, 22 April, https://www.weforum.org/agenda/2016/04/the-number-of-cars-world-wide-is-set-to-double-by-2040. Accessed 26 August 2018.

Stanley, J.K., Stanley, J.R., Balbontin, C. and Hensher, D. (2018), 'Social exclusion: The role of mobility and bridging social capital in regional Australia', *Transportation Research Part A: Policy and Practice*, https://doi.org/10.1016,j.tra.2018.05.015. Accessed 1 September 2018.

Stanley, J.K., Stanley, J.R. and Hansen, R. (2017), *How Great Cities Happen: Integrating People, Land Use and Transport*, Cheltenham: Edward Elgar.

Stevenson, M. et al. (2016), Land use, transport, and population health: Estimating the health benefits of compact cities, *The Lancet*, **388**(10062), 2025–2935.

Stiglitz, J. (2012), *The Price of Inequality*, London: Allen Lane.

UNESCAP (United Nations Economic and Social Commission for Asia and the Pacific) (2013), *Review of Developments in Transport in Asia and the Pacific*, Bangkok: UN.

United Nations (2015), *Sendai Framework for Disaster Risk Reduction 2015–2030*, Third UN World Conference in Sendai, Japan, 18 March.

Welch, D., Shepherd, D., Dirks, K., McBride, D. and Marsh, S. (2013), 'Road traffic noise and health-related quality of life: A cross-sectional study', *Noise Health*, **15**, 224–230.

# 4     Transport and the environment

*Robin Hickman and David Banister*

## 4.1   Introduction

Transport plays a central role in society, as production, business, leisure and everyday activities all depend on movement. It has been instrumental in allowing the increase in trade and globalisation to take place, and in allowing new forms of networking between people and businesses. This global mobility has been built on international aviation and shipping networks, enhanced by new communications technologies. At the more local level, there have also been substantial increases in mobility by all forms of transport as income levels have risen (Banister, 2011).

Whilst other sectors of the economy have decarbonised, transport has continued to increase its consumption of energy and $CO_2$ emissions. It now accounts for nearly 20 per cent[1] of global $CO_2$ and this is expected to increase to 50 per cent by 2030 (on 2005 levels), as most other sectors decarbonise and as transport emissions continue to grow (International Transport Federation, 2017). Transport $CO_2$ reduction targets need to be set at the global, national and city scales. A 50 per cent reduction in transport $CO_2$ emissions would be required by 2050 (on 1990 levels), if the transport sector were to make a significant contribution to the Paris Agreement (2015) of avoiding a +2°C in global temperature and substantial sea level rise[2] (IPCC, 2014). This means that the richer countries should be targeting an 80–90 per cent reduction over this period, but this would require wide-ranging policy interventions that cover extensive public transport investments, walking and cycling facilities, urban planning, traffic demand management and low emission vehicles (Hickman and Banister, 2014).

At the city level, the concerns are less about global environmental issues ($CO_2$) and more about the quality of life, clean air, safety, accessibility and affordability of transport, and the quality of the local neighbourhood. Long-term ecological

---

1 Transport is the second leading source of carbon dioxide emissions, contributing about 9 gigatonnes of $CO_2$ in 2015.

2 $CO_2$ concentrations are currently (June 2018) about 410 ppmv and with other greenhouse gases being included, this value increases to over 450 ppmv $CO_2$e (https://www.co2.earth/global-co2-emissions, accessed 10 July 2018). A level of 450 ppmv $CO_2$e means that there is a 40 per cent chance of exceeding 2°C by 2100. A level of 550 ppmv $CO_2$e means that there is a 50–60 per cent chance of exceeding 2°C, and the estimated sea level rise is estimated to be 18cm (2030) and 44 cm (2070) (IPCC, 2014).

sustainability needs to be addressed through technological innovation and the efficient use of (clean) energy. But sustainable mobility should also address individual needs for travel, together with ensuring greater equity in terms of access to transport, affordability and participation in activities. This means that the environmental and social dimensions of sustainable mobility need to be considered alongside the technological and efficiency dimensions.

Transport also contributes substantially to local air quality with detrimental health effects. The main pollutants are nitrogen oxides (NOx) and carbon monoxide (CO), and these are added to by particulate matter ($PM_{10}$ and $PM_{2.5}$). For example, in 2013, around 17 per cent of the EU-28 urban population was exposed to $PM_{10}$ above the EU daily limit value (the threshold is $50\mu g/m^3$, not to be exceeded on more than 35 days per calendar year, for short-term exposure). Transport accounted for 13 per cent of $PM_{10}$, 15 per cent of $PM_{2.5}$ emissions, and 46 per cent of NOx emissions across the EU-28 in 2013 (European Environment Agency, 2015). The health effects of poor air quality are related to short-term and long-term exposure. Short-term (exposure over a few hours or days) is linked with acute health effects, whereas long-term exposure (over months or years) is linked with chronic health effects. The disease burden is substantial, including many non-communicable diseases, such as heart disease, stroke, cancers and respiratory diseases (Hickman et al., 2017), and air pollution globally is estimated to account for 9 million premature deaths annually (Landrigan et al., 2018).

A further environmental concern is the economic and social costs of transport-related crashes. Globally, there are 1.25 million people killed and a further 20–50 million injured each year (World Health Organisation, 2015). This equates to around 3,400 deaths per day, a figure seemingly accepted by society as a cost worth paying for car-based mobility. In almost all cities, traffic congestion is problematic, and this further reduces the quality of life and the health of residents. Even though improvements are taking place through safety programmes, more efficient transport, cleaner fuels, and technological innovation, the aggregate levels of $CO_2$, air pollution, and crashes are all increasing, particularly in emerging economies which are rapidly increasing their levels of car ownership and mobility. The rate and scale of change is unprecedented, and this means that radical rather than incremental change is required.

This chapter addresses some of these debates and it explores the range of policy actions that need to be taken to address the environmental elements. These actions can be implemented individually, but it is only when there is a coherent vision of the sustainable city that real progress can be made, through putting mutually supporting policy measures together to achieve both the global objectives ($CO_2$ and energy efficiency) and the local objectives (air pollution, safety, quality of life, accessibility, affordability and urban quality). The chapter comments on the growth in travel, in particular travel distance, but its main focus is on the options for mobility in the low carbon city, where radical thinking is required on moving away from a reliance on the private car. An approach to meeting the mobility needs of all those living and working in the city is discussed, which at the same time respects environmental limits. The final section discusses the emerging research agenda.

## 4.2   Visions of sustainable transport

Massive growth is predicted in mobility over the coming decades, as the number of cars and light trucks is likely to grow from 1 billion in 2015 to 2.4 billion by 2050. Travel distance is forecast to double, from 50,000 billion passenger kilometres (bpkms) to 120,000 bpkms, and freight transport to triple (tonne-kilometres) to 2050. There is a corresponding forecast increase of 60 per cent in passenger and freight transport $CO_2$ emissions (International Transport Federation, 2017). Cars and trucks are a global business, involving the motor manufacturers, the oil industry, many suppliers, energy providers, the construction business, support and maintenance providers, and others. This in turn means that it plays a substantial role for economies in providing employment,[3] allowing the distribution of goods and services, and in its extension to many parts of everyday life. But so too does employment associated with public transport, and often this is overlooked.

The rationale for the city now and in the future is based on the continued importance of face-to-face contact, networking and social interactions. Location is seen as being central to the economic rationale of the city and the efficiency with which business can be carried out. If the intention is to create a sustainable city then it must have a high quality of life and it must become less resource intensive. This would include the movement of goods and people within the city, but it also needs to address the supply chains for the goods and services required by the city, and the infrastructure necessary for business and leisure activities to be undertaken by the city residents.

The net effects will not necessarily be a reduction in the use of energy or $CO_2$ emissions from transport. For example, much of the population increase will take place in cities in developing countries. McKinsey Global Institute (2012) estimates that 1 billion people will enter the 'global consuming class' by 2025,[4] with incomes high enough to significantly consume goods and services. These people are likely to have increased levels of mobility, as they acquire motorised transport, and this in turn will lead to additional pressures on resource consumption and the environment. The current inequality in the distribution of population and emissions is illustrated by the high income countries and China currently accommodating 36 per cent of the world's population, but accounting for 65 per cent of $CO_2$ emissions; whilst the low income countries accommodate 9 per cent of the world's population, but account for 1 per cent of $CO_2$ emissions (2014 data) (World Bank, 2018).

---

3 For example, transport employs about 9 million people directly in the EU27 (2010) or about 4.5 per cent of all employed people and a further 25 million are employed either directly or indirectly in the car manufacturing industry (ACEA, 2012).

4 Defined by MGI as individuals with incomes of more than $3,600 per annum.

More comprehensive and radical action is required to tackle the expected global rise and inequity in mobility. There is considerable inertia within the transport system and any substantial change takes time to be effective, with considerable path dependence and lock-in reinforcing the current situation (Schwanen, Banister and Anable, 2011). It is very difficult to move from one well-established system to another, even if the alternative is well defined and provides a much better way of moving around. Three complementary approaches offer ways forward to facilitate transport systems that explicitly address the scale of the problem being confronted and the speed of change taking place in terms of the growth in carbon-based mobility.

### 4.2.1   Transport scenario building

Transport decision-making has its roots in forecasting and extrapolation of existing trends to estimate future demand. Environmental objectives can be better achieved in transport by reframing the approach to transport policy and programme development. The first stage would be to agree a vision for the future city or neighbourhood, with a much stronger participatory and deliberative process used. Scenario analysis becomes much more central to decision-making, with preferred scenarios and strategies being chosen by stakeholders and the public. The process for transport planners would be to consider the appropriate projects that would achieve these future visions, and to develop a programme of investments that permit a pathway from where we want to be, back to where we are now. This is the concept of backcasting that allows transport to be better aligned to policy goals, and it has the added advantage that transformative change can be addressed (Hickman and Banister, 2014). The current emphasis on modelling of current trends and the meeting of demand works well for the short-term and relatively stable situations, but for longer-term, more radical futures that address environmental and social issues, a scenario-based approach offers flexibility, involvement and a consistent framework for analysis.

### 4.2.2   Environmental limits

There has been much debate over sustainability and how this might be achieved in transport. The conventional application of sustainability in transport is to assume that strategies and projects can be developed to achieve the three pillars: satisfying economic, environmental and social objectives. The difficulty in practice is that these objectives are often competing and there is no balanced strategy to be achieved. In this case, the economic objectives are often given precedence. Projects are undertaken that seek to promote economic goals, but environmental and social objectives are not met or are overlooked (Hickman, 2017).

Using the principle of environmental limits can assist us here (Holden et al., 2018; Meadows et al., 1972; Raworth, 2017). Strategies and projects would not be accepted if they did not achieve environmental and social goals, or had too great an adverse impact against agreed thresholds. Such an approach would help rebalance the current emphasis on a narrow set of economic objectives (e.g., time savings, employment and wider economic benefits), with greater weight being given to the wider environmental and social dimensions. This approach would allow public transport, cycling and walking projects to be more easily prioritised, together with other measures to help reduce the adverse impacts of transport projects and to improve the quality of cities (e.g., transit-orientated development, more local facilities and measures to reduce travel distance, improved streetscape and neighbourhood design).

### 4.2.3   Sustainable Mobility Paradigm (SMP)

The SMP gives an alternative approach to high levels of motorised mobility, with its high levels of associated environmental, safety and health costs (Banister, 2008). The SMP challenges the importance of speed and travel time savings, through emphasising the need for slower travel, reasonable travel times and travel time reliability. Although this approach has been applied mainly in the developed countries, similar arguments can be made for the rapidly growing Asian cities, as demonstrated by the Asian Development Bank's Sustainable Urban Transport paradigm (Asian Development Bank, 2009), and their development of the Avoid, Shift, Improve (ASI) framework that is now being widely adopted as a structure within which the wide range of sustainable mobility options can be adopted. The ADB makes explicit the importance of integration within transport and between land use and transport. The two most important elements in the ASI framework are firstly that demand-based approaches ('predict and provide') do not work and there is a need for demand management, and secondly that there is a need for a city vision that provides affordable, adaptable and implementable mobility. This can include a headline target for non-car modes, such as in London where policies are being introduced to provide for 80 per cent of trips to be made by walking, cycling and public transport in 2041 (Transport for London, 2018).

Hence the requirements of the SMP and ASI frameworks are to work across a wide range of policy areas to ensure deep transport $CO_2$ reductions are achieved. This may include controversial policy areas which can be difficult to implement (Hickman et al., 2017), and cover the following types of measures:

- AVOID: use of urban planning, affordable housing, development restraint in inaccessible locations, and reduced growth in international air traffic;
- SHIFT: improved walking and cycling facilities and networks, multimodal public transport; use of urban highway re-prioritisation, emissions-based road pricing, Mobility as a Service (MaaS), car parking supply restraint, and urban logistics management;
- IMPROVE: use of shared vehicle ownership schemes, low emission vehicles and alternative fuels.

As can be seen from these approaches to addressing the environmental issues in transport, there are measures that go beyond the technological 'fixes' that seem to dominate the current debates over the means to decarbonise the transport sector. Much of the current discussion (e.g., Intergovernmental Panel on Climate Change, 2014) has concentrated on the important role that technology can have in moving towards sustainable mobility, principally through the introduction of new lower carbon fuels, more efficient engine technologies, and a range of small improvements in materials, aerodynamics, tyres, and control systems. Innovation within the existing paradigm is central to reducing levels of carbon use in transport and the IPCC (2014) suggests that there is still considerable potential for further technological improvements. These could amount to between 40 and 70 per cent reductions in fuel consumption in cars, between 30 and 50 per cent reductions in fuel consumption in goods vehicles, about a 50 per cent improvement in efficiency in aviation and between 5 and 30 per cent reductions in fuel used in maritime shipping, over the period 2010–2035. But these levels of improvement may only reflect the potential for improvement. On their own they will not reach the target reduction levels for transport, particularly if the growth levels anticipated in mobility are realised. At best, these technological improvements will maintain overall carbon emissions levels in transport at their current levels, and changed behaviours are also required to reduce emissions (Hickman et al., 2010).

## 4.3   Reflections for research and practice

In discussing issues concerning sustainable mobility, it is not just a question of what can be done, but how such a transition or transformation can take place – often it is the implementation of effective policy measures that is most difficult. Giddens (2009) has stated that fear is not the best way to induce low carbon futures, and that there need to be positive alternatives and new path dependencies. Arthur (2009) suggests that innovation takes 30–40 years and depends on new combinations of elements working together, synchronously, to create new habits and imaginations. These two views do not suggest that the achievement of significant environmental improvement will be easy, but at present there is too much emphasis placed on the role that improvements in technology can play in achieving change. This perspective is too simple, as the scale of change required, the expected growth in mobility levels, and the inherent inertia in the system make the technological future attractive, yet unrealistic in terms of sufficiently reducing global transport carbon emissions by 2050, as well as addressing the other priorities such as safe, clean, healthy and high quality transport. This means that much more attention needs to be given to the Avoid and Shift parts of the ASI framework, and the first three elements of the SMP that cover the need to make the trip, shorter distances, and the use of public transport, walking and cycling. It is only through comprehensive and complementary approaches, using a range of available measures, that the carbon reduction targets will be achieved.

The quality of life in cities is central, as signified by improved streetscape design and by the provision of open spaces for recreation and for people to meet and spend time together (Gehl, 2010). Increased levels of cycling, walking and activity provide health and well-being benefits, and open space also offers a counter to the urban heat island effect. Clear zones can also be designated, where polluting vehicles are restricted or charged, as high levels of local pollutants have a direct effect on health. The promotion of active transport encourages healthy lifestyles, and the reallocation of space in cities to cyclists and walkers with their own segregated networks of routes would create the most suitable conditions for change. By altering the speed and scale of activity, many spaces would become places that people would want to spend time and money. The concept of the 20-minute neighbourhood can be used, where most activities for a 'good life' can be carried out by walking, cycling and public transport within 20-minute journey times (Stanley et al., 2017).

This is where urban structure, urban design and the use of space all become central in determining the means by which sustainable urban forms can be established. Complementary approaches are needed that would be based on increased levels of urban density and reduced levels of urban sprawl, so that journey lengths and the levels of car dependence can be reduced. The distribution of services and facilities would be organised to minimise trip lengths and increase accessibility, as many activities can then be undertaken on one journey (the linking of activities), and destinations would be close together, as this allows multi-purpose trips and less travel, as well as providing the flows for efficient public transport. The allocation of space would give priority to different uses to make it clear as to whose space it is – this has implications for pedestrianisation, residential and shopping areas, as well as providing networks for public transport, cyclists and pedestrians, and it relates to the ownership of urban space. This is where research can be directed in terms of addressing the physical problems of transport and the environment in the city, including issues of space, capacity and prioritisation, and this can be achieved through building on the three approaches introduced earlier. In addition, new policy measures will emerge, perhaps tackling the blockages to greater sustainable mobility. There may be much greater use of road space reallocation, giving much more space to public transport, walking and cycling, and restrictions on urban sprawl.

Complementary to the issues related to the physical environment are those related to the social environment and the decision-making process. It is here that new research should engage with citizens, businesses and politicians in the city to listen to their concerns and to build strong support and understanding about the importance of the environment. Transport planning can become a much more participatory and deliberative process, allowing visions, strategies and projects to be chosen that are supported by the public and consistent with societal goals. This means thinking about future priorities so that the scale of the problems can be assessed and the need for radical and immediate action accepted. Approaches to transport appraisal may need to be amended to allow improved participation and more effective prioritisation of non-car modes (Hickman and Dean, 2017). Transformation is more than driving around in electric, autonomous vehicles. It is about the development of attractive, flexible, safe and comfortable cities, where mobility is affordable and available to all, and mostly undertaken by different forms of public transport, walking and cycling. To achieve this requires an improved understanding of the different viewpoints and the mediation of interests, so that the SMP can be delivered at scale. The sustainable city includes access to transport systems and participation in activities which are open to all. Consequently there needs to be dynamic leadership and institutional and organisational change which can help to deliver this. Research must address the politics of transport and the environment, together with identifying the necessary conditions for transformative change. Transport can hence be viewed as a means to access activities, within environmental limits and equitably, rather than as a means for a few to consume more mobility.

## References

ACEA (European Automobile Manufacturers Association) (2012), *The Automobile Industry Pocket Guide*, Brussels: ACEA.

Arthur, B. (2009), *The Nature of Technology: What It is and How It Evolves*, New York: Free Press.

Asian Development Bank (2009), *Changing Course. A New Paradigm for Sustainable Urban Transport*, Manila: ADB.

Banister, D. (2008), 'The sustainable mobility paradigm', *Transport Policy*, **15**(2), 73–80.

Banister, D. (2011), 'The trilogy of distance, speed and time', *Journal of Transport Geography*, **19**(4), 950–959.

European Environment Agency (2015), *Air Quality in Europe—2015 Report*, Luxembourg: EEA.

Gehl, J. (2010), *Cities for People*, Washington, DC: Island Press.

Giddens, A. (2009), *The Politics of Climate Change*, Cambridge: Polity.

Hickman, R. (2017), 'Sustainable travel or sustaining growth?' In J. Cowie and S. Ison (Eds.), *The Routledge Handbook of Transport Economics*, Abingdon, Routledge.

Hickman, R., Ashiru, O. and Banister, D. (2010), 'Transport and climate change: Simulating the options for carbon reduction in London', *Transport Policy*, **17**(2), 110–125.

Hickman, R. and Banister, D. (2014), *Transport, Climate Change and the City*, Abingdon: Routledge.

Hickman, R. and Dean, M. (2017), 'Incomplete cost-incomplete benefit analysis in transport appraisal', *Transport Reviews*, https://doi.org/ 0.1080/01441647.2017.1407377.

Hickman, R., Smith, D., Moser, D., Schaufler, C. and Vecia, G. (2017), *Why the Automobile Has No Future: A Global Impact Analysis*, Hamburg: Greenpeace.

Holden, E., Linnerud, K., Banister, D., Schwanitz, V. and Wierling, A. (2018), *The Imperatives of Sustainable Development. Needs, Justice, Limits*, Abingdon: Routledge.

Intergovernmental Panel on Climate Change (IPCC) (2014), *Climate Change 2014. Synthesis Report. Contribution of Working Groups I, II and III to the Fifth Assessment Report of the Intergovernmental Panel on Climate Change*, Geneva: IPCC.

International Transport Federation (2017), *Transport Outlook*, Paris: OECD/ITF.

Landrigan, P. et al. (2018), 'The Lancet Commission on pollution and health', *The Lancet*, **391**(10119), 462–512.

McKinsey Global Institute (2012), *Urban World: Cities and the Rise of the Consuming Class*, MGI.

Meadows, D.H., Meadows, D.L., Randers, J. and Behrens, W.W. (1972), *The Limits to Growth: A Report for the Club of Rome's Project on the Predicament of Mankind*. London: Potomac Associates, Earth Island Ltd.

Raworth, K. (2017), *Doughnut Economics: Seven Ways to Think Like a 21st-Century Economist*, London: Random House.

Schwanen, T., Banister, D. and Anable, J. (2011), 'Scientific research about climate change mitigation in transport: A critical review', *Transportation Research Part A: Policy and Practice*, **45**(10), 993–1006.

Stanley, J., Stanley, J. and Hansen, R. (2017), *How Great Cities Happen*, Cheltenham: Edward Elgar.

Transport for London (2018), *Mayor's Transport Strategy*, London: GLA/TfL.

World Bank (2018), *World Development Indicators*, Washington, DC: World Bank.

World Health Organisation (2015), *Global Status Report on Road Safety*, Geneva: WHO.

# 5    Transport governance

*Greg Marsden*

## 5.1    Introduction

Governance should not be confused with government. Government can be understood as 'the formal institutions of the state and their monopoly of legitimate coercive power' (Stoker, 1998: 17). By contrast, governance is seen to be the 'steering and co-ordination of interdependent (usually collective) actors based on institutionalized rule systems' (Trieb et al., 2007: 3). The distinction places the state as one actor 'among a vast array of spatially and functionally distinct networks composed of all kinds of public, voluntary, and private organizations' (Rhodes, 2011: 434). The art of governing is then to deliver socially desirable outcomes by steering collective action through this network of actors.

This chapter looks at the governance of transport with the aim of discussing some enduring themes which have proven resilient across previous socio-technical transitions and identifying what recent developments in the sector tell us about the critical challenges of the coming decades. The chapter does not seek to elaborate on the range of public policy goals which transport connects to, such as climate change, productivity, health and inclusion, as these are covered elsewhere. However, it does draw on how these issues are mobilised as part of strategies to steer policy development and delivery across the system. The importance of framing and story-telling in establishing problems and the resultant solutions is certainly not a value-neutral exercise (Torfing et al., 2012).

As a final introductory observation, the definitions of both government and governance point to the importance of formal institutional systems and power and how those institutionalised systems work in practice. This varies hugely across contexts. Singapore, for example, is often held up as a beacon of international good practice in the integration of transport. However, the particular conditions of a compact island state with a fairly authoritarian rule are not mimicked elsewhere and so neither are reforms nor the outcomes sought from those reforms when they are applied (Kamal Batcha, 2013). The prevailing interpretation of the role of the public sector in a country is hugely important to transport. In some countries, such as the UK and Australia, a strongly neo-liberal marketised mindset places the private sector centre stage in reforms whereas in some countries (e.g. in Scandinavia) a more social welfare model of provision prevails with the state more strongly involved (Legacy et al., 2017; Paget-Seekins and Tironi, 2016). In this chapter I try to work with core concepts which are relevant everywhere. How they matter in different contexts should be the subject of empirical enquiry, although a recent review of journal articles on transport policy shows that it rarely is (Marsden and Reardon, 2017).

## 5.2   Networks of actors and modes

As noted above, governance is steering through a network of actors. What does this mean for transport? The first critical observation to make is that 'the transport system' is a system for the traveller, in the sense that one can make journeys across multiple modes of transport. However, from an operational and regulatory perspective it is a distinct set of technological systems, each of which developed over a different period and which has its own history and traditions. It is also a system which generates accessibility between land-uses and ought, therefore, to be planned and managed in a co-ordinated manner, a further challenge (Stead and Meijers, 2009).

Low and Astle (2009) reviewed 50 years of development of transport policy in Victoria State in Australia. In commenting on the separation of road and public transport planning, the authors identify that bus and tram operations are users of roads, immediately flagging an artificial separation of actors and remits. Whilst, over time, the separate functions of road management such as infrastructure design, management and vehicle regulation have been brought together under one organisation (VicRoads), the history of public transport reform has seen periods of integration and fragmentation. Critically, the decision to privatise rail and tram operations on a franchise model led to the dismantling of integrated public transport planning as the operations were then treated more as regulated industry (Low and Astle, 2009). This, they argue, places the network of actors around road expansion in a much stronger position to advocate for investment. The ability to integrate public transport services, once they are subject to distinct rule sets governed to some degree by market logics, has proven particularly difficult in most parts of the world, although how the private sector is involved makes a difference. In England, for example, most local bus services are run by private companies but it is only in London where the fares and service schedules are set and this is the only major metropolitan area that has not seen major declines in patronage (White, 2009).

## 5.3   Multi-level networks of actors

As well as considering networks across modes of transport there is a need to consider spatial configurations of actors and networks. Transport crosses administrative boundaries. Where this happens, issues of standardisation of approach matter both for practical operational reasons, fairness across governmental authorities and

to limit the regulatory burden on the private sector. As well as creating requirements to cooperate, boundaries create powerful tensions between decision-making
across and within different layers of government. Different powers and resources
are held by different governmental layers and the trade-offs between international,
national, regional and local politics often play out in the arguments for investments
of different sorts. This multi-level governance challenge has been highlighted as a
reason why national governments struggle to get alignment from local governments
to their priorities such as climate change (Marsden and Groer, 2016).

Differences in approaches between and within different countries is a key source of
our ability to understand 'what works?' and 'why?' It is also, as the introduction of
new mobility services demonstrates, both an opportunity and a risk, as the new providers seek to pilot their systems in the most favourable regulatory environments.
Whilst this enables innovation it might also contribute to competition between
places and a race to the bottom in regulatory quality. The global mobility of policies
creates pressure for the rapid diffusion and the adoption of policies and technologies even though they may not initially have been welcomed and were developed
for quite different implementation environments (DiMaggio and Powell, 1983).

## 5.4   Industrial actors

The private sector is a critical actor in the governance of transport, and one which
often works across multiple spatial scales. This can be as a service provider, an infrastructure constructor and a manufacturer of vehicles and associated sensors. To
be clear, the transport industry is a set of massive global industries. Each year, 90
million new vehicles are made and sold, and according to the OECD $1.5 trillion
(US) was spent on new infrastructure investment globally in 2015. Boeing has a
market value of $108.8 billion (US) and Maersk shipping $35 billion (US). Uber has a
market value of around $50 billion (US) despite operating at a loss. The scale of these
interests dwarfs that of the bottom-up grass roots transport campaign groups and
has significant influence on how transport policy gets framed, formulated and implemented (or not). The recent tightening of vehicle emission standards from voluntary
$CO_2$ targets to mandatory targets in the European Union and the ensuing gaming
of the vehicle-testing procedures shows the challenge of effectively influencing big
industries which are seen to be critical to employment and growth (Skeete, 2017).

One of the changing contexts for transport governance is the arrival of a whole new
set of actors managing data, service integration or new mobility services. These
firms are not necessarily asset holders (e.g. fleet managers) but are instead putting together different services for travellers such as bundles of mobility (Mobility
as a Service) or ticketing, information and journey planning linked to activities.
Looking ahead, however, there is much interest in autonomous vehicles which, if
they do come to pass, could create massive new industrial companies responsible
for running transport services in place of much of what is currently seen as 'private'
car ownership. These would be influential actors not just because of their size but

because of how they might need our cities to be adapted to make their systems work (ITF, 2018).

## 5.5    From rowing to steering

One of the defining characteristics of the shift from government to governance is a move from direct delivery of many aspects of public service to shaping delivery through the networks described above. This is often described as a shift from 'rowing' to 'steering'. Whilst it is undoubtedly true that the state has retreated from direct delivery of transport services in most settings, it is still the custodian of an important set of tools through which to orchestrate the wider networks involved in delivery. These include setting the overarching policy goals and the setting and application of rules and regulations and sometimes specifying the services to be run. This can sometimes be termed the 'hard power'. However, the state also plays a critical role in mediating the mutual dependency for financial resources and information which are also seen to be critical for network governance to work (Rhodes, 1996).

As discussed in detail in Docherty et al. (2017), the shift from rowing to steering is important in how governments go about trying to deliver public value from their transport systems. However, the fundamental challenges the state needs to address remain remarkably stable, such as tackling the external costs of transport, ensuring basic levels of provision across society, managing market power, ensuring safe interoperable systems and seeking integration. It is the changing context of new technologies and actors, more limited resources and challenges to government legitimacy to act which make this a dynamic area of study.

## 5.6    New governance context

The promise of the three revolutions (electrification, automation and mobility as a service) is seen to be both a major growth opportunity and a chance to tackle some of the negative outcomes produced through the current transport system with its reliance on fossil fuelled vehicles (Sperling, 2018). Two decades ago autonomous vehicles and electric vehicles were not even mainstream research conference topics. In 1998 300 million people had a mobile phone subscription and no one had mobile internet. Today 4.3 billion people use a mobile phone. Mobility as a service, where people integrate their journeys using multiple modes in real-time through their phone, was not even a pipe dream. So, whilst it is early days in the cycle of innovations uptake, these innovations now form part of the mainstream thinking about what transport is for in a way which they did not two decades ago. With that comes a set of firms such as Google, Apple, Uber, Didi, Tesla, Mobike, Baidu and Whim, either new or new to the mobility market, each promising to form part of the mobility revolution needed to solve transport's problems. Each competes with existing providers for the market for future mobility.

The next generation of transport researcher will be massively influenced by which of these innovations will come to the fore and in what order and in which combinations. From a governance perspective, the critical questions revolve around how any transition in the mobility system can be influenced by the state to deliver the public policy outcomes that society needs. Different countries took different policy paths in the face of the growth of the automobile and are now confronted with different levels of conflict between the benefits and negative side effects. So, although steering is acknowledged to be becoming increasingly difficult, the choices about how the next transitions are steered will matter.

It is also important to consider the context today in which these systems are being developed. Emerging economies may, for example, never reach the same levels of automobile dependence seen in the US as the mobility system becomes something different to that of the latter half of the twentieth century and individual ownership becomes less defining of social progress. Whilst it is tempting to talk about three revolutions and a transition to smart mobility there will be many innovations and they will play out quite differently across the globe.

## 5.7    New agendas

In a review of the state of the art of studying transport policy that I published with Louise Reardon in 2017 we found that 87% of the papers studied did not look at the process of policy-making and that 90% of the papers did not engage policy-makers in their research (Marsden and Reardon, 2017). If, as is set out in this chapter, you see transport policy to be an outcome of a set of struggles within a complex and multi-level network of actors then this distance between research about policies and research on policy-making has to be closed. I identify three directions which I see as important.

### 5.7.1    Understanding new mobility providers

The new mobility service providers represent a new set of actors, some of which are seen to have 'disruptive' business models. More needs to be understood about the strategies of these firms and how well aligned they are to public policy goals. Platform companies such as Uber and BlaBla car can develop and deploy their products relatively rapidly without requiring to own the assets that are needed to operate on their platforms. Other firms such as the dockless bike share and e-scooter firms deploy large numbers of relatively cheap assets. However, the extent to which these assets achieve utilisation rates or provide network coverage which fulfils more than just the dense central area markets remains to be seen. It is also unclear whether the initial business models are artificially subsidising services to gain market share (as is the case with on-line delivery subscription platforms) or indeed whether the business models are more about selling the data which users generate. It is necessary for governments to think about where their regulatory influences are over such firms and how best to bring the parties together. Even early test cases such as arguments over driver safety certification for Uber or careless parking and abandonment of dockless bikes in cities show the need for some form of collaborative governance to emerge.

### 5.7.2   Revising or rewriting regulation?

Particularly in urban areas, the failure to deliver integrated transport services in many settings is seen to be a critical failure in producing healthier cities. It is increasingly recognised that there are no car-based solutions to accommodate the growth of cities and so making transport more efficient in moving people will become an even more important challenge. But what might that look like? Do we simply find ways of categorising and legislating for new modes of transport alongside our existing categories? Will that exacerbate rather than resolve the complexity of integrating services? It is perhaps instructive to imagine a world where some autonomous vehicles are in operation which any user can hail. Are these public transport? If so, would the same degree of priority be afforded to a single-occupancy vehicle as a half-full bus or tram? Early simulation results seem to suggest the potential to make traffic conditions worse until these new systems are widespread and heavily shared (e.g. ITF, 2018). Ultimately we are faced with decisions about how best to regulate access to a scarce resource – roads and kerbsides – and we need to do that in a way which best aligns with our public policy goals. Similar arguments revolve around what sorts of beneficial access to give to users of electric vehicles both in access and parking/charging places. It seems necessary to start this thinking now, before we arrive at a situation where we have been privileging a group of users by accident and then seek to remove such rights when it has become politically difficult to do so. There is a debate about the extent to which pro-active regulation might stifle innovation. However, the counter to this would be to consider that pro-active regulation could create secure environments in which innovations which deliver public value are able to flourish.

### 5.7.3   Managing change

It is curious to me that at the same time that utopian visions of more shared and autonomous futures underpin the future transport strategies of governments, the everyday business of transport spending seems firmly rooted in our understandings of the past. There remains a strong belief about the relationship between network capacity enhancements and economic growth even though that relationship has always been difficult to establish. To what extent are investment priorities established by 'transport need' and to what extent by the desires of the construction sector? It is known to be institutionally difficult to change deeply embedded technocratic decision-making processes, particularly when resources are limited and there is fierce competition for those resources (Marsden and McDonald, 2017).

The other aspect of change which should be examined is how to manage industries and institutions during decline. The excitement is around new markets and growth, which marginalises existing markets and how their decline is managed. How should we, for example, manage the decline in fossil fuel use and the associated impacts on the fuelling network resulting from electrification of the fleet? What role does or could transport policy have in regenerating the high street in the face of the rise of on-line shopping? When might state intervention be justified to preserve bus transport in the face of alternative services?

## 5.8  Conclusion

There is an exciting future research agenda for transport governance. As governance is the steering of outcomes through a network of actors then the interacting dynamics of changing policy needs and rapidly changing networks of actors creates a myriad of research opportunities. The technical challenges to developing many of the technologies which are currently dominating the research landscape should not be underestimated. However, separately developing their capabilities and then thinking about how they fit with existing systems of provision will surely lead to more conflicts and missed opportunities than necessary. Here, research can help by identifying the key conditions and trade-offs that should be managed to ensure better outcomes can be achieved. This chapter put forward three areas where governance researchers might usefully extend their studies but there are many more (see, for example, Docherty et al., 2017; Hensher, 2017; Legacy et al., 2018; Marsden and Reardon, 2018).

However, as well as researching the 'what' of better policy outcomes, greater emphasis needs to be given to the 'how' of bringing them about. In what ways will new commercial interests seek to influence development and how does the state respond to these? Whilst there is a great deal of harmonisation of transport regulation and operations around the globe there remain important national and local differences. How do these differences impact on the governance strategies adopted and their effectiveness? What does this tell us about the transferability or otherwise of these approaches? To answer this requires a much greater commitment to hands-on engagement with the processes of adoption (and rejection) that are unfolding today and a recognition from research funders that the how matters at least as much as the what.

## References

DiMaggio, P. and Powell, W. (1983), 'The iron cage revisited: Institutional isomorphism and collective rationality in organisational fields', *American Sociological Review*, **48**, 147–160.

Docherty, I., Marsden, G. and Anable, J. (2017), 'The governance of smart mobility', *Transportation Research Part A: Policy and Practice*, https://doi.org/10.1016/j.tra.2017.09.012.

Hensher, D. (2017), 'Future bus transport contracts under a mobility as a service (MaaS) regime in the digital age: Are they likely to change?' *Transportation Research Part A*, **98**, 86–96.

ITF (2018), *The Shared-Use City: Managing the Curb*, Paris: International Transport Forum.

Kamal Batcha, S.F.B. (2013), *Understanding the Governance of Reforms to Urban Transport in Developing Cities*, Ph.D. Thesis, University of Leeds.

Legacy, C., Curtis, C. and Scheurer. J. (2017), 'Planning transport infrastructure: Examining the politics of transport planning in Melbourne, Sydney and Perth', *Urban Policy and Research*, **34**(6), 1–17.

Legacy, C., Ashmore, D., Scheurer. J., Stone, J. and Curtis, C. (2018), 'Planning the driverless city', *Transport Reviews*, https://doi.org/10.1080/01441647.2018.1466835.

Low, N. and Astle, R. (2009), 'Path dependence in urban transport: An institutional analysis of urban passenger transport in Melbourne, Australia, 1956–2006', *Transport Policy*, **16**(2), 47–58.

Marsden, G. and Groer, S. (2016), 'Do institutional structures matter? A comparative analysis of urban carbon management policies in the UK and Germany', *Journal of Transport Geography*, **51**, 170–179.

Marsden, G. and McDonald, N. (2017), 'Institutional issues in planning for more uncertain futures', *Transportation*, https://doi.org/10.1007/s11116-017-9805-z.

Marsden, G. and Reardon, L. (2017), 'Questions of governance: Rethinking the study of transportation policy', *Transportation Research Part A: Policy and Practice*, **101**, 238–251.

Marsden, G. and Reardon, L. (2018), *Governance of the Smart Mobility Transition*, Bingley, UK: Emerald Publishing.

Paget-Seekins, L. and Tironi, M. (2016), 'The publicness of public transport: The changing nature of public transport in Latin American cities', *Transport Policy*, **49**, 176–183.

Rhodes, R. (1996), 'The new governance: Governing without government', *Political Studies*, **44**, 652–667.

Rhodes, R. (2011), 'Policy network analysis'. In D. Levi-Faur (Ed.), *The Oxford Handbook of Governance*, Oxford: Oxford University Press, pp. 425–447.

Skeete, J.-P. (2017), 'Examining the role of policy design and policy interaction in EU automotive emissions performance gaps', *Energy Policy*, **104**, 373–381.

Sperling, D. (2018), *Three Revolutions: Steering Automated, Shared and Electric Vehicles to a Better Future*, Washington, DC: Island Press.

Stead, D. and Meijers, E. (2009), 'Spatial planning and policy integration: Concepts, facilitators and inhibitors', *Planning Theory & Practice*, **10**(3), 317–332.

Stoker, G. (1998), 'Governance as theory: Five propositions', *International Social Science Journal*, **50**(155), 17–28.

Torfing, J., Peters, B.G., Pierre, J. and Sørensen, E. (2012), *Interactive Governance: Advancing the Paradigm*, Oxford: Oxford University Press.

Treib, O., Bähr, H. and Falkner, G. (2007), 'Modes of governance: Towards a conceptual clarification', *Journal of European Public Policy*, **14**(1), 1–20.

White, P. (2009), 'Factors behind recent patronage trends in Britain and their implications for future policy', *International Journal of Transport Economics*, **36**, 13–31.

# 6    Road transport infrastructure funding

*Georgina Santos*

## 6.1    Introduction

Roads are essential for the movement of goods and people, and thus for the economy and the welfare of a country. From an economic point of view, too much road space – or in other words, excess capacity all the time – implies a wasteful use of resources, and too little road space, with excess demand, yields a deadweight loss to society, or a welfare cost, mainly due to delays and their associated congestion costs.

Governments throughout the world are strapped for cash and struggle to find the resources required to satisfy competing demands from the different sectors they need to fund, such as education, health, defence and transport.

This chapter focuses on optimal road capacity and funding mechanisms, and concludes with some thoughts looking into the future.[1]

## 6.2    Some micro-economic considerations

### 6.2.1    Optimal road capacity[2]

Determining the optimal level of capacity is an economic problem. Small and Verhoef (2007) solve this problem by maximising social welfare, defined as benefits minus costs, with respect to vehicle flows and to capacity. Investment takes places until the marginal cost of the last unit of investment on road infrastructure is equal to the marginal benefit from lower congestion (Small and Verhoef, 2007, p. 164), which primarily means time savings benefits but also includes changes in other costs that are a function of congestion levels (e.g. fuel costs, air pollution) (UK Department for Transport, 2014).

---

1  Another area where (typically local) governments often, though not always, contribute financially, either by providing the service or subsidising it, is public transport. Stanley and Ljungberg (2018) provide an excellent discussion on the basis of Workshop 5 from Thredbo 15, which took place in 2017.

2  The interested reader should refer to Small and Verhoef (2007) for a full mathematical demonstration of the optimal investment rule, the optimal pricing rule and the self-financing capital cost.

When there is no congestion charging, however, adding new capacity will attract new or latent traffic and thus decrease social benefits (Small and Verhoef, 2007, p. 173). This is known as induced traffic. Essentially, when a new road is built, travel times initially decrease because average speeds are higher, faster travel times then attract more drivers to that road and the final result is more traffic and higher congestion than there was to begin with (Goodwin, 1996; Hills, 1996).

First-best congestion charges, which in their simplest form for a single road and a single time period are equal to the difference between short-run marginal and average cost (or marginal congestion cost, MCC), can be viewed as charges for the use of capacity (Small and Verhoef, 2007, p. 164). This pricing rule can be combined with the investment rule (of investing until the marginal cost of investment is equal to the marginal time saving from lower congestion) and thus relate total revenue to total cost.

First-best congestion charges 'exactly cover the cost of providing capacity if there are neutral scale economies in capacity provision' (Small and Verhoef, 2007, p. 165). If there are economies of scale then there is a deficit and if there are diseconomies of scale then there is a surplus (Small and Verhoef, 2007, p. 165). When there is a deficit the system will lose money and will need a government subsidy and when there is a surplus the system will make money. These results were first developed by Mohring and Harwitz (1962) and Vickrey (1963) and further expanded by Strotz (1964), Mohring (1970) and Keeler and Small (1977).

This understanding of optimal road capacity is crucial for an efficient use of limited resources, but it should also go hand in hand with land use planning. On the one hand, travel decisions depend largely on location and the way land at those locations is used and, on the other hand, transport facilities affect land use (Small and Verhoef, 2007, p. 12). As a result of this, integrated transport and land use planning – as opposed to land use planning, on the one hand, and transport planning, on the other – allows these interrelationships to be taken into account and to plan transport facilities and land use accordingly.

### 6.2.2   Road damage and other externalities

The assumption underlying the results above is that the rental cost of the highway depends on its width, and not on traffic. Newbery (1989) extends the model by assuming that road damage depends on traffic. Rather than charging for congestion only, vehicles can also be charged for the road damage they cause. A first-best road user charge would then include a congestion charge element and a road damage charge element.

When road user charges include other externalities, such as air pollution, noise, climate change and accidents, on top of congestion and road damage, the self-financing result still holds (Small and Verhoef, 2007, p. 171). Optimal congestion and road damage charges 'exactly cover capacity costs' and the revenues from charges for other externalities 'create a financial surplus' (Small and Verhoef, 2007, p. 171). From an economic point of view charging for other externalities internalises them and achieves an efficient (and lower) level of traffic.

## 6.3   Funding mechanisms

The result that first-best charges are enough to fund highways is clear and robust but there is not a single country in the world that has first-best charges.[3] All countries in the world, however, have highways. How these highways are funded varies by country.

Road infrastructure throughout the world is not always guaranteed a stable flow of revenues. One option to guarantee road infrastructure funding is to set up a Road Fund, typically fed with earmarked taxes. Alternatively, fuel and/or vehicle excise duties can be earmarked to road transport infrastructure funding, without necessarily going through a Road Fund. It should be emphasised, however, that unless fuel and vehicle taxes equal first-best charges,[4] the final result may not be efficient. A third way in which road infrastructure is often financed is through Public Private Partnerships, also discussed below.

### 6.3.1   Earmarking of taxes

Earmarking of taxes, such as vehicle excise duties or fuel duties, is the allocation of the revenues from such taxes to a specific expenditure. The British Treasury has always resisted hypothecating or earmarking taxes to particular purposes, with only a few exceptions (Newbery and Santos, 1999). The Treasury's view is that hypothecation of revenues should be limited to a few specific instances for which there is a very good case.

There are a number of advantages and disadvantages of earmarking taxes for road expansion and maintenance, as summarised by Queiroz (2003, p.7) and Santos (2007). The advantages include: (a) road users benefit from paying road taxes related to road use, and can see a clear link; (b) there is no underinvestment in roads as there is a guaranteed (protected) flow every year; and (c) it may be a successful way to increase public acceptability of higher taxes. The disadvantages include: (a) the government loses flexibility to decide how tax revenues are spent each year; (b) there could be a reduction in financial discipline, rather than an increase in efficiency of the road sector; and (c) earmarking prevents the funds from being spent somewhere else where there might be greater urgency or need.

---

3   A widely recognised problem that has prevented the introduction of congestion charging in many towns and cities around the world has been the lack of public and political acceptability. Singapore, London and Stockholm, however, show that these problems are not necessarily insurmountable.

4   Santos (2017) estimates that fuel duties in Europe more than cover congestion costs, and in some cases, although not always, cover other road transport externalities.

Conditions on revenue, however, could be included in an earmarking agreement. For example, if revenues exceeded certain benchmarks, the excess could be allocated to other uses, and this would provide a certain degree of flexibility.

### 6.3.2    Road Funds

A Road Fund is a fund that receives revenues, typically from fuel and/or vehicle excise duties, and whose revenues are exclusively allocated to the construction and maintenance of roads. It is essentially a more structured way of earmarking taxes, and therefore the advantages and disadvantages described above apply to road funds as well. If a Road Fund is set to operate independently from public transport planning and land use planning, and especially if there is no integrated land use and transport planning framework in place, then a Road Fund may exacerbate disjoint planning on both fronts, transport and land use, and not yield a coherent outcome. The very existence of a Road Fund could potentially discourage the use of integrated land use and transport models, at a time when governments are trying to adopt more integrated approaches.

In this section we briefly discuss the defunct British Road Fund, and the still operational Highway Trust Fund in the US.

#### 6.3.2.1    The Road Fund in the UK

The Road Fund in the UK was established in 1920 and abolished in 1955 (Bracewell-Milnes, 1991). The revenues consisted of motor licences, driving tests and driving licences. Fuel duties went to the Treasury instead. Although the Road Fund was initially set up to dedicate its revenues to road building and maintenance, it was not long before the Road Fund started to make payments to the Treasury. In 1936/37, payments to the Treasury amounted to over 40% of all disbursement (Bracewell-Milnes, 1991). In 1937 the hypothecation of motor vehicle licence duties to the Road Fund was ended. Between 1937 and 1955 the Road Fund had no revenues of its own and became merely an administrator of the grant in aid.

The gap between road tax revenues and expenditure on roads in the UK has been very large for decades (RAC Foundation, 2018) and earmarking road taxes or having a Road Fund would cause a substantial reduction in tax revenues for the Treasury.[5] Fuel duties are high, and together with vehicle excise duties represented 5.9% of total tax revenue in 2016/17.[6] From that, only 28.6% was spent on roads (RAC Foundation, 2018).[7]

---

5  It is worth noting that revenues from fuel taxes are set to decrease and eventually disappear as electric vehicles penetrate the market.

6  This is exclusive of VAT receipts, and was computed as fuel and vehicle duties, £33.8 billion (UK Department for Transport, 2018), divided by total tax revenue, £569.3 billion for 2016/17 (HM Revenue & Customs, 2018, p. 3, Table 1).

7  In the UK petrol taxes cover just over 70% of external costs of petrol cars and diesel taxes cover 53% of external costs of diesel cars and 34% of external costs of lorries (Santos, 2017).

### 6.3.2.2    *The Highway Trust Fund in the US*

The Highway Trust Fund in the US was established in 1956 and is still in place today. The Fund has three main sources of income: federal fuel taxes, other federal taxes on truck users, and interest on invested balances (US Federal Highway Administration Office of Policy and Governmental Affairs, 2017). The revenues from these are dedicated to funding highways in the US, to other surface transport and to public transport.

In contrast with the UK, federal fuel taxes in the US are very low. Probably due to these low taxes, since 2008, the Fund's expenditure has exceeded its revenues. Because of this, it has received additional revenues, mainly from the Treasury. In 2015, for example, the Treasury transferred $6.1 (€5.2) billion to the Fund. Fuel taxes along with other less important income totalled $35.7 (€30.6) billion, after subtracting transfers to other funds. The expenditure, however, was $43 (€36.9) billion, or 120% of its receipts before the transfer from the Treasury. Declining fuel tax revenues over coming years, as the vehicle fleet increasingly electrifies, and the absence of fuel tax indexation, suggest that the US urgently needs a replacement revenue source to its current Highway Trust Fund.

## 6.3.3    Private Public Partnerships

Private Public Partnerships (PPPs)[8] offer an option for governments that cannot, or choose not to, invest in a financially viable project either due to shortage of funds or other priorities. These types of partnerships are becoming more and more common (World Bank, 2018a), not just in developing countries but also in the US (World Bank, 2018b) and in Europe (Parada and Laserna, 2017).

Typically in PPP projects, the large capital expenditure required is provided by private finance and the maintenance and operating costs, as well as the return on investment, are part of the private sector responsibilities (Brocklebank, 2014). Often these resources are funded by tolls paid by users, generally regulated or capped, shadow tolls, paid by the government to the concessionaire (Brocklebank, 2014), according to traffic volume and composition (Queiroz and Izaguirre, 2008), or availability fees, also paid by the government to the concessionaire according to capacity, or number of lanes in acceptable condition rather than to traffic volumes (Queiroz and Izaguirre, 2008).

Road concessions are essentially monopolies, and therefore 'good governance is essential, to ensure that the private sector's involvement brings the maximum benefits to the public' (Queiroz and Izaguirre, 2008, p. 3). A key question is how a government can retain sufficient control of the network for policy implementation if it contracts out large chunks for long-term PPPs, which usually include restrictive conditions. Such matters are discussed in detail in Chapter 19 of this volume.

---

8  PPPs are discussed in detail in Chapter 19 of this volume.

### 6.3.4   Tolling versus road pricing reform across the entire network

Having discussed the pricing rule and the investment rule as well as ways to finance road infrastructure and tolling linked to PPPs, the natural question that emerges is whether tolling could or should replace or be replaced by a true road pricing reform across the entire network.

In real-world transport policy first-best pricing across an entire network can be very difficult to implement due to lack of public and political acceptability, often linked to equity issues. The regulator may therefore opt to price some but not all the links on a network, so that there are untolled alternatives. In its simplest version, this can be modelled as the two-route problem, with two competing, congested, perfect substitute roads linking the same origin and destination. Verhoef et al (1996) show that the efficient congestion charge when only one of the roads is tolled is not equal to the MCC on the tolled road but is equal to the MCC on the tolled road minus a non-negative term, which is a fraction of the MCC on the untolled road in the second-best optimum.

Tolling in Australia, particularly Sydney, is more extensive than anywhere else in the world. Hensher (2018) provides an excellent overview of the current situation and potential policy actions that could be implemented to make the pricing mechanism more efficient. As electric vehicles replace combustion engine ones and the revenues from fuel taxes decrease, this is an area which will become of utmost importance for most governments. Network pricing in such a setting will be complex, with the prospect of significant compensation payments to private concessionaires if major contractual changes are required.

## 6.4   Looking into the future

Fuel taxes constitute an important source of revenues in many countries, such as the UK, and although low in relative terms, in the US as well. These revenues help fund highways, indirectly in the UK, through the Treasury, and directly in the US, through the Highway Trust Fund.

These fuel taxes are set to decrease substantially over the next few decades, and eventually disappear because the transport sector is already in the process of being decarbonised. Electric vehicles are replacing fossil fuel propelled ones. The International Energy Agency (2018) forecasts that the number of electric cars in the world will reach 125 million by 2030 and, under stringent government policies, could reach 220 million. Although this could still only represent between 10 and 20% of the total car fleet in the world, the percentage share in developed countries is likely to be much higher than in developing countries. Over time, however, the whole world vehicle fleet will be electrified.

Slowly but steadily, fuel tax revenues will decline and alternative sources of revenues will be needed, eventually, everywhere. The time may be ripe then to finally charge drivers for congestion and road damage, or using an even longer-term view, when automated vehicles reduce congestion to zero, simply charge drivers for the use of roads so that these can be built and maintained.

This idea, indeed, is essentially the concept behind toll roads from PPPs, which, provided there is good governance and regulation to avoid monopolistic behaviour, provide a practical and attractive option for governments in both developing and developed countries to fund road infrastructure, provided governments do not lose policy control over their transport networks in the process of implementing PPPs.

## 6.5   Research priorities in transport policy related to road funding

Future research should look into better estimates of external costs and benefits of road transport (both private and public transport) and the use of these as input into policy. Efficient pricing/funding models are now essential and new forward thinking is needed with the eyes set on an increasingly electrified vehicle fleet. Understanding the politics of road pricing reform to assist effective implementation, the role of land value capture in road infrastructure funding, and how government can retain network control while engaging in PPPs are all under-researched topics in need of practical solutions. The quantification of external costs should encompass externalities associated with accelerated urban sprawl, when major new road building leads to significant volumes of generated traffic, as is the case in cities like Melbourne and Sydney at present. This is an area with great research potential, including multiple urban efficiency and equity dimensions.

## References

Bracewell-Milnes, B. (1991), 'Earmarking in Britain: Theory and practice', Part 2 of Teja, R. and Bracewell-Milnes, B. (Ed.), *The Case for Earmarked Taxes*, London: Institute of Economic Affairs.

Brocklebank, P. (2014), *Private Sector Involvement in Road Financing*, Africa Transport Policy Program, World Bank, Working Paper No. 102, December. http://documents.worldbank.org/curated/en/776191468338369513/Private-sector-involvement-in-road-financing. Accessed 20 April 2018.

Goodwin, P.B. (1996), 'Empirical evidence on induced traffic', *Transportation*, **23**(1), 35–54.

Hensher, D. (2018), 'Toll roads – a view after 25 years', *Transport Reviews*, **38**(1), 1–15.

Hills, P.J. (1996), 'What is induced traffic?', *Transportation*, **23**(1), 5–16.

HM Revenue & Customs (2018), *HMRC Tax & NIC Receipts: Monthly and Annual Historical Record*, National Statistics, 24 April. https://assets.publishing.service.gov.uk/government/uploads/system/uploads/attachment_data/file/708094/Mar18_Receipts_NS_Bulletin_Final.pdf. Accessed 20 April 2018.

International Energy Agency (2018), *Global EV Outlook 2018*. https://www.iea.org/gevo2018/. Accessed 12 April 2018.

Keeler, T. and K. Small (1977), 'Optimal peak-load pricing, investment, and service levels on urban expressways', *Journal of Political Economy*, **85**(1), 1–25.

Mohring, H. (1970), 'The peak load problem with increasing returns and pricing constraints', *American Economic Review*, **60**(4), 693–705. Cited in Keeler and Small (1977).

Mohring, H. and M. Harwitz (1962), *Highway Benefits: An Analytical Framework*, Evanston, IL: Northwestern University Press. Cited in Keeler and Small (1977).

Newbery, D.M. (1989), 'Cost recovery from optimally designed roads', *Economica*, **56**(May), 165–185.

Newbery, D. and G. Santos (1999), 'Road taxes, road user charges and earmarking', *Fiscal Studies*, **20**(3), 103–132.

Parada, J. and M. Laserna (2017), *European Public-Private Partnership Transport Market*, Deloitte, Madrid, September. https://www2.deloitte.com/content/dam/Deloitte/es/Documents/infraestructuras-real-estate/Deloitte-ES-Infraestructuras-ppp-market.pdf. Accessed 20 April 2018.

Queiroz, C. (2003), 'A Review of Alternative Road Financing Methods', paper presented at the Transport Infrastructure Development for a Wider Europe Seminar, Paris, 27–28 November. http://unpan1.un.org/intradoc/groups/public/documents/UNTC/UNPAN013148.pdf. Accessed 10 April 2018.

Queiroz, C. and A. Izaguirre (2008), 'Worldwide trends in private participation in roads: Growing activity, growing government support', *Gridlines*, Note 37. https://ppp.worldbank.org/public-private-partnership/sites/ppp.worldbank.org/files/ppp_testdumb/documents/Gridlines-37-Worldwide%20Trends%20in%20Private%20-%20CQueiroz%20AIzaguirre.pdf. Accessed 6 April 2018.

RAC Foundation (2018), *UK public road expenditure and taxation.* https://www.racfoundation.org/data/road-user-taxation-highways-spending-data-chart. Accessed 31 May 2018.

Santos, G. (2007), 'Road User Charges and Infrastructure', 135 Round Table of the European Conference of Ministers of Transport on Transport Infrastructure Charges and Capacity Choice, Paris, 29–30 September 2005. https://www.oecd-ilibrary.org/transport/ecmt-round-tables_19900228. Accessed 6 April 2018.

Santos, G. (2017), 'Road fuel taxes in Europe: Do they internalise road transport externalities?', *Transport Policy*, **53**, 120–134.

Small, K. and E. Verhoef (2007), *Economics of Urban Transportation*, London: Routledge.

Stanley, J. and A. Ljungberg (2018), 'Bridging the benefit/funding gap: Report on Thredbo 15 Workshop 5', *Research in Transportation Economics*, **69**, 438–444.

Strotz, R. (1964), 'Urban transportation parables'. In Margolis, J. (Ed.), *The Public Economy of Urban Communities*, Baltimore, MD: Johns Hopkins Press. Cited in Keeler and Small (1977).

UK Department for Transport (2018), Table TSGB1311 (RDE0103), Road taxation revenue in the United Kingdom: 2016/17. https://www.gov.uk/government/statistical-data-sets/rdeo1-road-construction-and-taxation#table-rdeo101. Accessed 6 April 2018.

US Federal Highway Administration Office of Policy and Governmental Affairs (2017), Funding Federal-aid Highways: Publication No. FHWA-PL-17-011, January. https://www.fhwa.dot.gov/policy/olsp/fundingfederalaid/07.cfm. Accessed 6 April 2018.

Verhoef, E., Nijkamp, P. and Rietveld, P. (1996), 'Second-best congestion pricing: The case of an untolled alternative', *Journal of Urban Economics*, **40**, 279–302.

Vickrey, W. (1963), 'Pricing in urban and suburban transport', *American Economic Review*, **53**(May), 452–465.

World Bank (2018a), 'Public-Private Partnerships in roads'. https://ppp.worldbank.org/public-private-partnership/sector/transportation/roads-tolls-bridges/road-concessions. Accessed 30 May 2018.

World Bank (2018b), 'USA – Guidebook and case studies for transportation Public-Private Partnerships. https://ppp.worldbank.org/public-private-partnership/library/us-guidebook-and-case-studies-transportation-public-private-partnerships-2007. Accessed 30 May 2018.

# PART III

Modal perspectives

# 7    Public transport

*Chris Nash and Daniel Johnson*

## 7.1    Introduction

Public transport has long been seen as a solution to the environmental and congestion problems of car and air transport. For instance, the European Commission wishes to see rail as the main mode of medium-distance passenger transport in Europe (European Commission, 2011), whilst also arguing for an expanded role for public transport in urban areas. Yet public transport is often seen as bound to decline, with widening car ownership, and in the long run will come under pressure from new technologies such as autonomous electric cars. So a key issue is to understand better the demand for public transport and the influence of factors which may change it, such as changing tastes, land use and the sharing economy. Of course, advances in public transport technology are also crucial; further automation of operations, ticketing and information will open up new possibilities in terms of infrastructure capacity, pricing, service levels and quality of service.

A second major area is efficiency of public transport supply. In many countries, public transport has for many decades been a public sector monopoly. There has been much concern with its efficiency and calls for a greater role for the private sector. But even in bus transport, there remains no consensus on what this means in terms of the combination of competitive tendering, on road competition, regulation and negotiated quality contracts. For rail and light rail modes, the options are more complex, including whether infrastructure should be integrated with operations, contract length and asset ownership, which raise more issues in rail than bus because of longer asset life. Given severe public sector budget constraints, Public Private Partnerships (PPPs) are an attractive option, but the record of success in rail is not strong, and other ways of financing public transport must also be examined. It is also often argued that existing methods of investment appraisal undervalue the advantages of public transport over other modes, whilst there remain many uncertainties regarding other issues, such as wider economic impacts, in updated approaches to investment appraisal.

In this chapter we consider in turn public transport demand, technological change, supply and investment before reaching our conclusions.

## 7.2    Public transport demand

Many commentators assume that public transport is inevitably on a path of decline, attributable particularly to rising car ownership along with reduced motoring costs and improved car journey times, as a result of major investment in road systems. There is strong evidence of the impact of all these variables on bus and rail patronage (TRL, 2004). This was indeed the broad pattern of development in Britain from 1960 to 1990. However, many Western European countries did not experience such a decline, and even in Britain it has been reversed since 1990, at least for rail and for buses in London.

What are the major factors leading to this reversal? A study of rail in Britain (Wardman, 2006) concluded that by the 1990s car ownership growth had markedly slowed down (and even fallen in some younger groups of the population, for whom it is seen as less of a priority as lifestyles change and people start families much later), whilst higher motoring costs, particularly insurance, and longer car journey times (as rising congestion outweighed a slower pace of road investment) also played a part (Independent Transport Commission, 2016). Demographic change is also important, with rising proportions of older people in many countries. Other important factors have been changes in the structure of employment (the growth of services in place of manufacturing) and associated changes in land use, with more commuting into city centres and, in many jurisdictions, land use planning concentrating development into existing urban areas rather than allowing sprawl (ITS et al., 2016). Population density has been identified as a strong influence on public transport patronage (TRL, 2004).

Much of Western Europe has retained a higher population density in urban areas than Britain, with suburbanisation planned around public transit corridors and high investment in new public transport systems, especially metro and light rail. There has been a high level of integration of public transport in countries such as Switzerland, Germany and Sweden, with planning of all modes often in the hands of regional authorities (Van de Velde, 2001). In some countries, there has also been an explicit policy of backing public transport against the car, with restraint particularly on car parking (and in a few cities, including London, Stockholm and Oslo, road pricing). However, rural areas have seen a continuing growth in car ownership and use, with the problem of maintaining services for those without access to a car becoming more acute. Increasingly the solution is being seen as community transport, with volunteers providing scheduled or dial-a-ride on demand services (Mulley and Nelson, 2012). Ultimately the economics of these could be revolutionised by developments in communications and automated driving.

Looking ahead, the role of public transport will continue to depend heavily on government policy towards land use, public transport investment and the car, including parking and road pricing. Further research is needed on other factors, such as the causes and consequences of the lifestyle changes referred to above. But technological change is the cause of greatest uncertainty, as it now offers the prospect of considerable acceleration of change, and the future impact of this on public transport is perhaps the most urgent research need.

## 7.3    Technological change

Technological change has obviously played a major part in changes in the transport sector over the last 50 years, and particularly in rail transport. The replacement of steam by diesel and electric traction, and the introduction of power signalling systems that could be controlled from a remote control centre enabled major economies in labour and improvements in service. High speed rail technology has permitted rail to compete with air for journeys of up to 1000km (Nash, 2013). Automated metros have become common since the opening of the Lille Metro in 1983, and automation of main line services is foreseen in the next few years. Automation is not simply a means of saving labour; by making it possible to provide frequent short trains as cheaply as less frequent long trains, it permits a big improvement in service quality, and by eliminating variability in driver behaviour, it maximises capacity and reliability. Moving block cab signalling systems are starting to be introduced which offer a further prospect of improving capacity, and research is underway on virtual coupling of trains which could increase capacity and flexibility even more, permitting through services on a greater number of routes as trains join and split automatically. The vision of the European Shift2rail research programme is a 100% increase in capacity, a 50% increase in reliability and a 50% reduction in cost (Shift2rail, 2015).

Technological change to date has been less marked in the bus industry, but that may be changing. Already advances in battery design have permitted introduction of electric or hybrid vehicles, without the cost and inflexibility of overhead wires. Fully automated bus systems are already running on an experimental basis (in China and the US, for example) and, because they run to a fixed route, are simpler to achieve than fully automated cars. Priority at junctions and segregation from general traffic on congested sections by construction of bus lanes, busways or guideways enables buses to achieve speeds approaching those of light rail or metros whilst maintaining the flexibility to serve points off the segregated system by using local roads.

Technological change is also important in terms of information and ticketing. Already real-time information may be obtained via Google or journey planning apps like Citymapper and, for many rail and coach systems, ticket purchases and seat reservations may be made by smartphone. Research is proceeding on how to ensure that these systems cover all modes of transport and guide the passenger step-by-step through the journey, with exact information on where to go at stations and other interchanges (see, for instance, the Shift2rail Co-Active project). Smart card ticketing systems are spreading, and in London any contactless credit or debit card may be used, completely removing the need to spend time on line or at a machine topping up a smartcard.

But of course technology for the private car is not standing still either. Cars are rapidly improving in reliability, energy efficiency and technical aids to the driver, many improving safety. Electric private cars are spreading, although they remain expensive in terms of first cost, if cheap to run. Full automation of private cars may still be many years off, but there is enormous research effort on this, and – combined with growth in shared ownership – may ultimately make private car use effectively available to most people. When autonomous driving becomes so reliable that the driver no longer needs to supervise the system, then the big advantage of public transport that the traveller can usefully use the time spent travelling will be removed. Also, if vehicles become so safe that seat belts are no longer required, then greater flexibility of vehicle design will be possible (the car industry already dreams of cars designed as offices, meeting rooms and even bedrooms). Full automation will also enable more efficient use of road space (although not if the added flexibility of vehicle design leads on average to much larger vehicles and/or more vehicle time on-road).

At the same time, technology has permitted the development of taxi services such as Uber that may be called much more quickly, and with the increased possibility of sharing them. These are a clear challenge to traditional urban bus services; indeed research has suggested that both traditional urban bus services and private cars in urban areas may be completely replaced, in an efficient way, by demand responsive systems using shared taxis and minibuses (International Transport Forum, 2017a).

The concept of Mobility as a Service (see Mulley 2017, and Chapter 21 of this volume) packages these developments in digital and vehicle technologies to promise a single on-demand service tailored to users' needs, encompassing sharing, public transport and taxi-based services with a simple payment platform. Such services are now emerging across the US and Europe through apps such as Switch and Whim.

Researching the implications for the public transport sector of these technological developments is the most urgent requirement; yet it is also exceedingly difficult. It involves forecasting how passengers will respond to the availability of services which either do not exist, or only exist in limited trials. That means that there is limited scope for revealed preference methods, and stated preference methods, although they deal with hypothetical options, are known to be least reliable when dealing with the unfamiliar. Moreover, there remains enormous uncertainty as to exactly what the characteristics will be, of the services to which the technological developments will lead.

## 7.4  Supply

In recent decades, concerns about efficiency have led to the supply of public transport in many countries being moved away from a public sector monopoly to being contracted out to the private sector, or in some cases completely left to the private sector on a commercial basis. In Britain outside London, in 1986 the local bus market was completely opened up to the private sector on a competitive basis, with private operators able to provide whatever they wished in terms of routes, timetables and fares. Local authorities were confined to the role of providing subsidies, by means of competitive tendering, to fill gaps in the commercial network (either geographical gaps or gaps by time, such as evenings or Sundays). Debate continues over the degree of success of this approach (Preston and Almutairi, 2013). It certainly reduced costs (but so did competitive tendering, as adopted in London), but it did not immediately reverse the decline of patronage, whereas the planned, integrated competitively tendered system in London did (but of course there are many differences between London and the rest of Britain). Even in British cities where there is free market entry, there has been the development of partnership arrangements between local authorities and operators, with investment by local authorities in more bus priorities and information matched by improved services, and legislation does make the introduction of a franchising system possible under certain conditions. Most countries which have liberalised entry into the bus industry have followed the London model, whereby a transport authority defines routes, timetables and fares, but then goes out to competitive tender to secure services. However, open entry for commercial operators of long-distance services is now required under European Union law, and such services are developing as competitors for long-distance rail services in Europe.

In the rail industry there has also been the development of both competition in and for the market (Nash et al., 2016). The first country to privatise its rail passenger services was Japan in 1987, but it did so as a set of geographically based vertically integrated companies, with competition confined to places where there were competing routes run by smaller companies (quite common in suburban passenger transport in Japan). The European Commission adopted a policy more focused on introducing within-industry competition, by seeking the separation of infrastructure from operations, with open entry for new commercial operators and competitive tendering for public service contracts for subsidised services. In practice it could never get agreement to complete vertical separation, so a holding company model, in which the state-owned infrastructure and passenger train operators remain separate subsidiaries of the same holding company, exists in some countries (including France, Germany, Austria and Italy). This has advantages in terms of coordinating planning and investment (Mizutani et al., 2014) but raises fears of discrimination against new entrants. To deal with this, all EU member states are required to have a regulator with powers to investigate and take action in the case of alleged discrimination. So far, open access for commercial operators is only legally required for international services; this will come in for domestic services in 2020 and competition for public services contracts in 2023. But several countries have already introduced both these measures. In Italy, a private operator now duplicates the main high speed services on the new high speed lines, whilst intense on-track competition exists on the main conventional lines in Sweden, Austria and the Czech Republic. Whilst they have invariably led to better services at lower costs, there are also concerns that they may hamper efficient use of limited track capacity and, by reducing the profitability of incumbents, lead to other services being withdrawn. A number of the new entrants also operate long-distance bus services (as indeed do incumbents) and an interesting development is the formation of an alliance between some of the new rail entrants and private long-distance bus operators, leading to development of an integrated bus-rail network, competing with the network of the incumbent.

Where competitive tendering is practised, there is an enormous range of options, from short tightly specified gross cost contracts, where often the authority provides depots and vehicles, to long net cost contracts, where the operator has much more choice regarding timetables and fares and secures its own vehicles. Naturally the former is more likely for regional services and the latter for more commercial long-distance services. But competition may not be the only way to achieve an efficient public transport network. Switzerland is generally recognised to have a very efficient public transport network, with virtually no competition for or in the market. The Swiss success seems to come from decentralisation of local transport to the Cantons, with strongly incentivised contracts, but with the entire network integrated in terms of timetables and fares as a condition of government subsidies.

In low density areas, public transport is often still losing patronage, and in some countries, including Britain, budget constraints are leading to significant loss of services. There is a growing use of the voluntary sector providing car or minibus services, either scheduled or dial-a-ride, in such areas.

Again, there remains a need for further research on what approach works best in what circumstances, including high-level choices such as competition in or for the market, the role of shared taxi and minibus services and the details of the approach to contracts. But one important factor to consider in such decisions is how best to encourage the sort of technological developments outlined in the previous section. The vision for information and ticketing requires the participation of all operators, and is most likely to come about under the control of a single authority. Franchisees, particularly when franchised for short time periods, have little incentive to drive forward long-term innovations. Regulatory systems, such as control the monopoly public sector rail infrastructure companies in Europe, tend to emphasise short-term cost reductions rather than long-term innovations. So innovation may need to be driven by a combination of outside bodies providing funding for research and development and carefully designed incentives within the regulatory and franchising system.

## 7.5   Investment

In most countries, public transport investments are subject to a full cost-benefit analysis, considering costs to operators and government, benefits to users and benefits from diverting passengers from cars. Benefits to users have been expanded beyond simply time savings to take in aspects of comfort and convenience including better information, reliability and ability to get a seat. There is a need to keep valuation of time savings up to date, as it is often argued that technological developments making it easier to make effective use of time spent travelling will reduce the value of time savings. However, the latest study in Britain found no evidence of this for commuting and business journeys over 100 miles, whilst it did produce a lower value of leisure time and shorter-distance business journeys (as a proportion of the wage rate) than previous research (Arup et al., 2015).

In some countries, there has been research on other benefits of public transport, including reduced social exclusion (Stanley et al., 2011) and option values – the value that non-public-transport users place on having a public transport service available as a standby should they need it (Laird et al., 2009). Substantial benefits have been found in the former case, whilst in the latter case evidence of significant values has been obtained particularly for services to cities from small towns within commuting distance, where people may particularly value having the option of taking a job in the city and commuting by public transport. It does not make sense to pay a lot to have public transport available for very occasional use, such as when a car breaks down, as taxis would be a viable option here, but the possible need to commute every day is a more likely cause of substantial option values.

But in recent times there has been an emphasis on appraisal of wider economic impacts, the inclusion of which can significantly bolster the benefit-cost ratio of a project. Agglomeration effects (increased productivity from improved accessibility to other firms, customers and workforce) have formed a significant part of the case for recent public transport investments in London, such as the new Crossrail cross London rail service (Venables, 2007) and its proposed successor Crossrail2, both directly, from improved accessibility for existing locations, and indirectly by promoting concentration of jobs in city centres. There has been much more debate about whether intercity service improvements also have wider economic impacts, for instance by increasing specialisation and thus economies of scale (Venables et al., 2014). Other wider economic impacts include additional tax income from increased and more productive employment arising from reduced commuting costs and the additional value of increased output in imperfectly competitive markets. For an international review of wider economic impacts in appraisals see Wangsness et al. (2017). Another stream of literature focuses on land value impact as both a proxy for economic impact (see, for example, Debrezion et al., 2007) and as a potential means of financing large-scale infrastructure projects (e.g., Crossrail). What is clear is that major transport investments may set up significant land use changes and thus distributional effects even if these are not necessarily net benefits.

The other big issue with public transport investments is their affordability. There remains strong interest in value capture mechanisms and in Public Private Partnerships to fund investments, even if the history of these is relatively discouraging: this is particularly so for rail schemes, which, because of their long time scales and uncertain demand, have often needed renegotiation and the public sector has ended up taking on a greater responsibility than was originally foreseen (International Transport Forum, 2017b).

Despite the amount of work in these areas, wider socio-economic impacts and methods of financing investments remain priorities for further research.

## 7.6    Conclusions

This is a time of great uncertainty but also opportunity for the future of public transport. After a long period in which many saw decline as inevitable, some trends favourable to public transport have emerged, but more research is needed to understand fully their causes and sustainability. Major technological changes are underway in both public transport and the private car, but again the full implications of these for public transport are not yet understood. At the same time, longstanding research issues such as the best way to organise the provision of public transport and how to appraise investment remain subject to uncertainty. In particular, the best way of encouraging innovation in public transport and the issue of the wider socio-economic impacts of public transport investment remain a priority for future research.

## References

Arup et al. (2015), *Provision of Market Research for Value of Travel Time Savings and Reliability*, London: Department for Transport.

Debrezion, G., Pels, E. and Rietveld, P. (2007), 'The impact of railway stations on residential and commercial property value: A meta-analysis', *Journal of Real Estate Finance and Economics*, **35**, 161–180.

European Commission (2011), *Roadmap to a Single European Transport Area – Towards a Competitive and Resource Efficient Transport System*, Brussels: Author.

Independent Transport Commission (2016), *Recent Trends in Road and Rail Travel: What Do They Tell Us?* London: Author. http://www.theitc.org.uk/wp-content/uploads/2016/12/OTM2-Policy-Analysis.pdf. Accessed 3 October 2018.

International Transport Forum (2017a), *Shared Mobility Simulations for Helsinki*, Paris: OECD.

International Transport Forum (2017b), 'Public Private Partnerships for transport infrastructure: Renegotiation and economic outcomes', *Round Table report 161*, Paris: OECD.

ITS, Leigh-Fisher, Rand Europe and Systra (2016). *Rail Demand Forecasting Estimation: Final Report*, London: Department for Transport.

Laird, J., Geurs, K. and Nash, C.A. (2009), 'Option and non-use values and rail appraisal', *Transport Policy*, **16**, 173–182.

Mizutani F., Smith A.S.J., Nash C.A. and Uranishi, S. (2014), 'Comparing the costs of vertical separation, integration and intermediate organisational structures in European and East Asian railways', *Transport Economics and Policy*, **49**(3), 496–515.

Mulley, C. (2017), 'Mobility as a Services (MaaS) – does it have critical mass?', *Transport Reviews*, **37**(3), 247–251, DOI: 10.1080/01441647.2017.1280932.

Mulley, C. and Nelson, J.D. (2012), 'Recent developments in community transport provision: Comparative experience from Britain and Australia', *Procedia – Social and Behavioural Sciences*, **48**, 1815–1825.

Nash, C.A. (2013), 'When to invest in high-speed rail', *Discussion Paper No. 2013-25*, Paris: International Transport Forum.

Nash, C.A. et al. (2016), 'Liberalisation of rail passenger services', CERRE Discussion Paper, Brussels.

Preston, J. and Almutairi, T. (2013), 'Evaluating the long term impacts of transport policy: An initial assessment of bus deregulation', *Research in Transportation Economics*, **39**(1), 208–212.

Shift2rail (2015), *Strategic Master Plan*. Brussels.

Stanley, J.K., Hensher, D.A., Stanley, J.R., Currie, G. and Greene, W. (2011), 'Social exclusion and the value of mobility', *Journal of Transport Economics and Policy*, **45**(2), 197–222.

TRL (2004), 'The demand for public transport: A practical guide', *TRL Report 593*. Crowthorne: Author.

Van de Velde, D. (2001), 'The Evolution of Organisational Forms in European Public Transport'. 7th Conference on Competition and Ownership in Land Passenger Transport, Molde (Norway), 25–28 June 2001.

Venables, A., Laird, J.J. and Overman, H.G. (2014), 'Transport investment and economic performance: Implications for project appraisal', *Research Report*, London: Department for Transport.

Venables, A.J. (2007), 'Evaluating urban transport improvements. Cost–benefit analysis in the presence of agglomeration and income taxation', *Journal of Transport Economics and Policy*, **41**(2), 173–188.

Wangsness, P.B., Rødseth, K.L. and Hansen, W. (2017), 'A review of guidelines for including wider economic impacts in transport appraisal', *Transport Reviews*, **37**(1), 94–115, DOI: 10.1080/01441647.2016.1217283.

Wardman, M.R. (2006), 'Demand for rail travel and the effects of external factors', *Transportation Research Part E*, **42**, 129–148.

# 8    Active transport perspectives

*Stephen Greaves and Christopher Standen*

## 8.1    Introduction

This chapter provides perspectives on active transport, which covers walking, cycling and other variants operating under human power. Active transport provides an important alternative to the private motor vehicle, both in and of itself, and as a means for accessing public transport with increasingly well-touted health and wider sustainability benefits to the individual and broader society. However, these benefits continue to be compromised by safety concerns, the perceived limitations of active transport in meeting day-to-day mobility needs, and transport systems and policies justified using evaluation methods that privilege car use, often at the expense of active transport.

In the developed world, rapid motorisation and suburbanisation since World War II were associated with declining levels of active transport. However, beginning in the 1970s, governments of Western Europe, particularly the Netherlands, Germany and Denmark, invested heavily in infrastructure programs and policies, which significantly increased active transport shares. This provided impetus to many North and South American, European and Australian cities, struggling with the unsustainable costs of motorised travel (congestion, pollution, safety) and mounting public health concerns over sedentary behaviour to promote cycling and walking. This has seen large increases in cycling in cities without a cycling culture, including London, Paris, Vienna, Buenos Aires and San Francisco (Pucher & Buehler, 2017). Key to this process has been the development of evaluation methods that consider the travel, health and wider societal benefits of active transport.

Although this chapter is prepared primarily for a transportation-based audience, it is evident that active transport scholars must employ a cross-disciplinary lens drawing from areas including sociology, psychology, urban planning, environmental planning and public health. Acknowledging we cannot cover all the issues around active transport here, this chapter is organised around the following themes: (1) influencers of active travel choices; (2) health and wellbeing considerations; (3) policy interventions to increase active travel and evaluation approaches; (4) contemporary issues, including bike share, e-bikes and autonomous vehicles.

## 8.2   Active travel choices

A body of knowledge has built up around factors impacting active transport choices, in both the real-word (e.g., using travel surveys) and hypothetical settings (e.g., using stated preference surveys). Active transport comprises a variety of modes (primarily walking and cycling) that have differing determinants affecting participation (Blanco et al., 2009). For cycling, focus is primarily on mode and route choice, with the choice to cycle influenced to varying degrees by individual characteristics (gender, age, income, education, cycling experience, bicycle and car ownership), the trip (cost, time, distance, gradient, surface type, separated cycling facility, traffic mix/speed), end of trip facilities (parking/storage, shower), built environment and contextual factors (weather, day/night). Although the prevalence of walking is substantially higher than cycling, the former has received less attention in the academic literature. Most of the research on walking propensity has been around the influence of urban form, principally population density, land-use mix/ accessibility, quality open space and street connectivity (Saelens & Handy, 2008; Smith et al., 2017). Together, these factors influence the 'walkability score/index' of a neighbourhood, a useful tool for identifying barriers to walking participation.

While much is now known about the factors impacting mode and route choice, particularly of cycling, little is documented about other choices (e.g., the choice of bicycle type – road, mountain, hybrid, electric, etc.). We also have little evidence of how individual tastes change over time, and how they are shaped by policy interventions (Standen, 2017). It is also rare to validate stated preference experiments, i.e., verify the extent to which the forecasts manifest in reality; when done, there is evidently significant diversion from stated intentions or 'hypothetical bias' (Fifer, Rose, & Greaves, 2014).

## 8.3   Health and wellbeing considerations

A substantial body of evidence now exists demonstrating that active transport has positive benefits both for the individual traveller and broader society (Saunders, Green, Petticrew, Steinbach, & Roberts, 2013). Benefits largely accrue from increases in physical activity and other health/wellbeing outcomes associated with being active and decreases in negative externalities associated with reduced motor vehicle use (air quality, noise, amenity, road crashes). Physical activity benefits of active transport have been demonstrated for all-cause mortality, cardiovascular disease, obesity and type 2 diabetes (Andersen, Schnohr, Schroll, & Hein, 2000). Researchers have attributed a broader array of health and wellbeing benefits to active transport users, including improved quality of life, lower levels of social exclusion, and even feeling happier while commuting (Rissel, Crane, Wen, Greaves, & Standen, 2016). Several studies have documented the benefits of reduced motor vehicle use to the broader community, including increased community cohesion, more liveable communities, and reducing barrier effects of road infrastructure (Litman, 2018).

A correspondingly large body of evidence suggests that vulnerable road users are at greater risk of death or serious injury from road-related crashes. Globally, vulnerable road users constitute roughly half of road fatalities, although this is higher in lower-income countries. Even in higher-income countries like Australia, the relative risk of being injured as a cyclist/km is around 19 times higher than in a car (Garrard & Greaves, 2010).[1] We also know that, as levels of active transport rise, the relative risk of death or injury as a cyclist or pedestrian generally goes down (even more so if there is commensurate investment in safety measures), the 'safety in numbers' phenomenon (Jacobsen, 2003). We also know that, while there are unquestionable risks associated with active travel, often the main barrier to usage is the *perception* it is more unsafe than being in a car (Jacobsen, Racioppi, & Rutter, 2009). This extends to other dimensions of safety, which can be overlooked in the promotion of active transport (particularly walking) around personal safety/ stranger danger (Saelens & Handy, 2008).

Active transport is now as much a public health priority as a sustainable transport issue, given both the limited success of strategies focused on increasing leisure-time physical activity (e.g., only 40% of Australians meet daily recommended levels of physical activity) and the intrinsic appeal of incorporating physical activity into day-to-day travel. However, questions remain around the health/wellbeing impacts of active transport. First, despite recent evidence that all-cause mortality is reduced with active transport (Mueller et al., 2015), we assert that questions around the benefits versus risks of active transport (cycling in particular) remain and are highly context-specific. Questions also remain about other health impacts of active transport, including exposure to noxious pollutants (Schepers et al., 2015).

Second, despite the touted health benefits of active transport, it is often hard to establish causality between active transport levels and health outcomes – for instance, in their study of 14 developed countries, while Pucher, Buehler, Bassett, and Dannenberg (2010) suggest a negative association between active transport levels, obesity and type 2 diabetes, the results were insufficient to establish causality. This is largely down to challenges in measuring health effects and numerous confounders to isolating the effects of active transport, an issue we consider later.

Third, the raft of different approaches to safety interventions shows that, despite some general principles, there is much that divides us. For instance, an ongoing area of discourse is compulsory helmet laws, such as those in Australia, New Zealand and parts of North America. Questions continue to be raised around their effectiveness in reducing specific types of injuries (Elvik, 2011) and their impact on cycling rates (Fishman, Washington, & Haworth, 2012). Future studies could disaggregate low-speed transport/utility cycling and high-risk sport cycling. A finding that helmet use has no significant impact on the injury risk for utility cycling

---

1 When measured on a per trip basis, the relative risk is similar to driving given the shorter trip lengths on average for cycling and walking (Teschke et al., 2013).

would raise questions over policies to make them mandatory for all types of cycling – given that most sport cyclists use them anyway.

Fourth, while the proliferation of mobile devices throughout society has provided benefits (e.g., route guidance, emergency contact) for active travellers, we voice an urgent need to research distraction-related accidents and potential longer-term health and wellbeing impacts of our addiction to these technologies. Some authorities are taking actions to address distracted walking (e.g., in-ground walk signals).

## 8.4   Policy, forecasting and evaluation

Mounting scientific evidence suggests the key to increasing levels of active transport is the physical separation of cycling/walking and motor vehicles for highly trafficked roads, and comprehensive traffic calming in residential areas to slow motor vehicles (Pucher & Buehler, 2017). It is also evident that strong political will, supported by legal frameworks that provide protection/support for vulnerable road users and educational programs focused on both the active traveller and motorist awareness, are critical elements in achieving an 'active transport culture'. Despite this, many cities, particularly those largely built around the car, have struggled to justify active transport programs and policies, and end up with piece-meal solutions. The issue now is whether countries that followed this latter path, such as Australia and North America, have both the will and fortitude to re-visit land-use development and infrastructure to be more conducive to active transport. Neo-traditional developments such as Transit Oriented Development and the 20-minute city are largely a step in the right direction, in that they consider land-use/transport together (Stanley, 2014). However, without complementary restrictions on car use, their effectiveness wanes.

While much has been documented about policy interventions designed to increase active transport, their effectiveness continues to be hampered by incomplete/inconclusive evaluations (Pucher, Dill, & Handy, 2010). Critics will argue this reflects the prioritisation/bias given to vehicular travel, particularly the heavy focus on travel time savings, which tends to undervalue 'slower' modes – as an aside, there is evidence to suggest that cycling has become increasingly competitive with road-based modes as congestion continues to worsen (Ellison & Greaves, 2011). However, it also reflects a paucity of active travel data on both the demand and supply/infrastructure side, a lack of behavioural paradigms underlying the choice of active travel, and disagreement on how to define and quantify the wider benefits of active transport investments, particularly health and wellbeing (Porter, Suhrbier, & Schwartz, 1999).

### 8.4.1   Data collection/travel surveys

The known challenges of conducting travel surveys are exacerbated with active travel for various reasons. First, the prevalence among the population is low (particularly for cycling) and, while people generally do recall cycling trips, walking tends to be under/mis-reported as it is often incidental to another 'primary' mode. Second, walking/cycling duration and intensity are important for health valuations, yet are poorly captured from self-reported data. In response, researchers have equipped participants with an array of GPS devices, accelerometers and smartphones designed to better capture travel (Greaves et al., 2015). Third, measurement challenges are compounded when trying to assess changes in travel/health outcomes following a policy intervention, where changes are often marginal and may take some time to eventuate (Crane et al., 2017). While future research could focus on improving elements of the current processes, an alternate pathway could be to harness the abundance of 'big data' coming from smartphones, if we can overcome ongoing privacy/ethical concerns.

### 8.4.2    Forecasting active travel choices

The main advances in forecasting demand for active travel have come from nations with reasonable modal shares, such as the Netherlands. For many others, a fundamental challenge is trying to forecast change off a low base, particularly for cycling. Most operational travel forecasting tools have been developed for motorised modes. They are not well-suited for modelling short, active transport trips, for various reasons including: trip origins/destinations typically being approximated to zone centroids, networks assumed to be the same as for vehicular travel, which are too coarse and ignore paths, short-cuts, etc., and the use of shortest path traffic assignment algorithms that cannot capture the realities of cyclist/pedestrian route choice, which is often a less direct route to avoid busy roads, use a cycleway, go through a park, etc.

### 8.4.3    Appraisal

The appraisal process for a proposed project/policy involves two problems: (a) identifying and forecasting the benefits (and costs), and (b) putting these on a common scale, typically monetary, such that they can be assessed against other projects competing for finite resources. The process is more complex than appraising highway and public transport improvements, because many of the benefits are more subjective and difficult to quantify (Litman, 2018).

Health benefits, particularly those associated with increased physical activity, have received the most attention, but there is no consensus on the correct methodological approach, and valuations vary considerably (Mulley, Tyson, McCue, Rissel, & Munro, 2013). Future research could attempt to validate some of the forecast health benefits of active travel interventions, which typically take time to eventuate. Additionally, there are key questions around who really benefits and to what extent, the marginal health benefits, and the extent to which people consider health benefits when they make active transport choices.

Other dimensions underlying the positive utility of active travel are even more subjective and contentious. Standen (2017) demonstrates the use of the logsum measure of consumer surplus (an output of disaggregate demand forecasting models) to capture the negative and positive utility of all the mode choices available to a traveller. If the utility of an active travel option increases, for example through the provision of a new bicycle path, then the consumer surplus can increase, even if the travel time does also. He identifies several avenues for future research, including the need to assess if/how people's preferences for active travel change over time, and/or when significant changes are made to the walking/cycling environment, and how to effectively communicate this 'positive utility' of travel to decision makers.

## 8.5    Contemporary issues

This chapter would not be complete without some consideration of issues on the near (or far) horizon and how they might impact active transport. First is bikeshare, in which bicycles are made available for short-term rental typically at an affordable price or free with the purpose of providing a sustainable alternative to motor vehicles for short-distance travel in urban areas. The origins of bicycle share can be traced back to the 1960s in the Netherlands, and as of 2016 there were 1,000 schemes operational worldwide.[2] Most bikeshare schemes are 'docked', requiring users to pick up and return the bicycle to designated bicycle stations. More recently, we have seen GPS/app-facilitated dockless schemes emerge in cities such as Beijing and Sydney, albeit to mixed reaction.[3] The rapid growth in bikeshare schemes offers research possibilities around who uses them and for what purpose, optimal numbers/locations of bicycles, effects of different charging mechanisms, docked versus dockless, integration with electric-assist bikes (e-bikes), integration with public transport, impacts on other modes, and broader sustainability/health impacts (Fishman, 2016).

Second is the equally rapid growth of e-bikes, from 300,000 in 2000 to 35 million in 2016 (Pucher & Buehler, 2017). Although 90% of e-bikes are in China, we have seen significant increases in e-bike sales globally, as legislation catches up with known benefits of making cycling easier and faster than conventional bicycles for a larger proportion of the population. Again, this is a rich area of research, raising questions around who is using them, the extent to which they are contributing to sustainability goals, integration with bikeshare schemes, etc.

Third is technology, particularly that facilitated by the increasingly ubiquitous penetration of smartphones.[4] Apps focused around the provision of real-time travel options and the monitoring and changing of travel/health behaviour (e.g., Strava) all provide intriguing possibilities to study the determinants of active travel choices.

---

2  https://en.wikipedia.org/wiki/List_of_bicycle-sharing_systems provides a listing of bicycle share schemes as of December 2016. Accessed 10 October 2018.

3  https://www.afr.com/lifestyle/cars-bikes-and-boats/cycling/dockless-bikes-are-part-of-a-battle-between-chinese-tech-giants-20180420-hoz1m8. Accessed 10 October 2018.

4  88% of Australians owned a smartphone in 2017: https://www2.deloitte.com/au/mobile-consumer-survey. Accessed 10 October 2018.

Fourth is Mobility as a Service (MaaS), which involves the shift away from person-ally owned transportation to the bundling of mobility services. Cycling appears relatively well-placed given the growth of bicycle share and e-bikes and the poten-tial for integration as part of the 'last-mile' component of public transport travel.

Finally, we speculate on the possible shake-up for active travel if prophecies of autonomous vehicles (AVs) come to fruition. Plausibly, AVs may decrease the rela-tive disutility of car travel (and barriers to driving, e.g., young age) in comparison to active transport, attracting droves of cyclists and walkers. Policy-makers may exacerbate this trend by investing in infrastructure designed to facilitate the fast and efficient movement of streams of AVs at the expense of pedestrians/cyclists, underpinned by vehicles that prioritise occupant comfort and safety over that of vulnerable road users. Conversely, depending on how the safety promises of partial and full automation manifest, pedestrians and cyclists could feel safer in a world where there is less chance of driver error causing a crash. Some have argued this could take us to the other extreme where people will deliberately impede cars, for which there is some circumstantial evidence from recent Uber trials.

## 8.6    Concluding comments

As we approach 2020, what lies ahead on the active transport landscape? First, while perspectives are changing, active transport is evidently not a ubiquitous con-cept with very different issues afflicting cycling, walking and other active transport modes such as roller-blading, scootering and skateboarding. In fact, sometimes these modes do not exist harmoniously, such as with some of the shared pedestrian/ cycle paths in Australia.

Second, while we have seen a re-ignition of interest in active transport in many major cities for various sustainability/health reasons, it should be noted that active travel receives a fraction of road funding in many jurisdictions. Contemporary ini-tiatives such as bike-share and e-bikes, and the fact that congestion on both car and public transport is set to worsen, could provide further impetus for active travel.

Third, despite the fact it is the most widely used mode of transport, walking has received a paucity of research attention in comparison to cycling. We still have quite a poor handle on how much and at what intensity people walk, and this makes it problematic to evaluate the benefits of strategies that may lead to direct or indirect walking benefits such as public transport improvements.

Fourth, evidence-based assessments of active travel interventions remain rare, with continued disagreement on how to both measure and value benefits. It is worth asking whether we have become overly obsessed with evaluations of small, piece-meal initiatives that may create more questions than answers – perhaps a more strategic approach is needed, for example how to identify what kind of city people want to live in, and optimal approaches for achieving it. For example, the positive correlation between property prices and walkability scores suggests people value living in walkable neighbourhoods. Different strategies for improving walkability could be trialled in different neighbourhoods, and the results/impacts compared/ evaluated to inform future policy.

Finally, we face many unknowns in the coming years/decades, including automated vehicles, the effects of which are only just being considered and speculated on for active transport. Perhaps AVs will attract casual walkers and cyclists in droves or perhaps they offer the 'silver-bullet' solution to resolving many of the safety issues that continue to hinder active transport participation. Only time will tell.

## References

Andersen, L. B., Schnohr, P., Schroll, M. and Hein, H. O. (2000), 'All-cause mortality associated with physical activity during leisure time, work, sports, and cycling to work', *Archives of Internal Medicine*, **160**(11), 1621–1628. http://www.ncbi.nlm.nih.gov/pubmed/10847255. Accessed 15 July 2018.

Blanco, H., Alberti, M., Forsyth, A., Krizek, K. J., Rodríguez, D. a., Talen, E. and Ellis, C. (2009), 'Hot, congested, crowded and diverse: Emerging research agendas in planning', *Progress in Planning*, **71**(4), 153–205. http://doi.org/10.1016/j.progress.2009.03.001

Crane, M., Rissel, C., Standen, C., Ellison, A., Ellison, R., Wen, L. M. and Greaves, S. (2017), 'Longitudinal evaluation of travel and health outcomes in relation to new bicycle infrastructure, Sydney, Australia', *Journal of Transport and Health*, **6**, 386–395. http://doi.org/10.1016/j.jth.2017.07.002

Ellison, R. B. and Greaves, S. (2011), 'Travel time competitiveness of cycling in Sydney, Australia', *Transportation Research Record: Journal of the Transportation Research Board*, **2247**(1), 99–108. http://doi.org/10.3141/2247-12

Elvik, R. (2011), 'Publication bias and time-trend bias in meta-analysis of bicycle helmet efficacy: A re-analysis of Attewell, Glase and McFadden, 2001', *Accident Analysis & Prevention*, **43**(3), 1245–1251. http://doi.org/10.1016/j.aap.2011.01.007

Fifer, S., Rose, J. and Greaves, S. (2014), 'Hypothetical bias in Stated Choice Experiments: Is it a problem? And if so, how do we deal with it?', *Transportation Research Part A: Policy and Practice*, **61**, 164–177. http://doi.org/10.1016/j.tra.2013.12.010

Fishman, E. (2016), 'Bikeshare: A review of recent literature', *Transport Reviews*, **36**(1), 92–113. http://doi.org/10.1080/01441647.2015.1033036

Fishman, E., Washington, S. and Haworth, N. (2012), 'Barriers and facilitators to public bicycle scheme use: A qualitative approach', *Transportation Research Part F: Traffic Psychology and Behaviour*, **15**(6), 686–698. http://doi.org/10.1016/J.TRF.2012.08.002

Garrard, J. and Greaves, S. P. (2010), 'Cycling injuries in Australia: Road safety's blind spot?', *Journal of the Australasian College of Road Safety*, **21**(3), 37–43.

Greaves, S., Ellison, A., Ellison, R., Rance, D., Standen, C., Rissel, C. and Crane, M. (2015), 'A web-based diary and companion smartphone app for travel/activity surveys', *Transportation Research Procedia*, **11**, 297–310. http://doi.org/10.1016/j.trpro.2015.12.026

Jacobsen, P. L. (2003), 'Safety in numbers: More walkers and bicyclists, safer walking and bicycling', *Injury Prevention: Journal of the International Society for Child and Adolescent Injury Prevention*, **9**(3), 205–209.

Jacobsen, P. L., Racioppi, F. and Rutter, H. (2009), 'Who owns the roads? How motorised traffic discourages walking and bicycling', *Injury Prevention : Journal of the International Society for Child and Adolescent Injury Prevention*, **15**(6), 369–373. http://doi.org/10.1136/ip.2009.022566

Litman, T. (2018), *Evaluating Active Transportation Benefits and Costs*. http://www.vtpi.org/nmt-tdm. pdf. Accessed November 2018.

Mueller, N., Rojas-Rueda, D., Cole-Hunter, T., de Nazelle, A., Dons, E., Gerike, R., . . . Nieuwenhuijsen, M. (2015), 'Health impact assessment of active transportation: A systematic review', *Preventive Medicine*, **76**, 103–114. http://doi.org/10.1016/j.ypmed.2015.04.010

Mulley, C., Tyson, R., McCue, P., Rissel, C. and Munro, C. (2013), 'Valuing active travel: Including the health benefits of sustainable transport in transportation appraisal frameworks', *Research in Transportation Business & Management*, **7**, 27–34. http://doi.org/10.1016/j.rtbm.2013.01.001

Porter, C., Suhrbier, J. and Schwartz, W. (1999), 'Forecasting bicycle and pedestrian travel: State of the practice and research needs', *Transportation Research Record*, **1674**(1), 94–101.

Pucher, J. and Buehler, R. (2017), 'Cycling towards a more sustainable transport future', *Transport Reviews*, **37**(6), 689–694. http://doi.org/10.1080/01441647.2017.1340234

Pucher, J., Buehler, R., Bassett, D. R. and Dannenberg, A. L. (2010), 'Walking and cycling to health: A comparative analysis of city, state, and international data', *American Journal of Public Health*, **100**(10), 1986–1993. http://doi.org/10.2105/AJPH.2009.189324

Pucher, J., Dill, J. and Handy, S. (2010), 'Infrastructure, programs, and policies to increase bicycling: An international review', *Preventive Medicine*, **50**(Suppl 1), S106-1025. http://doi.org/10.1016/j. ypmed.2009.07.028

Rissel, C., Crane, M., Wen, L. M., Greaves, S. and Standen, C. (2016), 'Satisfaction with transport and enjoyment of the commute by commuting mode in inner Sydney', *Health Promotion Journal of Australia*, **27**(1), 80–83. http://doi.org/10.1071/HE15044

Saelens, B. E. and Handy, S. L. (2008), 'Built environment correlates of walking: A review', *Medicine and Science in Sports and Exercise*, **40**(7 Suppl), S550–566. http://doi.org/10.1249/MSS.0b013e31817c67a4

Saunders, L. E., Green, J. M., Petticrew, M. P., Steinbach, R. and Roberts, H. (2013), 'What are the health benefits of active travel? A systematic review of trials and cohort studies', *PLoS ONE*, **8**(8), e69912. http://doi.org/10.1371/journal.pone.0069912

Schepers, P., Fishman, E., Beelen, R., Heinen, E., Wijnen, W. and Parkin, J. (2015), 'The mortality impact of bicycle paths and lanes related to physical activity, air pollution exposure and road safety', *Journal of Transport and Health*, **2**(4), 460–473. http://doi.org/10.1016/j.jth.2015.09.004

Smith, M., Hosking, J., Woodward, A., Witten, K., MacMillan, A., Field, A., . . . Mackie, H. (2017), 'Systematic literature review of built environment effects on physical activity and active transport – an update and new findings on health equity', *International Journal of Behavioral Nutrition and Physical Activity*, **14**(1). http://doi.org/10.1186/s12966-017-0613-9

Standen, C. (2017), *The value of slow travel: An econometric method for valuing the user benefits of active transport infrastructure* (Doctoral thesis, University of Sydney, Australia), http://hdl.handle. net/2123/17914. Accessed 8 June 2018.

Stanley, J. (2014), *MOVING PEOPLE Solutions for Policy Thinkers*. http://sydney.edu.au/business/__ data/assets/pdf_file/0005/228785/Moving-People-3.pdf. Accessed 12 April 2018.

Teschke, K., Harris, M. A., Reynolds, C. C. O., Shen, H., Cripton, P. A. and Winters, M. (2013), 'Exposure-based traffic crash injury rates by mode of travel in British Columbia', *Canadian Journal of Public Health*, **104**(1), 75–79. https://doi.org/10.17269/cjph.104.3621

# 9     The future of urban roads

*Richard de Cani, Ritu Garg and Harrison Peck*

## 9.1   Introduction

At the risk of over-simplification, the emerging nature of urban road development in highly developed economies is increasingly becoming a story of the rise of major road-building programs, based on catering for the movement requirements of traffic growth, followed by the recognition that such an approach has unacceptably high societal costs. This has led to a focus on containing growth in motorised traffic, particularly car use, through measures such as integrated land-use transport planning, prioritising public and active transport and congestion pricing, while giving much greater emphasis to the place functions of road space. This chapter discusses this evolution, drawing mainly on London's experiences but also on experience elsewhere. The next section illustrates challenges to the freeway era in California and London. This is followed in Section 9.3 by discussion of how London has managed to contain growth in car travel and, in Section 9.4, by consideration of the place function of road space and some of the factors that have been important in this focus. Section 9.5 presents the chapter conclusions.

## 9.2   The evolution of roads in our cities: Challenging the freeway era

The relationship between towns and cities and their streets and roads has been subject to a constant process of transformation and evolution over hundreds of years. The contest between the movement and place functions of urban road space is a major theme of this chapter, which highlights how the solution to that contest has been changing over time in cities with a strong focus on sustainable development (Cervero et al. 2017). In many towns and cities, the basic road infrastructure that has been the backbone of their urban development started life as rights of way connecting areas of commerce and trade with civic buildings, neighbourhoods and other functions essential to daily life. For many decades, planning for the future of the motor vehicle was seen as the priority objective (Stopher and Stanley 2014). Towns and cities needed to adapt by making it easier to move around by motor vehicle, leading to an explosion of new road construction and an adaption of historic roads and streets into corridors for the movement of vehicles. Urban neighbourhoods, which at one point had enjoyed a more balanced and equal relationship with their streets, often became blighted by urban road corridors focused on the movement of vehicles, segregated from people. The impact of this urban transformation has been long lasting, with new patterns of travel established, focused on expectations of accessibility by car and impacting significantly on the public transport proposition in many towns and cities for decades.

Opposition to new road development started to appear in the 1960s. In London, for example, proposals for the development of an urban motorway network across the city, to improve access for road vehicles, were included in the Greater London Development Plan of 1969 (GLC 1969). The impacts of the plan, with its infamous 'Motorway Box' proposal for motorways around central London, were significant, with over 1 million homes estimated to be within 200 metres of a new urban motorway. Whilst initially supported by all political parties in London, the proposals received criticism from some academics and professional planners, who questioned the estimation of costs and benefits and raised the prospect of these new roads generating large quantities of extra traffic, which would have a negative effect on the road network across a much wider area. One section of the proposed network, the Westway, connecting Paddington to the west of Central London through North Kensington and to the west, was constructed in spite of the opposition it received. The 3.5 kilometre elevated route of the Westway followed the alignment of an existing railway line but involved major demolition of existing buildings, truncating roads below and creating a vast area of undeveloped land underneath the viaduct. There was fierce opposition against the construction of the road from local neighbourhood groups on noise and pollution grounds but also because it failed to have any relationship at all with its surrounding context. The completion of the Westway project mobilised the anti-road movement in London, who had formed a well-organised group called Homes Before Roads, and who led a series of protests against other urban road projects. This quickly influenced the political mood, which led to the Greater London Council abandoning its plans for an urban road program in favour of policies supporting investment in public transport. This led to urban road construction in London coming to an abrupt halt, a position that has remained largely the same for the past 40 years.

Similar adverse reactions against the imposition of new highway infrastructure on urban areas were taking place elsewhere in the world. In San Francisco, the Embarcadero Freeway once stood as an elevated double-decker highway along San Francisco's waterfront. The idea of the Embarcadero Freeway – a massive divider within the city, which severely segregated its waterfront and iconic Ferry Building – was met by strong opposition from its conception. In 1955, before the Freeway construction had begun, the *San Francisco Chronicle* featured an editorial with images of such a roadway in Seattle, to raise awareness among San Franciscans of the negative implications of a double-decker freeway in the city's central areas (Niekerken 2017). By 1958, a strong campaign calling for the removal of the Embarcadero Freeway had begun – more than 30,000 San Francisco residents gathered in the city's various districts and signed petitions against the freeway (Carlsson n.d.).

In 1959, with growing opposition against the freeway, San Francisco's Board of Supervisors voted to cancel 75 per cent of planned freeway routes through the city.

In 1961, a bill was put forward by the California Assembly, proposing *the use of gas-tax funds to demolish 'unwanted freeways' in general, and the Embarcadero in particular.* The demolition of the freeway was put to a vote in 1986 but, as a whole, San Francisco voted against the measure – many feared that the loss of the fast connections the freeway provided would disadvantage their businesses. In 1989, the Loma Prieta earthquake severely damaged the freeway and initiated a debate on the future of the Embarcadero Freeway (Vanderbilt 2010). In 1991, California State Department of Transportation engineers concluded that repairing the Embarcadero Freeway would be as costly as constructing a new freeway. This assessment led to a final decision calling for the removal of the Embarcadero Freeway, and the structure's demolition finally began in February 1991.

Today, the Embarcadero is San Francisco's prime walking path and a centre of activity for the city. The promenade along the waterfront offers open views of the San Francisco Bay, Treasure Island and the Bay Bridge, and is adorned by activity culminating from the Ferry Building, weekly farmers' markets, museums and endless shops and restaurants. Since the demolition of the freeway, dense commercial development has sprung up along the Embarcadero. Reports suggest housing in the area has increased by 51 per cent and jobs by 23 per cent. Major redevelopment projects and plans for continued densification and development of the waterfront continue to surge this central part of San Francisco with life and on-going transformation.

The mood continued to shift in the 1990s, through the growing awareness of the environmental impact of continued traffic growth, helped by the 1992 Rio Earth Summit and UK government research which demonstrated that new road schemes contributed significantly to the generation of additional vehicle trips. Taken together, these milestones helped reset the focus for transport policy in the UK, leading to the development of government policy focused on the integration of land use and transport, to reduce the need to travel where possible and encourage development that maximised the use of public transport.

Many other developed cities, however, remain more firmly embedded in the road-building stage, partly reflecting path dependency, albeit that some have a bet each way by adding freeways/toll roads and also major public transport infrastructure (e.g., Melbourne). The author expects that the balance in such places will increasingly shift towards containing growth in car use. Transport policy research can play a vital role in informing the implications of such choices and of measures to improve societal outcomes.

## 9.3   Encouraging modes other than the car

In London, there have been successive policies in place for decades to reduce travel by car and increase the volume of trips by public transport, walking and cycling. Through the creation of the position of Mayor of London and the formation of Transport for London in 2001, as a truly integrated transport authority with responsibility for setting the strategic direction for transport in the city and having the operational responsibility for its main networks, this policy has been largely successful (Stanley et al. 2017). Since 2001, London has had three Mayors, with the first two both serving eight years in office, from different political backgrounds but with a broadly consistent approach to transport in the city. Policies that support population and employment growth, whilst helping to secure a reduction in congestion and car trips, have underpinned the transport strategies of all three Mayors. Over this period in London we have seen a number of trends emerge. As the population of London has increased and the income levels of its population have increased overall, the volume of trips being generated has also increased. Figure 9.1 shows this growth in terms of daily motorised person kilometres of travel. Whilst the volume of trips has increased, the number of car trips has remained relatively constant, in spite of significant population growth.

Figure 9.2 shows that significant increases in travel demand have taken place for all types of public transport use over the 2001–2013 period, with bus and rail use increasing by more than 60 per cent and Underground use by over a quarter.

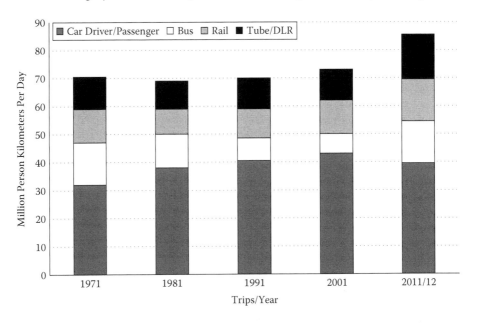

**Source:**   TfL (n.d.), Figure 3.

**Figure 9.1**   Daily trips with an origin or destination in Greater London: 1971–2011/12

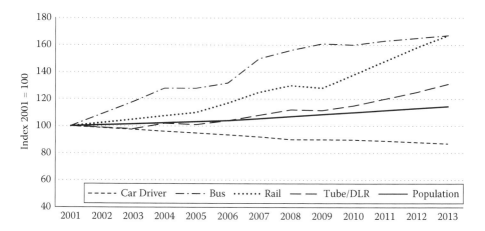

Source:    TfL (n.d.), Figure 7.

**Figure 9.2**    Daily travel trends in Greater London: 2001–2013

Cycling use (not shown in Figure 9.2) has doubled (from a low base) over this period (TfL n.d.).

The outcomes that have been achieved in London are in the direction that many cities around the world would like to be heading. However, in spite of these successes in London, over the same time period there has been a worsening of congestion and deterioration in air quality, partly caused by road traffic congestion. For example, data from Transport for London (TfL) shows that, over the period from 2001 to 2013, overall traffic speeds in London reduced across the whole of the city by around 20 per cent (TfL n.d.).

To understand these relationships, it is necessary to look back at the implementation of transport and planning policy in London over the period since 2001. Changes in travel behaviour have been secured through the implementation of policies targeted at reducing car trips and promoting other modes of transport, built on a number of basic principles. The first is through influencing the development of the city by integrating plans for urban growth with investments in public transport. London's population growth has been entirely supported by development within the city boundary. This is encouraged by policies which seek to limit the amount of parking available for new developments to very low levels in many cases, including zero provision where sites are accessible by public transport. Densification is promoted around transport nodes and analytical techniques such as TfL's Public Transport Accessibility Level (PTAL) tool identify areas that are highly accessible by public transport and where densification can be accommodated without leading to increases in traffic congestion (TfL 2015). It has been possible to implement and sustain such an approach because the Mayor of London has ultimate control over strategic land-use planning and transport, so the opportunity to align and integrate the approach across the city exists in London, something that is not always available in other cities.

The second principle has been to pursue policies which actively promote greater use of public transport, through investment in services, infrastructure and the integration of ticketing and fares, whilst at the same time restricting car use through the introduction of the London Congestion Charge and other policies which seek to reduce or limit road capacity. Throughout the whole period since 2001, when London has been governed by a Mayor, only one major road in the city has been progressed, a new road crossing under the River Thames in east London. However, over the same period, there has been a major expansion of the public transport network with new capacity introduced through services such as the London Overground network and a major expansion of the bus network. This has led to a substantial increase in operated kilometres on all parts of the public transport network and this has meant, for example, that a greater proportion of Londoners have easy access to bus services. Ninety-five per cent of households in London now live within 400 metres of a bus stop with a regular/frequent service.

In addition to the major increases in the capacity of the public transport network, the quality of service on public transport has improved dramatically, with customer satisfaction rising over the period following the introduction of TfL. This has been achieved through a number of targeted measures, including improvements in reliability but also through the roll-out of integrated ticketing and payment mechanisms. The introduction of the Oyster Smartcard in 2003, alongside the harmonisation and integration of fares, made it easier for people to use and move between different modes of public transport. The transition from Oyster into contactless payment technology means that many users of the transport network in London do not need to purchase a ticket – they can just use their bankcard, smart phone or smart watch to access the system.

Alongside the investment that has taken place in the capacity and quality of the public transport network in London, specific measures have been deployed focused on traffic restraint. The London Congestion Charge was a major manifesto commitment for the first Mayor, Ken Livingstone, who led his campaign to be London's first elected Mayor with proposals to introduce a new charging regime for vehicles driving into Central London. The objective of the policy was to reduce congestion and there was a clear requirement that any surplus revenue generated by the introduction of the scheme would be used to support investment in public transport and other complementary measures. Unusually so for a new charge, the policy was broadly welcomed by Londoners, including businesses who saw the benefits of specific and targeted policies to help reduce congestion, mainly from an economic perspective. The Congestion Charge was successful at reducing the volume of vehicles driving into Central London during the Monday to Friday period and was initially successful at helping to reduce traffic congestion.

Alongside the introduction of the Congestion Charge, significant investment in the London bus network took place, which helped deliver a major increase in bus usage. This meant that the introduction of the Congestion Charge, as part of a much broader package of measures which made travel in London not only quicker and easier but more enjoyable for many users of the system, was largely welcomed by stakeholders and the public as a positive step forward.

## 9.4    A greater role for place

Whilst the overall impact of the London Congestion Charge on mode share across the city has been positive and car use has continued to fall, congestion on London's roads has worsened, which has manifested itself through a reduction in speed. Alongside the reduction in speed, London suffers from poor air quality, caused predominantly by diesel engines, which have increased in volume, and the impact of slower speeds means that parts of Central London breach European limits for nitrogen dioxide. There has also been a change in who is using London's roads, with a major increase in freight and servicing traffic, which now makes up over 30 per cent of all vehicles on some London streets. This has been caused by an increase in deliveries, in part due to growth in on-line retailing and commerce.

The increase in congestion has also been partly fuelled by a program of capacity removal on many streets and roads, reallocating space for public transport, pedestrians and cyclists, largely supported by changes in public perception and attitudes. In London, roads and streets constitute a significant proportion of public space and many residents value their streets and roads as essential components of their urban neighbourhoods, fully integrated into the urban fabric, without having the divisive impact of the past. Alongside this, property owners, businesses and investors are increasingly focused on factors that represent the liveability of a city. Increasingly this has come to apply to the quality of streets and spaces in a neighbourhood and ease of access by foot and cycle.

Given the fixed nature of road space in a city like London, constrained by buildings on each side, any decision to give more space to one road user will result to a degree in a reduction in capacity for another. This has been highlighted most recently when decisions taken to reallocate substantial amounts of road space on major roads in London to deliver a network of new 'Cycle Super Highways' led to consequential impacts on the capacity available for other road users. The situation in London is always one of balancing competing needs, understanding 'trade-offs' and pursing policies that reflect the priorities of the Mayor of the day.

The current Mayor of London, Sadiq Kahn, has gone further by introducing a clear hierarchy of users and outcomes focused on health, which invariably benefits the pedestrian and cyclist above the motor vehicle user. The introduction of the 'Healthy Streets' approach seeks to place health and wellbeing outcomes at the heart of decision making around future investment in London's streets and roads, with emphasis on the human experience from a user perspective. This ground-breaking approach identifies 10 indicators against which streets will be assessed and investment will be prioritised. Factors such as noise, air quality, ambience and activity are considered alongside traditional criteria such as safety (Mayor of London and TfL 2017).

This change in approach has been supported through a combination of positive support and strong pressure to transform London's streets and roads from specific user groups, pressure groups, local communities and business. There is widespread recognition from some groups that improving the quality of urban streets and roads in London, to provide better facilities for pedestrians and cyclists, whilst leading to a direct reduction in the operational performance of the road for some users, is the only way forward. However, there remain areas of disagreement and conflict and proposals for transforming road space in accordance with the Mayor's 'Healthy Streets' approach do not receive the support of all.

Experience from New York demonstrates how a transformation can take place relatively quickly, through a series of targeted measures delivered in a timely manner and with significant effect. In 2007, through PlaNYC, New York City's long-term comprehensive plan, former Mayor Michael Bloomberg made an ambitious commitment: all New Yorkers will live within a 10-minute walk of an open space (City of New York and Mayor Michael Bloomberg 2011). Home to some of the most densely populated neighbourhoods in the United States, with a notorious shortage of vacant land, exorbitant real estate prices and largely fixed street grids, New York provided a particularly challenging setting for the creation of new public spaces. The New York City Department of Transportation (NYCDOT) launched the NYC Plaza Program *to transform underused streets into vibrant, social public spaces* (NYCDOT n.d.) and, since its launch in 2007, the NYC Plaza Program has created more than 70 new public open spaces in all five boroughs, with another dozen projects currently under development. New York City's public plazas have hardly been delivered without their share of controversies, with some residents expressing concern about the loss of parking spaces, the potential for intensified congestion levels on adjacent streets and impacts to local businesses. To help allay these fears, NYCDOT often constructs new plazas using temporary tools such as planters, gravel, movable furniture and other materials that are relatively quick and inexpensive to introduce into the street environment – as well as easy to remove. Times Square underwent a wholesale conversion from perpetually clogged vehicle artery to the pedestrianised centrepiece of Midtown Manhattan, measuring over 1 hectare, in a span of seven years. Just in time for the 2016 New Year's Eve celebrations, Broadway in Times Square was permanently pedestrianised and, since then, injuries have dropped by 40 per cent, crime has decreased by 20 per cent and air pollution has reduced by 60 per cent (Designbloom 2017).

## 9.5   The future

Looking to the future, the transport industry is subject to on-going change and disruption through the introduction of new trends and changes in technology, including a shift away from internal combustion engines to electric vehicles and the development of autonomous technology. However, no matter what form urban mobility takes in the future, we can expect transport systems to continue to shape cities' physical, economic and social landscapes, as transport is increasingly seen as the answer to multiple policy objectives, from health, economic development and social inclusion to environmental improvement. City policy needs to reflect this new normal, informed by transport policy research programs.

The major focus of the current chapter has been on the movement versus place functions of roads, matters related thereto, and ways to alter this balance towards more sustainable outcomes, in economic, social and environmental terms. These areas provide innumerable research opportunities to inform better policy choices. This research needs to span a wide range of matters, such as improved identification and valuation of the place function of roads and streets, the costs of increasing motorisation, opportunities arising from improved land-use transport integration and the place of emerging digital technologies, and policies related thereto, in shaping more sustainable futures.

Rather than overregulating and dissuading the spread of private transport companies, cities must collaborate with the private sector and embrace a research and development role for new technologies. However, in so doing, they must also strike a delicate balance between technological foresight and inclusion and equity, working to create legislative frameworks that deliver positive outcomes for residents. For example, the proliferation of bike share schemes and the introduction of new dockless systems create multiple benefits for the city and its residents, through choice and accessibility to a broader range of transport. However, benefits could easily be outweighed by negative impacts on users of the public realm and streets due to the accumulation of bikes in locations that impact on pedestrians and/or the natural environment (e.g., bikes dumped in rivers in cities like Melbourne). Similarly, considering the increasing appetite for autonomous passenger and freight technologies, cities must pave the way for a sustainable, autonomous future that avoids exacerbating congestion, network inefficiencies and urban sprawl. These areas are ripe for transport policy research.

## References

Carlsson, N. (n.d.), 'The freeway revolt: Historical essay', *Found.* http://www.foundsf.org/index.php?title=The_Freeway_Revolt. Accessed 5 October 2018.

Cervero, R., Guerra, E. and Al, S. (2017), *Beyond mobility: Planning cities for people and places*, Washington, DC: Island Press.

City of New York and Mayor Michael Bloomberg (2011), *PlaNYC Update 2011: A Greener, Greater*

*New York*, New York: Authors. http://www.nyc.gov/html/planyc/downloads/pdf/publications/planyc_2011_planyc_full_report.pdf. Accessed 5 October 2018.

Designbloom (2017), 'Snøhetta opens pedestrian plaza at times square, doubling its amount of public space'. https://www.designboom.com/architecture/snohetta-times-square-pedestrian-plaza-opens-new-york-04-19-2017/. Accessed 8 October 2018.

(GLC) Greater London Council (1969), Greater London Development Plan, London: Author.

Mayor of London and TfL (2017), *Healthy Streets for London: Prioritising Walking, Cycling and Public Transport to Create a Healthy City*, London: Authors. http://content.tfl.gov.uk/healthy-streets-for-london.pdf. Accessed 5 October 2018.

(NYCDOT) New York City Department of Transportation (n.d.), NYC Plaza Program. http://www.nyc.gov/html/dot/html/pedestrians/nyc-plaza-program.shtml. Accessed 5 October 2018.

Niekerken, N. (2017), 'An ode to the Embarcadero Freeway, the blight by the bay', *San Francisco Chronicle*. https://www.sfchronicle.com/thetake/article/An-ode-to-the-Embarcadero-Freeway-the-blight-by-11543621.php. Accessed 5 October 2018.

Stanley, J., Stanley, J. and Hansen, R. (2017), *How Great Cities Happen: Integrating People, Land Use and Transport*, Cheltenham: Edward Elgar Publishing.

Stopher, P. and Stanley, J. (2014), *Introduction to Transport Policy: A Public Policy View*, Cheltenham: Edward Elgar Publishing.

(TfL) Transport for London (2015), *Assessing Transport Connectivity in London*, London: Author. https://files.datapress.com/london/dataset/public-transport-accessibility-levels/2017-01-12T15:59:45/connectivity-assessment-guide.pdf. Accessed 5 October 2015.

(TfL) Transport for London (n.d.), *Drivers of Demand for Travel in London: A Review of Trends in Travel Demand and Their Causes*, London: Author. http://content.tfl.gov.uk/drivers-of-demand-for-travel-in-london.pdf. Accessed 5 October 2018.

Vanderbilt, T. (2010), 'Unbuilt highways', *Slate*. https://www.sfchronicle.com/thetake/article/An-ode-to-the-Embarcadero-Freeway-the-blight-by-11543621.php. Accessed 5 October 2010.

# 10 A maritime research agenda in transport policy

*Michael Bell*

## 10.1 Introduction

Maritime transport is about to undergo its next big technological revolution. After the shift from sail to steam, and then from steam to oil, the advent of containerisation and intermodal transport in the 1960s ushered in an era of globalisation. Supply chains benefitted hugely from the efficiencies offered by intermodal transport and the mechanised handling of containers. The economies of scale in shipping led to larger ships, constrained by the dimensions of ports and canals and eventually by the value of inventory carried by ships (higher-value cargo goes in smaller shipments).

We are now, however, witnessing some shrinkage of supply chains, brought about by the basket of technologies referred to as the Fourth Industrial Revolution, or Industry 4.0 for short. These include the internet of things, automation, digitalisation, the proliferation of app-based services and the switch to electric propulsion for all modes of transport. Automation and digitalisation are reducing the significance of labour cost, enabling some production to locate closer to consumers, driven by the desire to reduce inventory costs and customise production. This is weakening the growth of container flows and leading to chronic over-capacity in the container shipping industry.

Automation will at some point impact on shipping itself, raising the prospect of crewless ships. In addition to automation, concern about the emissions generated by burning high sulphur oil for power combined with the falling cost of LNG is driving a shift to cleaner fuels. For short sea shipping and towage, there is a growing interest in hybrid and battery propulsion, helping to reduce the direct environmental impact of shipping on coastal communities and port cities. The following sections review these developments in greater detail, leading to the three key research themes.

## 10.2    Shrinking supply chains and digitalisation

Industry 4.0 technologies are gradually reshaping supply chains, and in some cases shortening them. By reducing the dependence on large pools of cheap labour, production is becoming more mobile. As a consequence, there is a trend to 'reshoring' or 'near shoring' as some forms of production seek to locate closer to consumers to reduce inventory and transport costs, and facilitate greater customisation of products. This trend is reducing the rate of growth of container flows on the high seas and through ports. The digitalisation of some products, like books and music, and the miniaturisation of electronic goods, are further reducing the rate of growth of container flows.

The ratio of the rate of growth in TEU flows through world ports, as measured by Drewry Shipping Consultants, to the rate of growth in GDP, obtained from World Bank data, has changed over time, as shown by Rodrigue (2017). This ratio, referred to as the TEU-to-GDP multiplier, has weakened to values less than one since the Global Financial Crisis of 2008/9. Further headwinds faced by global TEU flows that will eventually show up in the TEU-to-GDP multiplier include a growing opposition to free trade resulting from populist movements, particularly in the US and Europe, driven by sections of society that feel left behind by globalisation.

While globalisation has been a clear win for the world economy as measured by GDP, it has come at a cost to welfare and equity. The concentration of certain industries in limited locations has reduced the range of jobs available to those who lack freedom of movement, and this freedom is increasingly restricted by tighter immigration controls where activities are concentrated. Globalisation has increased wealth inequality as capital moves internationally to where the greatest return can be earned and as a result labour is squeezed by international competition.

Industry 4.0 is accentuating the squeeze on labour by creating new but poorly paid and insecure app-driven service jobs (Uber drivers, Foodora bikers, etc.). This development is in part behind the persistently slow growth in productivity in many developed countries, as intense competition in the job market keeps employment up and earnings down, enabling app-driven services to be offered at lower prices. Statistically it therefore appears that the value of output per person-hour worked is stagnant. One reaction to this is rising opposition to immigration, as immigrants are perceived as undercutting locals in the job market, along with opposition to free trade, which is seen as undercutting local industries and traditional jobs. In total, these trends constitute a headwind to the growth of international containerised trade, container flows through ports, and international container shipping.

A countervailing trend is a digital revolution in freight forwarding and shipping. The electronic exchange of documents, like the bills of lading, letters of credit, certificates of origin, manifests, warranties and bonds, coupled with the spread of trusted databases, like port community systems and single window systems, is reducing the delays from paperwork, improving inventory management, cutting waste and reducing the cost of international trade. Trusted databases, in particular, ensure that all the stakeholders involved in international trade, like shipping lines, freight forwarders, cargo owners, and customs and excise, have access to accurate data on a need-to-know basis, thereby preserving commercial confidentiality and reducing the risk of rekeying errors when data is transferred from one document or system to another.

The increasing reliance of shipping lines, freight forwarders and cargo owners on IT systems is making them more vulnerable to hacking. A 'ransomware' cyber attack in 2017 on the email system of the largest container shipping line, Maersk, cost the company between $200m and $300m (Milne, 2017). The COSCO shipping line is currently (August 2018) recovering from a cyber attack to its email system. However, blockchain and distributed ledger technology is offering the potential to reduce fraud and errors while enhancing the transparency and security of information sharing between trading partners. Maersk and IBM are currently partnering to develop a neutral blockchain and distributed ledger technology platform for shipping named Tradelens (2018).

Digitalisation is also increasing the efficiency of shipping in other ways. For example, ship registries are gradually moving toward the issuing of e-certificates of sea worthiness, increasing the efficiency and effectiveness of port state control, whereby national agencies, such as the Australian Maritime Safety Agency (AMSA), make ship inspections. Shipping lines increasingly optimise their networks dynamically by 'weather routing' (navigating around storms) or modifying schedules in response to port congestion, equipment breakdown, trade fluctuations or even changes in fuel prices. OOCL (a Hong Kong container shipping line, currently being acquired by the Chinese shipping line COSCO) is working with Microsoft Research Asia (MRSA) on deploying Artificial Intelligence (AI) research to improve network operations and achieve efficiencies in shipping (OOCL, 2018).

The depressed state of demand for container shipping and intense competition between lines is in part behind the current wave of consolidation among container shipping lines, whereby larger, stronger lines take over smaller, loss-making lines in the search for cost savings through synergies and improved market power (Maersk's recent takeover of Hamburg Süd is such an example). Container shipping lines have coalesced into three large alliances that enable the smaller lines to benefit from greater geographic and temporal coverage. Regarding vertical as opposed to horizontal integration, container shipping lines have always had a commercial interest in terminal operation, but the recent takeover of Unifeeder, a line providing feeder and shortsea shipping services in northern Europe and Scandinavia, by the global terminal operator DP World marks a new development, enabling DP World to extend the catchment areas of its terminals (Unifeeder, 2018).

## 10.3    Reducing the environmental footprint of shipping

Although shipping is the most efficient of the modes of transport in terms of emissions per tonne carried, there is considerable potential to reduce its environmental and health impact. Heavy fuel oil, the residue from oil distillation, has traditionally fuelled shipping, but contains up to 3.5% sulphur (the upper limit set by the International Maritime Organisation in 2012). When burned, this fuel produces black clouds of particulates, sulphur oxides and nitrogen oxides, which are unpleasant, cause acid rain and are deleterious to human health.

As a result, Emission Control Areas (ECAs) have been introduced on the North American eastern and western seaboards as well as in the North Sea and Adriatic Sea. In these areas, the sulphur content of fuel burned is capped at 0.1%. As of 2020, the International Maritime Organisation (IMO) will cap the sulphur content of fuel burned on the high seas at 0.5%, unless the ship is fitted with an exhaust gas cleaning system, referred to as a 'scrubber'. Low sulphur fuel oil is around 50% more expensive than heavy fuel oil, giving ships fitted with scrubbers an operating cost advantage to set against the cost of installing scrubbers.

To date, Hapag Lloyd and Maersk favour low sulphur fuel oil while MSC, Evergreen and HMM favour fitting scrubbers. Globally it would be more sustainable to remove sulphur from fuel oil at the refinery rather than to clean the exhaust gases later. Furthermore, the safe disposal of the residue from scrubbers raises issues, leading some to question how long and where scrubbers will remain legal. Scrubbers, where chosen, have been most popular for new very large crude oil carriers (VLCCs) and Capesize dry bulk carriers (Wackett, 2018).

There is increasing interest in the use of Liquified Natural Gas (LNG) as a fuel for ships, driven in part by the absence of sulphur oxides and particulates in the emissions when burned and in part by economics. LNG output is ramping up rapidly, with the US switching from being a net importer to a net exporter and Australia increasing its output. Although gas reserves around the world appear to be plentiful, with a number yet to be tapped, the technology used to extract gas from rock, referred to as 'fracking', has proved unpopular in Europe and Australia because of the risk of ground water contamination. Despite this limitation, the global prospects for LNG output look secure enough for ships propelled by LNG to be ordered. Cruise ships and barges are leading the way, because they come close to coastal communities and port cities, but the added expense of either switching to low sulphur fuel or fitting scrubbers from 2020 will encourage the switch to LNG as a fuel for all types of new ship. The Carnival Corporation has ordered four large LNG-powered cruise ships (Grey, 2018), Brittany Ferries takes delivery of an LNG-powered cruise ferry, the Honfleur, in 2019 (Greenport, 2017), Unifeeder has launched a retrofitted LNG-powered shortsea container ship, the Wes Amelie (Whiteman, 2017), and Shell has taken delivery of an LNG-powered barge for use on inland waterways (LNG World News, 2018).

In addition to LNG, there is also increasing interest in battery and hybrid propulsion for shortsea shipping. An all-electric ferry, the Ampere, is now in operation in Norway on a relatively short route (Corvus Energy, 2018a). Similarly, an all-electric car ferry, the Elektra, is operating a short route in the Finnish Archipelago (Greenport, 2018). For longer distances and larger ships, hybrid propulsion is an attractive option. Scandlines is operating diesel-electric car ferries with battery storage in the Baltic (Corvus Energy, 2018b). Hybrid propulsion is also an attractive option for tug boats where short bursts of power are required. Batteries can supplement the bursts of power and be recharged during idle times. Kotug operates hybrid Rotortugs, a particular design of tug, in the ports of Rotterdam, Bremerhaven and London (Greenport, 2014).

While the days of sail propulsion for large commercial ships are long gone, there is renewed interest in the use of auxiliary wind power to save fuel. A German manufacturer of wind turbines is operating a cargo ship with four Flettner sails (vertically spinning cylinders that rotate to generate a forward force from the wind), which it claims saves around 15% of fuel oil (Enercon, 2018). A Hamburg company, SkySails (2018), is producing giant kites designed to help ships reduce their fuel consumption by catching the wind and pulling the ship.

Another source of pollution from ships is ballast water. Bulk carriers, once they have discharged their load at the destination port, need to take on ballast water in order to remain stable on their journey to the next port for reloading. As they reload, they discharge their ballast water including any marine life in it, potentially introducing alien species which may go on to cause environmental damage. The Ballast Water Management (BWM) Convention, which requires ships to remove, render harmless, or avoid the uptake or discharge of aquatic organisms and pathogens within ballast water and sediments, entered into force in September 2017 (Port Technology, 2017).

Reducing greenhouse gas (GHG) emissions across the shipping sector is work in progress. The Marine Environment Protection Committee of the IMO is working on the sector-wide adoption of a framework for all IMO member states, which sets out the guiding principles for international shipping with reduced GHG emissions (Port Technology, 2018a). Part of this framework is the lowering of the maximum permissible sulphur content in fuel oil to 0.5% from 2020, unless the ship is fitted with a scrubber.

As well as reducing the environmental footprint of shipping at sea, big advances are being made on reducing the environmental footprint in ports. The electrification of port equipment constitutes a major step forward in cutting emissions, provided the electricity is sourced renewably (from wind, sun or the waves). The APM Terminals Maasvlakte 2 development at the Port of Rotterdam is claiming to be a zero-emission terminal, because the cranes that load and unload containers to and from ships are electrically powered, the cranes that stack the containers in the yard are also electrically powered, the automatic guided vehicles that move the containers around the yard are battery powered, and the electricity is sourced from a zero-emission generator (Schuler, 2015). In addition to the electrification of the port, ships when in port and berthed can be plugged into a shore-based power supply and switch off their generators in a process known as 'cold ironing'.

Beyond the port on the landside, container flows can impose significant costs and damage on port cities through pavement wear and tear as well as noise and exhaust emissions. One strategy, referred to as port-centric logistics, is to locate warehouses and distribution centres adjacent to the port so the need for containers to be transported by road is minimised. However, this strategy is often infeasible because of the absence of suitable space close to the port, so an alternative strategy is to shift containers from the road to rail and construct intermodal terminals close to the ultimate origins and destinations of the cargo. Containers would be transported between the port and intermodal terminal by rail, removing a significant source of traffic congestion and emissions in the vicinity of the port, and would only use the road network around the intermodal terminal, which will typically lie in a less congested area. This strategy is being pursued in Sydney, Australia, where a number of inland intermodal terminals are either in operation or under construction. However, so far only around 20% of containers enter and leave Port Botany (Sydney's port) by rail.

## 10.4    Automation in ports and at sea

Advancing automation is not only a feature of production but also of ports, and in the future, shipping. The automation of container terminals has been a slow process, starting in 1993 with stacking cranes and now extending to automatic guided vehicles, automated straddle carriers (Autostrads©), the gates to the container terminal and the quay cranes on the landside. The loading and unloading of ships has yet to be successfully automated, so a twin trolley system has been devised whereby a crane driver transfers containers between the ship and an intermediate platform on the quay crane and a second trolley working in parallel transfers containers automatically between the intermediate platform and the quay. By 2014, there were 32 automated container terminals around the world (Van Jole, 2014). As the technology becomes standard, this trend can be expected to continue, driven by the electrification of port equipment, greater safety since dock workers are excluded from automated yards, the ability to work 24 hours, improved reliability in terms of equipment and labour, and to a lesser extent by operational cost savings.

The next step in automation will be the ships themselves, driven by potential cost savings, safety, and difficulties with the recruitment of seafarers. The technology is mostly there, but the regulatory framework is currently lacking. Autopilots on commercial ships and the remote monitoring of marine engines are becoming increasingly sophisticated, facilitating the reduction of the crew. The IMO has identified four steps to full automation (Port Technology, 2018b):

1.  *Ship with automated processes and decision support*: Seafarers are on board to operate and control shipboard systems and functions. Some operations may be automated.
2.  *Remotely controlled ship with seafarers on board*: The ship is controlled and operated from another location, but seafarers are on board.
3.  *Remotely controlled ship without seafarers on board*: The ship is controlled and operated from another location. There are no seafarers on board.
4.  *Fully autonomous ship*: The operating system of the ship is able to make decisions and determine actions by itself.

The first step is underway, the second step is imminent. Traditionally, pilots are sent out by small boat or helicopter to ships as they approach a port, in both cases with an element of risk involved, so remote control by shore-based pilots would be a safer option. The final step will see the complete removal of crew and life-support systems (crew quarters, provisions, kitchens, life boats, etc.), freeing up significant space on board for extra cargo.

Crewless ships will have lower fixed costs, particularly when the hard- and software required for ship automation becomes standardised and therefore cheaper. The optimal size of the ship depends on many factors like the fixed cost, the value of the cargo, the quantity of the cargo to be shipped, the distance over which the cargo is shipped, and the cost of storing the cargo at either end. An important consequence of a lower fixed cost is that ceteris paribus the optimal ship size is smaller. More specifically, when the fixed cost is halved, the optimal size of the ship falls by the square root of a half.

The potential consequences of smaller cargo ships are significant. Smaller regional ports with shallower approach channels, swing basins and berths can be accessed, increasing the viability of coastal and shortsea shipping. Cargo flows, whether containerised or otherwise, can become more continuous, reducing inventory in the supply chain. This development fits well with the trend to all-electric and hybrid propulsion. Norway is currently taking the lead with the delivery in 2019 of the Yara Birkeland, the first all-electric autonomous container ship designed for coastal use (Skredderberget, 2018).

The initial trials with autonomous ships will be restricted to coastal waters, as there are as yet no conventions to govern autonomous shipping on the high seas. IMO regulations currently specify the minimum crew levels, effectively banning crewless ships on the high seas. However, the IMO's Maritime Safety Committee has launched meetings to discuss rules for the safe operation of MASS (Maritime Autonomous Surface Ships). This could lead eventually to the addition of regulations to the key IMO conventions governing the safety of shipping on the high seas (Port Technology, 2018b).

## 10.5    Research agenda for shipping

Given the vast scope and scale of the shipping industry, identifying a maritime research agenda is necessarily a selective exercise. However, the trends outlined above point to the following research agenda for shipping:

1.  While technological changes associated with Industry 4.0 will have a depressive effect on world trade, its efficiency will be improved through greater digitalisation. However, as document exchanges become electronic, new cyber security threats materialise. There is therefore great interest in blockchain and distributed ledger technology to improve the transparency and security of electronic document exchange. A number of platforms are on offer (Tradelens was mentioned earlier), but the full potential of this technology will not be realised until one platform achieves widespread acceptance. Apart from issues of interoperability, the level of security offered by the technology depends on the number of participants, as each participant checks changes made to the blockchain. *An important research theme is therefore the best use of blockchain and distributed ledger technology to support international maritime trade and the appropriate policy settings to encourage the wide-scale adoption of this technology.*

2.  LNG is proving to be an increasingly popular choice of fuel for ships, because the exhaust emissions are free of particulates and sulphur oxides and IMO regulations relating to sulphur emissions are making the use of fuel oil more expensive. LNG supply at a global level is growing, however the LNG bunkering (refuelling) infrastructure is still in its infancy, limiting the deployment of LNG-powered ships. All-electric ships are being trialled, but battery power is only suitable for smaller ships over shorter distances. To bridge the gap, there is interest in hybrid power, with the first hybrid car ferries operating in the Adriatic Sea and hybrid tug boats operating in some northern European ports. The move to cleaner fuels is driven by increasing IMO regulation, ECAs and port-specific regulations as well as a genuine wish by the industry to reduce its environmental impact, particularly where it comes into contact with coastal communities and port cities. *An important research theme is thus the policy that would encourage the rolling out of an LNG refuelling infrastructure to support a growing fleet of LNG-powered ships.*

3.  The automation of container ports is advancing steadily, with the next logical step being the automation of shipping. The technology is largely there, but IMO regulations currently prohibit the operation of crewless ships on the high seas. The first step to automation will be the remote piloting of ships into ports, followed later by the removal of crew on the high seas. Automation, however, is only relevant for certain types of shipping, namely containers and bulk cargo, so the global employment implications will be limited, at least initially, and may alleviate difficulties in the recruitment of seafarers. Crewless ships are expected to be smaller than their conventional counterparts, in part due to the removal of the crew and their life-support systems and in part due to the lower fixed cost and the effect of that on optimal ship size. *An*

*interesting research theme is therefore a policy to maximise the benefits of the eventual arrival of smaller crewless ships for coastal and shortsea shipping, supply chains and the regeneration of port cities like Newcastle NSW (a large coal port faced with the long-term decline in the coal trade).*

# References

Corvus Energy (2018a), 'World's first all-electric car ferry', www.corvusenergy.com/marine-project/mf-ampere-ferry/. Accessed 24 August 2018.

Corvus Energy (2018b), 'Scandlines shares experiences with hybrid and electric ferry technology', www.corvusenergy.com/scandlines-shares-experiences-with-hybrid-and-electric-ferry-technology/. Accessed 24 August 2018.

Enercon (2018), 'Class renewal for the "E-Ship 1"', www.enercon.de/en/news/news-detail/cc_news/show/News/class-renewal-for-the-e-ship-1/. Accessed 24 August 2018.

Greenport (2014), 'New hybrid Rotortug for Kotug', www.greenport.com/news101/lng/kotug-takes-delivery-of-new-hybrid-rotortug. Accessed 24 August 2018.

Greenport (2017), 'LNG ferry for Brittany Ferries', www.greenport.com/news101/lng/brittany-ferries-confirms-lng-ferry. Accessed 24 August 2018.

Greenport (2018), 'Battery electric ferry wins hybrid ship award', www.greenport.com/news101/energy-and-technology/battery-electric-ferry-wins-hybrid-ship-award. Accessed 24 August 2018.

Grey, E (2018), 'Carnival's LNG fleet: Ushering in a new generation of cruise ships', www.ship-technology.com/features/carnivals-lng-fleet-ushering-new-generation-cruise-ships/. Accessed 24 August 2018.

LNG World News (2018), 'Shell takes delivery of LNG-powered barge', www.lngworldnews.com/shell-takes-delivery-of-lng-powered-barge/. Accessed 24 August 2018.

Milne, R (2017), 'Moller-Maersk puts cost of cyber attack at up to $300m', *Financial Times*, 16 August 2017.

OOCL (2018), www.oocl.com/eng/pressandmedia/pressreleases/2018/Pages/23apr18.aspx. Accessed 24 August 2018.

Port Technology (2017), 'New IMO rules Introduced to fight invasive aquatic species', www.porttechnology.org/news/new_imo_rules_introduced_to_fight_invasive_aquatic_species. Accessed 25 August 2018.

Port Technology (2018a), 'IMO set on slashing industry emissions', www.porttechnology.org/news/imo_set_on_slashing_industry_emissions. Accessed 25 August 2018.

Port Technology (2018b), 'IMO begins validating autonomous ship operations', www.porttechnology.org/news/imo_begins_validating_autonomous_ship_operations. Accessed 24 August 2018.

Rodrigue, J-P (2017), *The Geography of Transport Systems*, New York: Routledge.

Schuler, M (2015), 'APM Terminals open high-tech, zero emissions Maasvlakte II container terminal in Rotterdam', www.gcaptain.com/apm-terminals-opens-high-tech-zero-emissions-maasvlakte-ii-container-terminal-in-rotterdam/. Accessed 24 August 2018.

Skredderberget, A (2018), 'First ever zero emission, autonomous ship', www.yara.com/knowledge-grows/game-changer-for-the-environment/. Accessed 24 August 2018.

SkySails (2018), www.skysails.info/en/. Accessed 24 August 2018.

Tradelens (2018), www.tradelens.com. Accessed 24 August 2018.

Unifeeder (2018), 'The Unifeeder Group becomes part of the DP World Group', www.unifeeder.com/C1257026006095A6/0/D632DB230E6E35BDC12582E2001CA814. Accessed 24 August 2018.

Van Jole, J A (2014), 'Control of automated container terminals: A literature review on automated container handling equipment', mararchief.tudelft.nl/file/38043/. Accessed 24 August 2018.

Wackett, R (2018), 'Rotterdam deal ensures low-sulphur fuel supply for Maersk box ships', www.theload star.co.uk/maersk-ensures-low-sulphur-fuel-supply-box-ships-rotterdam-deal/. Accessed 24 August 2018.

Whiteman, A (2017), 'Unifeeder launches first retrofitted LNG-powered shortsea box ship', www. theloadstar.co.uk/unifeeder-launches-first-retrofitted-lng-powered-shortsea-box-ship/. Accessed 24 August 2018.

# 11 Long-distance transport service sustainability: Management and policy directions from the airline perspective

*Rico Merkert and James Bushell*

## 11.1 Introduction

Airlines have seen significant expansion from their initial role as a mail carrier, to providing hundreds of thousands of seats and connections daily. Aviation has been globally transformative in its ability to quickly connect parts of the world. Replicating previous efforts by sea and rail, aviation is able to move more people further, quicker, allowing them to conduct business or enjoy leisure time. Increasing efficiency of aviation services is only serving to increase the demand. This has, in part, facilitated economic growth in a range of geographies (Baker et al. 2015; Hakim and Merkert 2016). If aviation was a country it would be the 21st largest when measured in Gross Domestic Product (ATAG 2016). The industry has grown on average 4.4 per cent annually and is expected to double within the next 10 years (Airbus 2018). Given this growth, the industry has reached limits, including bilateral air services agreements, airport congestion (airside and landside) and environmental limits. Whilst the industry has developed voluntary mechanisms related to reducing its carbon footprint (e.g., Carbon Offsetting and Reduction Scheme for International Aviation (CORSIA), which will come into force in 2019; ICAO 2018), new ways of integration may be required to ensure that the contributions of aviation are not diminished. Research is required to better understand the role that previously outclassed modes may play in the current transport task and how, in their entirety, all forms of transport can be more effectively connected to enhance the sustainability of the system.

The increase in air travel brings new management challenges, policy directions and research opportunities across a range of areas. Research efforts have begun to examine some of these, including air-rail intermodality, incorporation of aviation into urban transport systems and management of the environmental impacts of air transport (Merkert et al. forthcoming), with initial policies of integrating air and rail services for environmental and congestion benefits perhaps not yielding the desired results. Indeed, a number of follow-on effects have been identified, consistent with the linkage that air travel has with the broader economy (Baker et al. 2015). These topics may represent new areas for research efforts and management focus for value creation that are worthy of investigation, and may require new policy to govern (unintended) side effects.

In this chapter, we discuss areas where, in our view, additional focus is required to provide meaningful inputs into the policy process for government, and to the strategic management process by airlines.

## 11.2    Air-rail intermodality

Rail (and sea) modes traditionally dominated the long-haul passenger transport task, until the advent of aircraft overtook them. Given rail's geographically constrained route options and the long travel times of sea modes, they were limited in their ability to compete with air to provide faster, point to point journeys at a lower cost to the passenger.

However, the advantages of these previously 'outclassed' modes, particularly rail, have recently been more appreciated (Givoni and Bannister 2017), especially for short-/medium-distance trips and journeys. Recently both rail and air have seen changes in their thinking on integration, particularly where the cost of integration is low (Albalate et al. 2015). Research has shown that connected rail services may alleviate airport congestion (Sun et al. 2017), through passengers choosing rail options and reducing demand for air travel. Policy directives have therefore looked to rail as a policy solution to help solve congestion and environmental problems, caused by increasing travel demand. With the broadening of the High Speed Rail (HSR) networks in Europe, China, and other areas, HSR can feed passengers to, and distribute passengers from, air services at large airports and reduce the need for air travel over shorter distances (Clewlow et al. 2012). Airlines have also seen integration with rail operators as a strategy to operate to more destinations without contravening restrictive airspace agreements.

Some tentative steps to more fully integrate air transport with land modes have been taken (e.g., Merkert et al. forthcoming), where railways have agreements with airlines to extend passenger route options, offering booked, timetabled services between distant places. Investment in medium and HSR has let it compete with short-haul flights, particularly for trips of less than a few hours (Dobruszkes et al. 2014; Jiang and Zhang 2016). Given its ability to deliver passengers to the heart of cities, instead of airports on their outskirts, and provide better passenger amenity (including seat comfort, on board service, short/no check-in and reduced security screening), rail transport is becoming more and more attractive to consumers who value the travel time and convenience savings (Brida et al. 2017). Rail may also have lower fares than comparable journeys by air (Socorro and Vincennes 2013). Therefore there are situations where rail may complement air and provide value to passengers.

AirRail, a successful partnership between Lufthansa and Deutsche Bahn (DB; which has similar agreements with 50 other airlines marketed as Rail and Fly), utilises a fully integrated rail terminal in Frankfurt airport, offering an airline-like transfer, baggage check-in, lounge access and journey disruption management.

Other similar arrangements exist in Europe between airlines and SNCF (France), Trenitalia (Italy), Renfe (Spain) and ÖBB (Austria). Another noteworthy air-rail arrangement exists between United Airlines and Amtrak, for connections from Newark Airport to various stations in the US North East. Air Canada and Via Rail have an agreement where rail is offered as an alternative in cases of significant disruption experienced by the airline.

Passenger preferences will impact the overall success of air-rail policy directives. Transfer/transit experience is a well-known driver of passenger choice of airline/route/flight (e.g., Merkert and Beck forthcoming) which applies to air-rail transfers. Lower passenger connection times make intermodal transfers more likely, through improved passenger convenience (Xia and Zhang 2017). The minimisation of transfer cost will influence whether air-rail partnerships will form. Jiang et al. (2017) found that high pre-cooperation service levels (including low passenger transfer costs) led to partnership formation. The presence of co-located terminals can be the most significant determinant of whether an air-rail partnership will form (Lia et al. 2018). Thus there has been focus on efficient physical integration to improve passenger connection experience. Provided with an easy, convenient transfer route and a short transit time, consumers may be more willing to make the transfer.

A first-best policy response appears to be to co-locate air and rail terminals to reduce passenger transfer cost. Decisions made to not integrate air and rail in future developments are therefore interesting: for example, High Speed 2 in the United Kingdom which does not connect directly to Heathrow and would reduce the attractiveness for air-rail transfers to other locations in the UK or Europe. This is especially interesting considering the debate around the third runway at Heathrow and its significant capital cost and disruption to local residents. Transport researchers may wish to examine the assumptions underlying the business case and compare these to proven experiences.

However, high-quality physical terminal integration in China has, as yet, failed to develop meaningful air-rail partnerships. Absent effective institutional integration, the benefits of this physical integration can be limited or indeed unachievable (Givoni and Chen 2017). Integration efforts appear to have been airline driven (and indeed many publications on this matter appear in aviation rather than railway journals). Railway operators do not market these arrangements to any significant degree and seem to be a passive participant in the agreement. Indeed, DB requires that the booking be handled and managed by the airline, rather than marketing the ticket itself. Airlines use these options to extend the already successful integration experienced between airlines through integrative institutions in air transport.

Airlines cooperate with each other through a range of institutional mechanisms including the International Air Transport Association (IATA), an airline member led organisation. IATA has led the development of standardised agreements that reduce transaction cost between airlines, and helps in their execution through services such as clearinghouse transaction settlement. Airlines have looked to extend this behaviour into the rail space to provide new destination options to their passengers, using someone else's network. Working with each other, forming alliances and joint ventures to their mutual benefit (Wang 2014), value is created for passengers through collaborative service provision, including ticketing, seating, journey management and fare integration (which is valued by passengers (Román and Martín 2014)).

Attempting to replicate this with rail operators has been a natural strategy for airlines; however, for rail operators it is perhaps a strategy they do not yet see value in. Up to the early 2010s the number of these arrangements was increasing but their number has not grown in any substantial manner, at least in comparison to the continued proliferation of airline-airline agreements since then. The terminal/transfer experience will be an explanator for the low number of these arrangements. There may be strategic and structural considerations that warrant research to explain the low uptake and adoption of air-rail partnerships.

Chiambaretto and Decker (2012) note that competition regulators have not yet assessed such relationships. There may be some hesitance to enter into potentially non-compliant agreements from the perspective of bilateral air service agreements. These agreements restrict carrier services (such as those in Germany where airlines like Qantas and Emirates can only operate to four airports). Should air-rail partnerships be viewed as a means of subverting these agreements, they may be less attractive for both parties to enter into. There is hence potential for research and policy initiative to clarify air service agreements further, so that air-rail partnerships are appropriately incentivised.

Airline travel has also changed strategically. With newer fuel-efficient aircraft, and competition from low cost carriers, airlines have changed their strategy, which may now be inconsistent with previous policy directives. Recognising that passengers prefer direct flights to connecting flights (Johnson et al. 2014), airlines have transitioned from a hub and spoke operating model to a point to point model (e.g., Qantas' new B787 service between London and Perth). This reduces the transfer cost by eliminating the transfer in its entirety. Low cost carriers are not interested in being part of the passenger's journey outside the section of the journey that they operate. Instead they prefer to leave passengers to manage their own journeys to and from airports.

Concentration of rail operators may reduce ability for airlines to form partnerships. For air travel, airlines can enter into contracts with a range of other airlines. But the dominance of rail operators such as DB/SNCF/Acela in their home markets means airlines are somewhat beholden to these carriers when negotiating agreements. Rail market liberalisation is prevalent in the UK market, but the lack of physical infrastructure integration makes it difficult to test if higher volume of rail operators leads to greater air-rail partnership formation. There are signs that there are rail operators wanting to try new approaches to service provision (e.g., low cost HSR (Delaplace and Dobruszkes 2015)), although these approaches are limited by the underlying railway fundamentals. Investigating why alternative services are not present, and the oligopolistic nature of the rail industry in general, may help understand how policy makers may make entry into the market more approachable for cooperation.

Air and rail operators offer a similar product but are different commercially. Airlines are increasingly commercially driven, given their privately held nature and reducing government intervention. Rail operators generally remain part of government transport policy execution (including accessibility) and usually receive funding from government budgets. Commercially, they operate differently, given that they do not need to generate all of their own income to cover costs. Linked with entrenched geographic monopolistic positions, the commerciality of management is arguably less focused on returns than it is for airlines. Chiambaretto and Decker (2012) reported that air-rail agreements involved airlines paying a fee to rail operators for the use of their services. This is in contrast to forms of airline-airline cooperation, where deep commercial negotiations have led to a range of fare-sharing arrangements. This area is ripe for research attention. Overall, research into the commerciality of rail compared to airlines may illustrate differences for consideration when forming partnerships and by policy makers when developing integration policy.

More research is needed into the broader integration of air-rail services into the networks and target passengers of the respective operators. Rail and air may serve different passenger groups, and the degree of overlap, and therefore complementarity of air and rail, requires analysis. Having integration without any real destination to get to limits the attractiveness of a connected service, and so the broader network that operators use to serve passengers may warrant consideration.

Finally, given the significant capital cost involved in terminal integration (a first-best policy), second-best policy options may be better to consider for more effective policy achievement and, from a management perspective, the achievement of greater passenger value. Policy makers might examine ways of reducing the transfer discomfort experienced by passengers through other means. Researchers and policy makers may wish to examine the role of the third operators and their place in passenger journeys. More integrated incorporation into air-rail transfers may increase the attractiveness of transfers. Linked with the next section, better use of third operators, often part of urban transport networks, may enhance the overall journeys for passengers.

## 11.3   Connecting air to the urban transport network

Ground congestion at airports continues to increase pressures on urban transport networks. Increased air transport volumes deliver passengers to concentrated airport nodes, from where passengers need to be distributed to final destinations. Encouraged in some jurisdictions (e.g., Europe) to manage these externalities, better integration of air into different modes will provide solutions to these problems. A lesser studied aspect of aviation is the impact that it has on transport systems in the cities and regions that they serve. Airports are seen as economic zones in their own right, with many air-related businesses located near them. In Sydney, the new Western Sydney Airport is being termed an 'aerotropolis' and is seen as the foundation of a new economic growth area (Australian Government 2018). Managing future transport and congestion issues that these facilities will generate should be a policy focus for governments now, rather than when the problems arise. These apply not only to the passengers who will use the terminals but also to the workers who will be commuting to and from the airport, their workplace (Orth et al. 2015).

In recognition, urban transport planners have increasingly linked urban transport services to airports. These have seen significant patronage increases, after urban rail operators have invested in reliability and punctuality, such as in Sydney where patronage on the Airport Line has increased significantly with increased reliability. Passengers are choosing to use these services over private modes. Researchers have shown that well-designed public transport is preferred by passengers when journeying to and from airports (Tam et al. 2011). Reliability, travel time, flexibility, cost and amenity are key variables that impact preferences for public transport (Akar 2013). Projects such as the proposed Underground Suburban Rail Loop in Melbourne that connect the airport to broad sections of the city are worthy of further study in this context. Policy makers could investigate changes to pricing systems, such as discounts when using public transport for airport journeys (Gokasar and Gunay 2017). Policy makers may see fit to investigate how airports may help to manage this congestion, through being tasked with managing some of the demand that they create (Ison et al. 2014). However, given the inherent conflict due to (sometimes substantial) profits being derived from parking charges and the substantial share that taxi operators may have in airport traffic, research may also need to focus on political factors and market power elements of transport linkages to airports. These impacts may prove challenging to quantify, if not address and/or manage.

Some airports do see the benefit in having better ground transport links. Gatwick Airport is working more closely with Govia Thameslink Railway to improve connectivity to the rest of the Greater London public transport network (although this is also a competitive response to Heathrow, which is well served by urban transport links). An important difference is how Gatwick and Govia share data to develop better services to meet demand and manage services more cooperatively in the case of demand interruptions. This coordinated approach may provide useful insight to networks management functions, which are often highly reactive in the face of disruption. The Gatwick/Govia interaction may be a worthwhile case study into disruption management, should sufficient disruption be experienced to test the partnership.

Commercially there are extensions to this air-ground transport coordination. Consumers show preferences for integrating air and land transport into one ticketed journey and are willing to pay for this convenience (Merkert and Beck forthcoming). Stated preference modelling shows that consumers value integrated services, which resemble integrated air services in that transfers are managed by transport operators, not the consumers. Cooperation between airlines and ride-share being witnessed in Australia between Qantas and Uber is an example of this. Investigating how such coordination may more broadly occur, or why it isn't already, will prove useful in developing policy and strategy options. This could provide useful insight into how operators may work together to provide more resource-efficient first- and last-mile journeys to airports, reducing congestion and the total cost of travel for consumers.

As noted, an important part of this research should be understanding how operators share data to improve their operations and/or improve their customer service. Airlines use passenger data (such as check-in data, intra-airport transfer data) to manage airline operations during the passenger's journey. Expanding this to ground operators and linking information about where passengers are in their total journey and their origin/destination points may provide significant insight into the impact of the total journey on airport congestion management. As IATA plays a role in the coordination of airlines, similar systems and processes warrant investigation in the public transport sector. Data ownership and the role of central public transport authorities need to be key features of this research.

Better management of airport congestion will aid in the reduction of urban congestion but will also facilitate the reduction of environmental costs incurred by private transport options on society.

## 11.4   Airlines and the environment

The above sections have mainly discussed reducing the total consumer journey cost and reasons why operators should work with each other in delivering service (and why they might not do so). An equally important facet of airline research is the environmental impacts of air travel and how better integration may reduce the negative environmental impacts of air travel – particularly through reducing greenhouse gas emissions (aviation $CO_2$ emissions are approximately 2 per cent of global emissions and are expected to grow around 3–4 per cent per year; ICAO 2018).

Research into the environmental impacts of air-rail integration has focused on rail services substituting for air services – termed the substitution effect (D'Alfonso et al. 2016) – given that rail has lower environmental costs than air travel. This is true from an operational perspective (Sicorro and Vincennes 2013). Research has not resolved whether the total lifetime cost of rail versus air travel is indeed lower. Research has also identified that airlines react to rail substitution at airports by increasing long-distance services. Rail services replace shorter-distance flights, leaving airports, particularly capacity constrained ones, to use these slots for longer-distance services which increase environmental impacts of transport

– termed the generation effect (D'Alfonso et al. 2016). Indeed, transitioning short-distance, lower-volume air services to rail services may be a profitable strategy for those constrained airports to free up slots for longer-distance, higher-volume ones (Dobruszkes and Givoni 2013). Dobruszkes et al. (2016) concluded that HSR as an environmental panacea may be somewhat overstated.

Accordingly, using rail to reduce air emissions is not a perfect policy response, and indeed, as second-best policy, it perhaps cannot hope to be. The first-best solution, introducing a global carbon emission trading scheme for aviation-related greenhouse gas generation (as with CORSIA from 2019), is a step in the right direction. A holistic transport approach integrating all modes including HSR, ground access transport at airports and private vehicles into such a scheme (or to set other incentives) should perhaps be the primary policy focus for longer-term success, as reduced private/increased public transport at airports has significant potential to reduce aviation's carbon footprint. Whilst fraught with political implications, the use of pricing mechanisms to influence air and rail costs, fares, and ultimately operator supply and consumer purchase decisions is more consistent with the achievement of economic efficiency. Integration with rail may be just one of the policy options.

## 11.5   Conclusions and final views

We have shown the substantial scope for research into more effective aviation-ground transport integration. This may create more sustainable services that meet passenger needs more effectively. Whilst significant attention has been placed on air and HSR cooperation, more impactful solutions may develop through integrating air and urban transport at the airports they serve, to address growing levels of localised congestion. Better integration through information systems may open new avenues for cooperation between ground and air operators to improve services. Better physical integration of public transport and air terminal infrastructure may be a good starting point but the integration should go beyond that and is an area where transport policy makers may be able to assist.

This is not to say that air and HSR do not have research futures, but assuming that air and rail terminal infrastructure is all that is needed to allow successful cooperation is not sufficient. Other facets of the relationship need consideration. The function of combined networks, complementarity or not of market structures and strategies, relative market presence of rail and air operators, and coordination mechanisms that they may use are all areas that will provide interesting insight into forming better relationships for a joint aim to improve sustainability of long-distance mobility.

Underlying all of this, fundamental economic market adjustment, as it pertains to aviation, and its integration into the broader transport landscape, should be an ongoing research area, particularly pertaining to key areas such as environmental charging, road user charging and congestion charging. With different price signals, cost structures of transport options will become different and impact on mode choice behaviours by passengers. Attention to these prices will aid in the development of economically efficient decision making by all participants in the transportation value chain.

# References

Airbus (2018), *Global Market Forecast 2018–2037*, Toulouse: Author.

Akar, G. (2013), 'Ground access to airports, case study: Port Columbus International Airport', *Journal of Air Transport Management*, **30**, 25–31.

Albalate, D., Bel, G. and Fageda, X. (2015), 'Competition and cooperation between high-speed rail and air transportation services in Europe', *Journal of Transport Geography*, **42**, 166–174.

ATAG (2016), *Aviation Benefits beyond Borders*, Geneva: Air Transport Action Group.

Australian Government (2018), *Western Sydney AEROTROPOLIS Investor Guide*, Canberra/Sydney; available at: https://www.industry.nsw.gov.au/__data/assets/pdf_file/0009/161694/Western-Sydney-Aerotropolis-investor-guide.pdf. Accessed 3 October 2018.

Baker, D., Merkert, R. and Kamruzzaman, M. (2015), 'Regional aviation and economic growth: Cointegration and causality analysis in Australia', *Journal of Transport Geography*, **43**, 140–150.

Brida, J.G., Martín, J.C., Román, C. and Scuderi, R. (2017), 'Air and HST multimodal products: A segmentation analysis for policy makers', *Networks and Spatial Economics*, **17**(3), 911–934.

Chiambaretto P. and Decker C. (2012), 'Air–rail intermodal agreements: Balancing the competition and environmental effects', *Journal of Air Transport Management*, **23**, 36–40.

Clewlow, R., Sussman, J. and Balakrishnan, H. (2012), 'Interaction of high-speed rail and aviation: Exploring air-rail connectivity', *Transportation Research Record: Journal of the Transportation Research Board*, **2266**, 1–10.

D'Alfonso, T., Jiang, C. and Bracaglia, V. (2016), 'Air transport and high-speed rail competition: Environmental implications and mitigation strategies', *Transportation Research Part A: Policy and Practice*, **92**, 261–276.

Delaplace, M. and Dobruszkes, F. (2015), 'From low-cost airlines to low-cost high-speed rail? The French case', *Transport Policy*, **38**, 73–85.

Dobruszkes, F., Dehon, C. and Givoni, M. (2014), 'Does European high-speed rail affect the current level of air services? An EU-wide analysis', *Transportation Research Part A: Policy and Practice*, **69**, 461–475.

Dobruszkes, F. and Givoni, M. (2013), 'Competition, integration, substitution: Myths and realities concerning the relationship between high-speed rail and air transport in Europe'. In Budd, L., Griggs, S. and Howarth, D. (Eds) *Sustainable Aviation Futures*. Bingley: Emerald Group Publishing, 175–197.

Dobruszkes, F., Givoni, M. and Dehon, C. (2016), 'Assessing the competition between high-speed rail and airlines: A critical perspective'. In Ablate, D and Bel, G. (Eds) *Evaluating High-Speed Rail: Interdisciplinary Perspectives*, London: Routledge, 159–174.

Givoni, M. and Banister, D. (2017), 'Realising the potential of HSR: The United Kingdom experience'. In Henríquez, B.L.P. and Deakin, E. (Eds) *High-Speed Rail and Sustainability*, London: Routledge, 33–49.

Givoni, M. and Chen, X. (2017), 'Airline and railway disintegration in China: The case of Shanghai Hongqiao integrated transport hub', *Transportation Letters*, **9**(4), 202–214.

Gokasar, I. and Gunay, G. (2017), 'Mode choice behavior modeling of ground access to airports: A case study in Istanbul, Turkey', *Journal of Air Transport Management*, **59**, 1–7.

Hakim, M.M. and Merkert, R. (2016), 'The causal relationship between air transport and economic growth: Empirical evidence from South Asia', *Journal of Transport Geography*, **56**, 120–127.

ICAO (International Civil Aviation Organization) (2018), *Carbon Offsetting and Reduction Scheme for International Aviation* (CORSIA) – Implementation. Available at: https://www.icao.int/environmental-protection/CORSIA/Pages/default.aspx. Accessed 3 October 2018.

Ison, S., Merkert, R. and Mulley, C. (2014), 'Policy approaches to public transport at airports – some diverging evidence from the UK and Australia', *Transport Policy*, **35**, 265–274.

Jiang, C., D'Alfonso, T. and Wan, Y. (2017), 'Air-rail cooperation: Partnership level, market structure and welfare implications', *Transportation Research Part B: Methodological*, **104**, 461–482.

Jiang, C. and Zhang, A. (2016), 'Airline network choice and market coverage under high-speed rail competition', *Transportation Research Part A: Policy and Practice*, **92**, 248–260.

Johnson, D., Hess, S. and Matthews, B. (2014), 'Understanding air travellers' trade-offs between connecting flights and surface access characteristics', *Journal of Air Transport Management*, **34**, 70–77.

Lia, X., Jiang, C., Wang, K. and Mac, J. (2018), 'Determinants of partnership levels in air-rail cooperation', *Journal of Air Transport Management*, **71**, 88–96.

Merkert, R. and Beck, M.J. (forthcoming), 'Can a strategy of integrated air-bus services create a value proposition for regional aviation management?', *Transportation Research Part A: Policy and Practice*.

Merkert, R., Bushell, J. and Beck, M. (forthcoming), 'Collaboration as a service (CaaS) to fully integrate public transportation – lessons from long distance travel to reimagine Mobility as a Service', *Transportation Research Part A: Policy and Practice*.

Orth, H., Frei, O. and Weidmann, U. (2015), 'Effects of non-aeronautical activities at airports on the public transport access system: A case study of Zurich Airport', *Journal of Air Transport Management*, **42**, 37–46.

Román, C. and Martín, J.C. (2010), 'Potential demand for new high speed rail services in high dense air transport corridors', *International Journal of Sustainable Development Planning*, **5**(2), 114–129.

Román, C. and Martín, J.C. (2014), 'Integration of HSR and air transport: Understanding passengers' preferences', *Transportation Research Part E: Logistics and Transportation Review*, **71**, 129–141.

Socorro, M.P. and Viecens, M.F. (2013), 'The effects of airline and high speed train integration', *Transportation Research Part A: Policy and Practice*, **49**, 160–177.

Sun, X., Wandelt, S. and Cao, X. (2017), 'On node criticality in air transportation networks', *Networks and Spatial Economics*, **17**(3), 737–761.

Tam, M., Lam, W. and Lo, H. (2011), 'The impact of travel time reliability and perceived service quality on airport ground access mode choice', *Journal of Choice Modelling*, **4**, 49–69.

Wang, S.W. (2014), 'Do global airline alliances influence the passenger's purchase decision?', *Journal of Air Transport Management*, **37**, 53–59.

Xia, W. and Zhang, A. (2017), 'Air and high-speed rail transport integration on profits and welfare: Effects of air-rail connecting time', *Journal of Air Transport Management*, **65**, 181–190.

# 12 Freight transport and logistics

*Alan McKinnon*

## 12.1 The evolution of freight transport research

Freight transport was for many years a subject of minority interest in the transport research community. It received token representation at transport conferences and in transport journals typically dominated by research on the movement of people, infrastructure planning and traffic safety. University transport departments and transport consultancies would often have a solitary freight specialist. In transport policy circles, much lip service was paid to the importance of freight but this was seldom matched by the amount of public research funding provided.

This comparative neglect of freight transport can be attributed to a number of factors. Perhaps the movement of inanimate objects is inherently less interesting than the movement of people. As researchers are travellers themselves they directly experience the challenges and frustrations and see the potential for improvement. Personal users of the transport system can also be more easily surveyed than businesses managing the distribution of goods, offering greater opportunity for empirical research and behavioural analysis. In many countries, government transport statistics offered much deeper insight into patterns of personal travel than into the workings of the freight transport system. The lower priority accorded to freight research may also have been related to the fact that it doesn't vote and usually gets limited exposure in national and local media.

Over the past 20–30 years, the study of freight transport has ceased to be the 'poor relation' and instead become one of the main growth areas for transport research. The transformation of its research prospects has been the result primarily of three developments.

### 12.1.1 Growth of logistics and supply chain management

The emergence of logistics/supply chain management in the 1970s and 1980s brought a new business perspective to the study of freight transport. This presented freight transport as an integral part of logistics systems also comprising inventory management, storage, materials handling and related information processing. It emphasised the inter-relationship between freight movement and all the economic activities it connects across the supply chain. In so doing it addressed one of the major deficiencies of previous academic research on freight transport, namely that it focused on individual freight trips and paid too little attention to their wider logistical significance. It saw them as vehicle movements in a traffic flow rather than as links in a supply chain. Freight journeys were subjected to the same four-stage modelling procedure used by highway engineers to simulate and forecast flows of other categories of traffic (i.e. trip generation, trip distribution, modal split and vehicle routing). While this offered consistency, it failed to capture the logistical complexity underpinning the movement of goods. To understand why particular products were moved between particular locations at particular times by particular modes in vehicles with particular load factors one needed an appreciation of business processes and distribution channels. Forty years of research on logistics and supply chain management has provided the necessary insights into the workings of the freight transport system. Much of this research has been done in business schools rather transport departments and its results published in the managerial rather than transport literature.

### 12.1.2   Increasing concern about the environmental and congestion impacts of freight traffic growth

The growth of freight traffic has exacerbated environmental and congestion problems, arousing greater public and political concern and often stoked by the campaigning of environmental pressure groups. In many countries economic growth and freight tonne-kilometres growth have remained closely aligned while road freight services have captured an increasing share of the freight market from more environmentally friendly rail and waterway networks. The resulting increase in freight-related externalities has stimulated research into ways of decoupling the adverse effects of freight traffic growth from economic development. Much of this effort has been concentrated in urban areas, where high levels of logistical activity and dense populations coincide, especially in the megacities of the developing world. While the impact of freight traffic on air quality has tended to dominate research agendas in developing countries, in Europe and North America, continents with a longer history of regulatory controls on exhaust emissions of NOx and particulate matter, freight's contribution to greenhouse emissions and global warming has become the main focus of environment-related research.

### 12.1.3   Development and refinement of public policy on freight transport

Governments at international, national, regional and local levels have, to some extent, been provoked into devising specific policies for freight transport by the negative trends outlined in the previous paragraph. It would be wrong, however, to suggest that the main objective of public policy in this field has been to minimise negative externalities. Governments recognise that freight transport plays a vital role in promoting economic growth and social well-being and must be supported with infrastructural investment and sound regulatory and fiscal policies. The move to more evidence-based policy-making on freight and logistics created a demand for new studies on topics such as freight modal shift, urban freight consolidation, eco-driving and the relaxation of truck size and weight limits.

Having reviewed the recent history of freight transport research, we will now examine some promising areas for future, policy-relevant research in this field. They will be reviewed under three headings: freight traffic growth, environmental sustainability and last-mile logistics.

## 12.2    Freight traffic growth: Modelling disruptive scenarios

The demand for reliable long-term freight traffic forecasts has never been greater. Governments require them for the formulation of economic and environmental policy and the planning of infrastructure, energy supply, employment, land use, etc. The private sector also needs them for strategic planning and investment appraisal. Mounting pressure on governments and businesses to decarbonise freight transport over the next few decades has further strengthened the need for accurate forecasts of baseline trends.

Freight modelling capabilities have greatly improved over the past decade with the development of new tools, access to new data sources and vast increases in computing capacity. The main challenges today, however, are not so much statistical and computational. They stem more from fundamental changes in the way goods are produced, traded and distributed, which prevent the extrapolation of past trends and undermine traditional assumptions upon which much long-term freight forecasting has been based. In some countries, one can no longer assume continued close coupling of GDP and tonne-kilometres while, in the case of international freight flows, analysts are unsure if the steep drop in the trade-GDP multiplier post-2008 is a temporary aberration or a 'new normal' (ECB, 2016). Forecasters are currently debating why GDP-trade-freight elasticities have sharply deviated from their historic trends and how they might incorporate new disruptive forces into their modelling. Many of these forces are at an early stage but likely to intensify in the coming decades. They include the following matters.

*Reshoring of production:* it is anticipated that some manufacturing capacity may return from low-labour-cost countries to North America and Europe, effectively reversing the process of globalisation (Wiessman et al., 2017). This would be encouraged by a combination of wage inflation in the Far East, a proliferation of protectionist policies and automation of production processes. If so-called reshoring gathers momentum it would further depress the trade multiplier and dampen the future growth of long-haul, cross-border freight. A much-quoted projection by OECD/ITF (2017) that globally freight tonne-kilometres will triple between 2015 and 2050 might then prove to be a substantial over-estimate.

*Additive manufacturing:* the long-term impact of this technology is one of the great uncertainties in freight transport planning. Surveys of expert opinion on this issue have yielded results that are fairly inconclusive (e.g. Boon and van Wee, 2017) or barely credible (ING, 2017). There are two key questions: (a) what will be the effect of additive manufacturing on supply chains and (b) what will be its likely uptake? The answer to both questions largely depends on the extent to which this technology offers economics of scale. In the current 3D printing phase of additive manufacturing, scale economies are limited and unit production cost relatively high, tightly constraining its impact on supply chain structure and tonne-kilometres. It is now entering a new phase when processes such as digital light synthesis offer much greater opportunity for mass customisation and the streamlining and relocalising of supply chains. How will this key element in the 4th Industrial Revolution affect the nature, pattern and scale of freight movement by 2030 and beyond?

*Circular economy:* the re-use, remanufacturing and recycling (the 3Rs) of products are well established but still only exploit a small fraction of the value remaining in much consumer and industrial waste. Applying the principles of the circular economy, as increasing numbers of businesses and organisations are committed to doing, would cause a step change in the 3Rs, reducing reliance on resource extraction and waste disposal and reconfiguring supply chains across a range of industrial and retail sectors (Ellen MacArthur Foundation and McKinsey & Company, 2014). This could dramatically change both the volume and pattern of freight movement over the next few decades.

*Dematerialisation:* the digitisation of news, education and entertainment media, product downsizing and the substitution of lighter materials for heavier ones have significantly reduced freight volumes in particular sectors. To what extent are these dematerialisation trends likely to continue over the next few decades and what will be their logistical consequences?

*Decarbonisation of energy:* The G7 countries have committed to abandoning fossil fuels by the end of this century. Recent climate modelling suggests that this fossil fuel phase-out will have to be completed much sooner if we are to meet the 2015 Paris Climate Change targets by 2100. As fossil fuels account for a substantial proportion of freight tonne-kilometres worldwide, this will have a significant impact on the global freight market (McKinnon, 2018). The substitution of fossil fuels by renewable and nuclear energy and the need to install carbon capture and storage systems on legacy fossil fuel plants will generate new forms of freight traffic which will at least partly replace coal, oil and gas movement. This fundamental transformation of the global energy system will also influence the freight transport system through its effect on the price of energy used in the logistics sector. This nexus of energy-related issues will merit close scrutiny in future analyses of freight traffic growth.

*Climate change adaptation, negative emissions and geo-engineering:* Even if climate change targets are met, which seems unlikely, there will still be a need to adapt our built environment to all the adverse meteorological and geophysical effects already 'in the pipeline'. This is likely to be both material- and transport-intensive, as revealed by preliminary modelling of the freight demands of infrastructural climate-proofing (Becker et al., 2016). Failure to stay within global carbon budgets will require the deployment of negative emission options to remove greenhouse gases already in the atmosphere. One of these options, bio-energy with carbon capture and storage (BECCS), will require the movement of vast amounts of biomass and liquefied carbon dioxide. It may ultimately be necessary to resort to various forms of geo-engineering, all of which would have to be applied at a planetary scale and impose heavy strains on the freight transport system. The logistical practicality of the various negative emission and geo-engineering options has yet to be fully investigated.

Each of these developments on its own has the potential to seriously disrupt long-term freight trends. Combining their effects adds an extra layer of complexity, making forecasting, road-mapping and scenario-building in the freight sector all the more daunting. It also encourages research on the inter-relationship between freight transport policy and wider government policies on trade, competition, technology, energy and the environment.

## 12.3   Sustainable freight transport: Plugging gaps and opening new horizons

Sustainability has become one of the dominant themes in freight transport research, being the subject of numerous journal papers, reports, theses and books, receiving significant research funding and featuring prominently in conference programmes. Although none of the UN Sustainable Development Goals specifically relate to freight transport, or indeed to transport as a whole, many of them will only be achievable if logistics systems function properly. The environmental policies of some countries and international organisations make more explicit reference to freight transport. The EU, for example, is requiring new trucks sold after 2025 to emit 15% less $CO_2$ than their 2019 equivalents and aims to achieve 'zero-emission city logistics' by 2030 (European Commission, 2011).

The greening of freight transport has generated a large literature, but this does not equip policy-makers with all the information and tools they require. Gaps exist in a number of areas.

*Assessment of freight transport externalities:* most of the available emissions data for the freight sector is calculated on a tank-to-wheel basis, giving only a partial view of its true environmental impact. The calculation boundary needs to be extended to include emissions from the energy supply chain, the construction and maintenance of vehicles and infrastructure and related administrative and IT activities. Only when assessments of freight externalities become truly holistic will policy-makers have the comprehensive evidence base that they require, particularly if and when they decide to fully internalise the environmental costs of freight movement.

*Freight modal shift:* despite 50 years of research on ways of promoting greater use of greener modes, particularly rail, and wide implementation of related public policy initiatives, there are still few examples of modal split trends moving in an environmentally friendly direction. This is clearly a source of disappointment and frustration but not a reason for abandoning modal shift as a pertinent research topic. Advances in intermodal technology, new concepts such as synchromodality (Dong et al., 2018), digitalisation and the rapid expansion of transAsian rail freight services offer new avenues for research and policy development on the modal split issue.

*Energy use in the freight sector:* reducing exhaust emissions of noxious and green-house gases across the freight sector in line with public policy objectives will necessitate both energy efficiency improvements and a major switch to alternative energy sources. Both options have already been actively researched, particularly with respect to trucking and shipping, though there remains great uncertainty over the most cost-effective pathways to deep decarbonisation (McKinnon, 2018). In the case of long-distance road freight, for example, batteries, hydrogen and highway catenary systems are all being promoted as carriers of the low carbon electricity that trucks will need to decarbonise, though it is not clear what their relative contributions will be. Likewise, the International Maritime Organisation's commitment to cut total emissions from international shipping by 50% between 2008 and 2050 (IMO, 2018) is provoking intense debate on how, in energy terms, this will be achieved.

*Routing, scheduling and loading of freight vehicles:* the optimisation of vehicle routing is one of the longest-established and, in terms of journal papers, most prolific fields of freight research. This has been largely the preserve of mathematicians and operations researchers, much of whose work has prioritised algorithm refinement over relevance to the real worlds of logistics management and transport policy. Research in this area has recently redefined optimisation criteria to include the minimisation of vehicle emissions in the expanding field of 'pollution routing' (Bektaş and Laporte, 2011). The rescheduling of freight deliveries into off-peak periods, long debated as a policy option, has been shown to yield large environmental and economic benefits (Holguín-Veras et al., 2018), but its wider impact on logistics systems has yet to be fully appraised. In the longer term, more radical reorganisation of freight transport could offer quantum improvements in the utilisation of freight vehicles. The Physical Internet has been presented as a 2050 vision of the future development of logistics, effectively transferring the principles of the digital internet into the physical world of freight transport (Ballot, Russell and Montreuil, 2014). It has attracted the attention of public policy-makers, particularly in Europe. Already roadmapping studies have examined migration paths from our current freight transport system to a PI one characterised by open access, shared use of assets, devolved control, data transparency and modularised consignments. These studies are likely to be the precursors of a major research effort to assess the practicality, scalability and sustainability of this major new logistical paradigm.

## 12.4    Last-mile logistics: Identifying potential game-changers

The last link in a supply chain, over which so-called 'last-mile' deliveries are made, has been the focus of much policy discussion and logistics innovation in recent years. The innovation has been both demand- and supply-driven. On the demand side, online retailers, and the carriers to whom they outsource their logistics, have been looking for new ways of providing rapid, reliable and secure home delivery at minimal cost. Online retailing, which effectively transfers responsibility for last-mile logistics from the consumer to the retailer, has been growing globally at annual rates of 20–25% (Emarketer, 2018). This has been dramatically increasing the amount of van traffic in urban and rural areas and helped to make vans the fastest-growing category of road traffic in many countries. For companies, the online logistics challenge involves not only accommodating high volume growth but also doing it within shorter order lead times and tightening delivery windows. Having conditioned consumers to expect delivery at little or no cost, they must also achieve this as efficiently as possible. For governments and municipal authorities it raises a host of issues relating to traffic growth, land use planning, the environment and working conditions in the delivery sector.

On the supply side, new modes of delivery and new business models are being trialled which, if they prove commercially viable and scalable, could transform the movement of freight in urban areas. On the other hand, they may remain little more than curiosities confined to a few cities. Research is required on the likely uptake rates for these logistical innovations and the wider implications for public policy. The innovations include the following.

*Domestic unattended delivery:* the concept of using reception boxes to allow unattended delivery to the home is not new. Trials and modelling conducted almost 20 years ago demonstrated that it could substantially improve delivery efficiency and cut traffic levels. The adoption rate for this technology has, nevertheless, remained very low. The steep growth of online retailing is now raising the frequency of home delivery beyond the break-even level for investment in reception boxes, while new secure home access systems for parcel deliveries might obviate the need for external boxes. The time is therefore ripe for a reappraisal of the potential contribution of unattended delivery to the rationalisation of last-mile delivery.

*Drones:* there has been much discussion in recent years about the use of drones to deliver parcels and numerous small-scale trials held around the world. In most countries aviation regulations currently require drone operation within line-of-sight, preventing their use as autonomous vehicles and hence stifling their commercial use as a parcel delivery mode. Relaxing these regulations would allow last-mile logistics to take to the air. Preliminary research has been undertaken on the potential usage of drones for this purpose (SESAR, 2016; McKinnon, 2016) but much more is needed to inform policy-making on the environmental and traffic impacts of this new freight mode. The use of drones to deliver emergency supplies in developing countries with poor surface infrastructure is also a research priority in the field of humanitarian logistics.

*Droids:* These surface delivery robots are being trialled in urban areas in several countries and advertised as offering a fast, efficient and secure means of distributing fast food and parcels within a 2–3km range. The implications of a mass uptake of droids for vehicular and pedestrian traffic and the urban environment have yet to be fully examined.

*Crowdshipping:* this involves the online crowdsourcing of delivery services from people willing to carry consignments for others often in the course of their normal travel. It was originally seen as part of the share economy operating within local communities and exploiting synergies between personal and freight movement (Marcucci et al., 2017). With the entry of companies like Uber and Amazon into the market, it has become a more commercial activity though still offers new opportunities for integrating personal and freight movement, with all the transport risks and benefits that might bring.

*Urban portering:* analyses in London and elsewhere have revealed that a large proportion of van drivers' time is spent walking to final delivery points, leaving the vehicles parked for around two-thirds of their time. This suggests that the efficiency of last-mile logistics might be significantly enhanced by decoupling vehicular movements from manual portering using outbased porters (or 'concierges') in strategic locations to provide 'micro-deliveries' on foot or by cargo-cycle (Bates et al., 2018). This suggests that the promotion of non-vehicular transport should feature in urban transport policies for freight as well as personal movement.

## 12.5   Conclusion

Plotting possible directions for future research in a field is inevitably a subjective process in which one exhibits biases in favour of particular topics and methodologies. In this chapter, however, I have taken a quite a broad view of the subject area to give readers a sense of the diverse range of policy-relevant research questions that still need to be answered. There are more than enough questions to keep the expanding community of freight and logistics researchers busy for the foreseeable future.

## References

Ballot, E., Russell, M. and Montreuil, B. (2014), *The Physical Internet: The Network of Logistics Networks*, Paris: PREDIT.

Bates, O. et al. (2018), 'Transforming last-mile logistics: Opportunities for more sustainable deliveries', *Proceedings of 2018 CHI Conference on Human Factors in Computing Systems* (paper 526), Montreal. https://dl.acm.org/citation.cfm?doid=3173574.3174100. Accessed 3 October 2018.

Becker, A., Chase, N.T.L., Fischer, M., Schwegler, B. and Mosher, K. (2016), 'A method to estimate climate-critical construction materials applied to seaport protection', *Global Environmental Change*, **40**, 125–136.

Bektaş, T. and Laporte, G. (2011), 'The pollution-routing problem', *Transportation Research Part B: Methodological*, **45**(8), 1232–1250.

Boon, W. and van Wee, B. (2017), 'Influence of 3D printing on transport: A theory and experts judgment based conceptual model', *Transport Reviews*, **38**, 556–575.

Dong, C., Boute, R., McKinnon, A. and Verelst, M. (2018), 'Investigating synchromodality from a supply chain perspective', *Transportation Research Part D: Transport and Environment*, **61**, 42–57.

ECB (2016), *Understanding the Weakness in Global Trade: What is the New Normal?* (Occasional Paper Series), Frankfurt: European Central Bank.

Ellen MacArthur Foundation and McKinsey & Company (2014), *Towards a Circular Economy: Accelerating the Take-up Across Global Supply Chains*, London: Author.

Emarketer (2018). 'Retail ecommerce sales worldwide, 2016–2021'. http://www.emarketer.com/Chart/Retail-Ecommerce-Sales-Worldwide-2016-2021-trillions-change-of-total-retail-sales/215138. Accessed 3 October 2018.

European Commission (2011), *White Paper: Roadmap to a Single European Transport Area – Towards a Competitive and Resource-efficient Transport System*, Brussels: Author.

Holguín-Veras, J. et al. (2018), 'Direct impacts of off-hour deliveries on urban freight emissions', *Transportation Research Part D: Transport and Environment*, **61**, 84–103.

IMO (International Maritime Organisation) (2018), 'UN body adopts climate change strategy for shipping'. http://www.imo.org/en/MediaCentre/PressBriefings/Pages/06GHGinitialstrategy.aspx. Accessed 3 October 2018.

ING (2017), *3D Printing: A Threat to Global Trade*. https://think.ing.com/reports/3d-printing-a-th reat-to-global-trade/

Marcucci, E., Le Pira, M., Carocci, C.S., Gatta, V. and Pieralice, G. (2017), 'Connected shared mobility for passengers and freight: Investigating the potential of crowdshipping in urban areas', In *Proceedings of 5th IEEE International Conference on Models and Technologies for Intelligent Transportation Systems (MT-ITS)*. https://ieeexplore.ieee.org/xpl/mostRecentIssue.jsp?punumber=7999202. Accessed 3 October 2018.

McKinnon, A.C. (2016), 'The possible impact of 3D printing and drones on last-mile logistics: An exploratory study', *Built Environment*, **42**(4), 617–629.

McKinnon, A.C. (2018), *Decarbonizing Logistics: Distributing Goods in a Low Carbon World*, London: Kogan Page.

OECD/ITF (2017), *Transport Outlook 2017*, Paris: OECD Publishing.

SESAR (2016), *European Drones Outlook Study: Unlocking the Value for Europe*, Brussels: European Union and Eurocontrol.

Wiesmann, B., Snoei, J. R., Hilletofth, P. and Eriksson, D. (2017), 'Drivers and barriers to reshoring: A literature review on offshoring in reverse', *European Business Review*, **29**(1), 15–42.

# PART IV

Regional perspectives

# 13 North America

Michael Roschlau and Josipa Petrunic

*The pace of change has never been so fast . . . but it will also never be this slow again.*
(Trudeau, 2017)[1]

## 13.1 Introduction

This insightful comment from the Canadian Prime Minister sets the stage for research trends in transport policy across North America and globally. The pace at which digital technological advances and social change are disrupting transport is unprecedented and shows no signs of abating. In coming years and decades, transport will face more uncertainty than at any time in recent history. The theme of policy and planning in a highly uncertain future will be central to any research agenda, specifically as it relates to emerging technology, new mobility, demographic change and the complementary or competing roles of the public and private sectors (Lyons and Davidson, 2016; WSP, 2017).

Many of the key issues for transport policy research in North America are common around the world as addressed in the thematic chapters. There are, however, areas dealing with funding and governance, the role of the private sector, new technology and transport-land use interactions that are particularly relevant to North America. Additionally, much of the mobility landscape will depend on how a connected, autonomous, shared and electric (CASE) future is embraced. These themes form the structure of this chapter.

## 13.2 Funding and governance

Canada and the United States have long struggled with the concept of sustainable funding for transport infrastructure. Whether this involves the periodic reauthorization process and the Highway Trust Fund in the United States or ad hoc municipal-provincial-federal funding patchworks in Canada, public transit agencies and transport authorities have lurched from feast to famine through uncertain

---

1 Comment on Twitter by Canadian Prime Minister, Justin Trudeau, on the progress of Artificial Intelligence, October 2017. https://www.technologyreview.com/the-download/609239/why-artificial-intelligence-should-be-more-canadian/. Accessed 27 April 2018.

periods, while changes in government or administrative conditions have determined frameworks within which decisions are made (Slack and Tassonyi, 2017).

In Canada, public transit is constitutionally defined as a municipal service. Therefore, it is the exclusive mandate of provincial and territorial governments. Some provinces have taken a more active role than others in management and operations, but mostly services have been delegated to municipalities, resulting in wide variations in the amount of funding available. As public transit is inherently a visible political issue, policies regarding its operating frameworks tend to be influenced by the ideological leanings of political parties. In provinces such as Nova Scotia, Quebec, Ontario and Manitoba, significant swings in funding and infrastructure investment have occurred because of changes in elected government.

Progressive funding and pricing policies, including congestion charges and road pricing, have also served as political lightning rods in North America with any attempt to replicate examples from Singapore, London and Stockholm stalled in first gear or defeated by voters. But new approaches to equity in road space allocation will be required. These may be driven by a transition away from fuel taxes to other forms of road user charges and mobility pricing.

Traditionally, Canada's federal government has not been involved in public transit, as its domestic transport-related mandate is restricted to inter-provincial air, rail and marine mobility. In recent years, however, federal policy has shifted to a more active role in capital investments for transit, justified by economic, environmental and social equity goals. Provinces have typically welcomed this new federal role, which has allowed for modernization and expansion of transit infrastructure. Examples include Skytrain expansion in Vancouver as well as light rail projects across Edmonton, Toronto and Ottawa – the latter case involving the world's first BRT to LRT conversion. It has also led to more consistent funding across the country. What remains to be seen is how sustainable these arrangements are in the face of future changes in government. It is in this context that approaches to policy research on interjurisdictional funding models and opportunities could prove valuable, both in terms of creating more predictable funding environments and insulating project investments from purely politically motivated decisions.

By contrast, in the United States the federal government has been a more active traditional funding partner, although budget approvals have been inconsistent and long delays in reauthorization have created short-term extensions pegged to concerns over predictability. As the US Highway Trust Fund faces shortfalls and an ongoing inability to cover investment needs, a more sustainable revenue stream, better tethered to the social costs of transport use, will be needed. Every year since 2008, the Fund's outlays have exceeded revenues with over $US 140 billion transferred from the general fund and other sources in the succeeding 10 years simply to maintain solvency.[2] As

---

2  US Department of Transportation (2017), pp. 44–46.

fossil fuels are replaced by other sources of propulsion energy, such as electricity from renewable sources, governments will necessarily shift from consumption-based fuel taxes to road user charges, such as vehicle-kilometres travelled and other forms of urban and rural mobility pricing.

Transport governance, meanwhile, remains open for debate and further research, especially as it applies to regional or metropolitan transport authorities. In the United States, metropolitan planning organizations (MPOs) and regional transit authorities operate based on independent governing structures. But MPOs are threatened today by declining ridership and funding instability. In Canada, municipalities typically share public transit capital investments with provincial and federal governments; but they are required to cover nearly all net operating costs after accounting for fare revenue, the bulk of which comes from property taxes. This funding formula is proving increasingly unstable due to insecure provincial and federal funding sources, even though Canadian transit systems recover, on average, a much higher proportion of operating costs from fares compared to US systems (54 per cent in Canada vs. 36 per cent in the US).[3] Since governance and funding formulae can be highly politicized, transit-related decision-making processes are often disconnected from sound, evidence-based planning principles. While this phenomenon is not unique to North America, it is especially pronounced in situations of weak governance. Recent examples include those in New York and Toronto, where conflict between local and state/provincial governments has resulted in delayed and poorly planned transport investments.

The swing towards populist governments in North America will further exacerbate the question of governance and provide significant challenges in maintaining land use and transport policies that have been developed over decades by forward-thinking planners and decision makers. While the impact of the smart growth agenda on transport policy and the relationship to land use is slow to take root, finding the right balance between market forces and government direction remains an elusive goal. The scarcity of affordable housing in high-priced urban areas such as Vancouver, San Francisco, Toronto and New York, coupled with the rising cost of mobility and competition for scarce road space, makes research into governance models that can achieve this balance, with effective integration across a number of functional areas, a high priority.

Experience from Vancouver shows that grounding metropolitan land use and transport policy in community values and insulating them from the short-term vagaries of provincial/state or municipal politics has been a successful recipe in making transit-oriented development and compact growth successful in the long run. The success of entities such as the Greater Vancouver Regional District (now Metro Vancouver) and the South Coast British Columbia Transportation Authority (TransLink) in thinking and planning at the metropolitan scale demonstrates the

---

3 Canadian Urban Transit Association (2017), p. G3; Federal Transit Administration (2017), p. 21.

value of this approach to transport governance. Research into the conditions that enable such success promises to yield substantial societal value (Stanley et al., 2017).

## 13.3    Public and private sector roles

From an operational perspective, public transit in North America has been largely the purview of the public sector with a relatively small role for private sector involvement. This may change in the future with the advent of new technologies. It is critical that decision makers are fully aware of the advantages and drawbacks of different approaches. Canada has been a world leader in the use of public-private partnerships (PPP) in the delivery of major infrastructure projects, largely because this form of turnkey construction and operation was favoured by some federal and provincial funding jurisdictions. Much can be learned from Canadian experience with PPPs. If carefully structured, the additional costs of borrowing capital based on private profit can be more than compensated by increased efficiencies and managerial focus. PPPs can also be useful in guarding against project changes and cancellations due to political swings (Siemiatycki, 2015).

## 13.4    Digital disruption – connected, autonomous, shared and electric

As digital connectivity, big data and Artificial Intelligence begin to offer new opportunities for transport planning, traditional policy mindsets will need to change as well, to ensure these opportunities improve efficiency and effectiveness as well as social equity and public mobility. A paradigm shift began several years ago with the broadening of scope associated with traditional public transit to embrace integrated urban mobility and new technologies. This work focused on policy development and innovation and was instrumental in creating Transit Vision 2040 in Canada (Canadian Urban Transit Association, 2015) and TransitVision 2050 in the United States (American Public Transportation Association, 2008). These generational frameworks have been supplemented by Smart City Challenge competitions in both countries promising to act as catalysts for local government innovation and unconventional thinking.

New technologies, such as connected and autonomous vehicles, herald the possibility of reducing private car ownership through Mobility-as-a-Service (MaaS) tools and the sharing economy. One part of this trend will depend on technology and the other part on policies encouraging a shift away from personal ownership of vehicles. The trend can be expressed as connected, autonomous, shared and electric (CASE) mobility. A CASE future envisions fewer cars per person, less road space dedicated to single passenger trips, smart-enabled curb and road use by public and private fleets, and transit systems that are consistently faster, greener, cheaper, more convenient and accessible across all spectrums of civil life – from individual childless urban residents to family-based suburban and rural home dwellers.

Further research is needed into the role played by policies that encourage or discourage shared mobility and their effect on future transport options. Some North American cities are leading the way in experimenting with these principles. An example includes the joint effort by Waterfront Toronto and Alphabet's Sidewalk Labs to create a new type of mixed-use community on Toronto's Eastern Waterfront (Sidewalk Toronto, 2017).

'Smart' vehicle technologies are composed of a variety of components that contribute to the multifaceted network of stakeholders involved in the adoption and commercialization of CASE mobility. But despite evidence of multiple 'smart' vehicle research and commercialization efforts across Canada, there has been no effort to unify or consolidate those projects in the form of an integrated National Smart Vehicle initiative or strategy. Coordination among the multiple 'smart' mobility research and commercialization projects across Canada could improve technology outputs allied to the standardization of digital communications systems that enable Smart Cities development overall. The pathways of development allied to transit and shared mobility systems are entwined, given that transit systems will need to be able to procure competitive and interoperable vehicle products in the future. The interoperability and standardization of 'smart' communications tools may be best pursued through a series of integrated, nationally aligned demonstration and commercialization projects. These efforts may help commercial entities develop interoperable communications and infrastructure technologies relevant to a global marketplace, while also testing new opportunities for revenue generation, such as direct advertising to smart vehicle and transit riders.

Research analyzing the effects that automated and connected vehicles will have on congestion currently shows mixed results (National Academies of Sciences, Engineering, and Medicine, 2017). If connected automated vehicles (CAVs) gain penetration as personally owned vehicles, they may increase congestion due to empty CAV driving, unless properly priced or restricted. If travel costs and travel times are reduced, people may choose to live farther away from their workplaces in more rural and low-priced areas. Conversely, shared CAVs that are deployed from a centralized city-perspective could reduce the need for parking spaces in dense urban cores, allowing more surface space for new housing and residences, green spaces, transit-privileged routes, and other active and passive uses.

CAVs could also provide critical mobility services to youth, seniors and people with disabilities who currently have limited mobility. Existing public transit systems in North America often do not offer wide enough services to meet the needs of these populations, while private transport services may not be available or affordable, especially with the rapid decline of intercity and rural coach services. A CASE future offers new opportunities to serve these populations and could provide social and economic benefits to communities through the development of secure and affordable transit options using CAVs. This futuristic vision of mobility would change many aspects of how a community's needs are met. In the longer term, a complete paradigm shift could occur that replaces most lower-frequency fixed-route transit services.

Critical policy research for shared on-demand mobility innovation includes: (a) standardization of cross-competitor interoperable communications systems; (b) optimization of shared mobility applications to avoid under-utilization of road vehicles; (c) smart curb modelling and development to ensure shared ride fleets utilize road and curb space effectively and avoid detrimental impacts on other services; (d) business development to support the integration of shared ride and shared mobility software tools into traditional transit systems, including fare integration and pricing to account for external costs; and (e) transformation of existing transit systems into mobility managers.

## 13.5   Energy, fuels and vehicle technology

A CASE future in North America is hindered today by the lack of alignment between transport policies and technology innovation policies that bring CASE mobility to the marketplace. Typically, both Canada and the United States have treated policies focused on vehicular innovation and procurement as distinct and untethered. In an era of technology transformation towards low-carbon smart mobility, this division is problematic and contributes directly to the delay in adoption and integration of advanced next generation technologies. Incentives, targets, mandates and funding programs aligned with emissions reductions have not mapped onto incentives, targets mandates or programs aligned with the technology innovation required to achieve those targets. This creates a blind spot with regards to technology standards development, which should no longer be treated as distinct from transport policy.

Technology standards form the basis upon which new forms of low-emissions and low-carbon energy can be integrated into advanced vehicular design. Without a shift in thinking on this front, governments risk continuing the fragmented, antiquated and largely ineffective approach to transportation innovation and transit disruption that has defined the bulk of the past 60 years of automotive, trucking and transit development. In addition, governments across North America typically fail to link policies aimed at increasing transit ridership to technology innovation that reduces emissions, improves efficiencies or optimizes rider services. The creation of ridership mandates that include 'technology performance standards' could constitute a new means of generating informed, modern and advanced transport policy, as it would motivate alternative propulsion technologies, operational cultural shift at transit agencies, MaaS developments, and energy and asset allocation efficiency.

Currently, the transport sector is frequently caught in a chicken-and-egg scenario: being required to reduce emissions and achieve environmental objectives while not having experience with the technologies available to achieve those goals. As an example, innovation associated with low-carbon smart mobility technologies has been driven primarily by investments in fuel economy improvements, vehicle light-weighting, and high-power charging systems development to achieve vehicle emissions reductions associated with Corporate Average Fuel Economy (CAFE) standards. However, procurement policies for public transit agencies have only aligned with these innovations in an ad hoc way as transit agencies usually lack the engineering and technology integration skill sets to understand these technological developments, as they emerge in real-time, and their integration requirements in fleets. In Canada, federal funds are making billions of dollars available to provinces for transit capital programs, but these funds are not linked to new technology integration metrics or economic, environmental and social performance measures.

A low-carbon smart mobility world implies a wholesale transformation away from energy-intense transit systems and other motorized mobility systems towards energy-efficient systems. This requires future transportation policies to be formulated as 'transportation-energy policies' or 'transportation-innovation policies' which view vehicle platforms, their source of propulsion energy, and their digital communications platforms as nodes within a new transportation matrix. For example, procurement policies will need to be overhauled to accommodate renewable energy systems integration, so that charging systems, energy storage systems, demand management systems and electric buses are procured as turn-key 'energy systems' rather than as individual or compartmentalized units.

As transportation constitutes 25–30 per cent of all greenhouse gas emissions (GHGs) in both Canada and the US, the elimination of emissions from vehicular sources has figured prominently in many federal and state/provincial carbon pricing policies. However, the impact of climate change policies, including carbon pricing, on transit system innovation has been marginal outside of California, where environmental policies and carbon pricing, stringent emission reduction targets for vehicles, and local job creation through e-vehicle manufacturing have merged to create a formidable eco-system for battery electric, hydrogen fuel cell and other alternative propulsion vehicles (International Council on Clean Transportation, 2018).

In addition, further policy analysis is required to assess legal implications of CASE technologies with regards to automated driving. For transit, this issue crops up in automated charging that reduces or eliminates driver engagement for temporary periods of time to enable optimal high-powered charging episodes while buses are on route. It also appears in the matter of automated electric buses which could travel in platoons along rapid transit ways. Several 'smart cities' initiatives have attempted to touch on these legal matters, but none has explored the design of cities and cityscapes that are 5G-enabled to support the robust digital architecture required for partial or full bus connectivity and automation. More policy research is also needed to explore city-led automated fleets operating within mixed traffic, given that municipal fleets are often operated using command-and-control models with centralized offices managing vehicular deployments.

In parallel, alternative fuels that will fuel the 'electric' part of CASE mobility constitute an important pillar supporting a 21st-century energy-transportation matrix (Daimler AG, n.d.). Critical systems research related to hydrogen fuel cell bus technologies in North America includes seasonal climatic effects on efficiency life cycle performance, fuel supply chain interruptions and – for carbon priced jurisdictions – the development of a standardized carbon number for hydrogen to ensure emissions reductions are actually made. Research exploring how to achieve these goals based on differing policy mechanisms will be key to future progress.

Governments, universities and vehicle manufacturers have initiated much research around batteries, power electronics, electric motors, charging systems, vehicle-to-grid communications, digitized communications for CAVs, alternative fuel sources and propulsion technologies. These are all part of a CASE mobility future. There is need for additional policy research governing these areas, including analyses of electricity rate structures for transit electrification, particularly in jurisdictions with publicly owned utilities. The development of standards supporting technology integration at transit facilities will be critical as well.

## 13.6   Conclusion

Much effort has been devoted to better coordinating land use-transport policy in urban areas to encourage more sustainable modes of mobility over single-occupancy automobiles. Some success has emerged with MPOs in the United States and in Canadian cities such as Vancouver, where regional planning and transport authorities have worked in close collaboration. Unfortunately, these experiences are far from the norm. Much work remains to be done with relation to creating better policy frameworks for land use-transport integration. Achieving a future of connected, autonomous, shared and electric (CASE) mobility will also require policy research in areas of technology development as well as regulation and other allied policy measures. The patchwork of provincial and state policies surrounding these themes and the lack of a unified federal approach threatens to be a major impediment, particularly in Canada where there is continued resistance from the federal government to establishing a uniform urban policy or attaching technological, economic, environmental or social equity conditions to infrastructure funding. These fissures become more challenging with emerging technologies that herald a paradigm shift in mobility, so the inclination of policy toward or away from a CASE future will be critical in shaping the fabric of North American cities and communities. As such, effective transport policy will increasingly depend on better integration across an ever-expanding set of policy arenas, as rapid technological change compounds already significant challenges in integrating transport and land use policies.

## References

American Public Transportation Association (2008), *TransitVision 2050: Final Report of APTA's TransitVision 2050 Task Force*, Washington, DC: Author. http://www.apta.com/gap/transitvision/Documents/transit_vision_2050.pdf. Accessed 3 May 2018.

Canadian Urban Transit Association (2015), *Transit Vision 2040 – Five Years of Progress*. http://cutaactu.ca/sites/default/files/cuta_eng_2015_01-low.pdf. Accessed 3 May 2018.

Canadian Urban Transit Association (2017), *Canadian Transit Fact Book – 2016 Operating Data*. http://cutaactu.ca/en/resources/research-reports-data/canadian-transit-fact-book-conventional-operating-data. Accessed 3 May 2018.

Daimler AG (n.d.), 'CASE – Intuitive Mobility'. https://www.daimler.com/case/en/. Accessed 3 June 2018.

Federal Transit Administration (2017), '2016 National Transit Summary and Trends', Office of Budget and Policy, Washington, DC. https://www.transit.dot.gov/sites/fta.dot.gov/files/docs/ntd/66011/2016-ntst.pdf. Accessed 3 May 2018.

International Council on Clean Transportation (2018), 'California's Continued Electric Vehicle Market Development', *ICCT Briefing*, San Francisco: Author.

Lyons, G. and C. Davidson (2016), 'Guidance for Transport Planning and Policymaking in the Face of an Uncertain Future', *Transportation Research Part A* **88**, 104–116.

National Academies of Sciences, Engineering, and Medicine (2017), 'Advancing Automated and Connected Vehicles: Policy and Planning Strategies for State and Local Transportation Agencies', *NCHRP Research Report 845*, Washington, DC: Author. https://doi.org/10.17226/24872. Accessed 3 June 2018.

Sidewalk Toronto (2017), Press Backgrounder, Sidewalk Labs, Toronto. https://sidewalktoronto.ca/wp-content/uploads/2018/04/Sidewalk-Toronto-Backgrounder.pdf. Accessed 3 May 2018.

Siemiatycki, M. (2015), 'Public-Private Partnerships in Canada: Reflections on Twenty Years of Practice', *Canadian Public Administration* **58**, 343–362.

Slack, E. and A. Tassonyi (2017), 'Financing Urban Infrastructure in Canada: Who Should Pay?', Institute on Municipal Finance & Governance, Munk School of Global Affairs, University of Toronto. https://munkschool.utoronto.ca/imfg/research/doc/?doc_id=442. Accessed 3 June 2018.

Stanley, J., J. Stanley and R. Hansen (2017), *How Great Cities Happen: Integrating People, Land Use and Transport*, Cheltenham: Edward Elgar.

US Department of Transportation (2017), 'Funding Federal-aid Highways', *Federal Highway Administration, Publication No. FHWA-PL-17-011*, Washington, DC: Author. https://www.fhwa.dot.gov/policy/olsp/fundingfederalaid/FFAH_2017.pdf. Accessed 3 May 2018.

WSP (2017), 'Navigating Uncertainty: Exploration of Alternative Futures for the Greater Toronto and Hamilton Area', *Technical Paper, Greater Toronto Area Transportation Plan*, Toronto: Metrolinx. http://www.metrolinx.com/en/regionalplanning/rtp/technical/NavigatingUncertainty.pdf. Accessed 3 May 2018.

# 14 South America: The challenge of transition

*Alejandro Tirachini*

## 14.1 Introduction

Economies of scale and agglomeration induce the emergence of cities, and transport is crucial to sustain their economic and social growth. This is particularly so in South America, where cities face a myriad set of challenges. The ownership of private cars grows faster than road infrastructure and faster than the availability and quality of public transport services, while the infrastructure for non-motorised travel is generally poor. Not surprisingly, the result is a sustained increase in car use (and in some countries motorcycle use) and traffic-related externalities like congestion, pollution and accidents, as has been observed in several South American cities. Hidalgo and Huizenga (2013) estimated the external cost of travel time, pollution and accidents to be between 900 and 1200 USD/person-year (2007) in cities like Bogotá, Buenos Aires, Caracas, Lima, Rio de Janeiro, Santiago and Sao Paulo. At the same time, South American countries are characterised by high inequality in the distribution of wealth, scarcity of public funds and the coexistence of formal and informal markets in the economy. A common factor in developing countries is the poor regulation of the private sector that provides infrastructure and public transport supply, usually with several deficiencies (Gwilliam, 2013). These elements should be considered in the economic, financial and social analysis of the transport sector, especially when studying the convenience of transport innovations.

Most South American cities are at an intermediate stage of development; therefore, if well led, they have the opportunity to develop their transport systems in a way to encourage sustainable mobility patterns (Hidalgo and Huizenga, 2013). In this chapter, we discuss a selected number of issues about urban mobility in South America. We focus the analysis on current and expected future mobility trends, the modernisation of public transport that has taken quite different forms in different cities and the issue of social exclusion and transport. We close the chapter with a discussion on the institutional challenges that add complexity to the continuation of sustainable mobility solutions, in a moment of rapid changes with the emergence of disrupting mobility technologies.

## 14.2  Urban mobility trends in South America

In South America it is usual to have a high share of trips by public transport, which in several cases is met by a myriad number of low-quality informal transport providers, that might be significant contributors to pollution, congestion and accidents themselves. CAF (2016) surveyed the modal share of private motorised transport (car, taxi, motorbike) and public transport (bus and rail) in different cities across Argentina, Bolivia, Brazil, Chile, Colombia, Ecuador, Peru, Uruguay and Venezuela. Including only public and private motorised transport, the share of private transport is around 30% in Rio de Janeiro, Quito, Caracas and Lima, around 40% in Santa Cruz de la Sierra, Bogotá and Medellín, and 50% or larger in Buenos Aires, Rosario, Brasilia, Sao Paulo, Santiago and Montevideo. Detailed modal split information for a selected group of South American cities is presented in Table 14.1, which includes all modes (not just car and public transport). The main outlier is La Paz, where public transport and car modal shares are 72.3% and 4.4%, respectively.

The broadly equal car and public transport modal split that is currently present in cities like Santiago or Buenos Aires is also observed in London, whereas other European capitals like Paris and Madrid have more trips by public transport than by car (EMTA, 2016). The trends are the main difference between some European capitals and South America. While London, Madrid and Paris have managed to reduce car trips and increase public transport trips, in South America the opposite trend is usual. Modal shares, measured with origin-destination surveys performed every 10 years or so, show an increase of car trips and a sharp reduction of public transport trips in cities like Santiago (SECTRA, 2014b) and Valdivia (SECTRA,

**Table 14.1**  Modal split (percentage of trips) in selected South American cities

| Mode | La Paz, Bolivia | Santiago, Chile | Bogotá, Colombia | Sao Paulo, Brazil | Quito, Ecuador | Lima and Callao, Peru |
|---|---|---|---|---|---|---|
| Public transport | 72.3 | 27.9 | 42.2 | 37.8 | 52.0 | 50.8 |
| Car | 4.4 | 25.7 | 11.2 | 25.8 | 19.8 | 15.2 |
| Motorcycle | – | 0.6 | 4.8 | 2.2 | – | 6.4 |
| Walking | 20.4 | 34.5 | 31.1 | 28.0 | 14.0 | 24.3 |
| Bicycle | 0.1 | 4.0 | 4.3 | 0.7 | 0.3 | 0.3 |
| Taxi | 2.7 | 1.7 | 4.6 | 0.3 | 3.4 | 2.6 |
| Others | 0.1 | 5.6 | 1.8 | 5.3 | 10.6 | 0.4 |
| Total | 100 | 100 | 100 | 100 | 100 | 100 |
| Total trips (millions per day) | 2.72 | 18.46 | 14.8 | 43.7 | 5.09 | 22.3 |
| Year of data | 2012 | 2012 | 2015 | 2012 | 2015 | 2012 |

**Source:**  Author's elaboration from the following sources: La Paz (GAMLP, 2012), Santiago (SECTRA, 2014b), Bogotá (AMB, 2016), Sao Paulo (GESP, 2013), Quito (SGP, 2015), Lima and Callao (MTC, 2013).

2014a) in Chile. A similar pattern is observed between 1992 and 2007 in Buenos Aires (Brennan, 2010). The reduction of trips by public transport in favour of motorised private transport gives rise to increased traffic congestion that in turn activates the downward spiral of deterioration of public transport. Also, in countries like Colombia, there has been a sharp increase of trips by motorcycle, with cities such as Pereira and Barranquilla having more trips by motorcycle than by car (CAF, 2016). The rate of growth of motorcycles is more than double the rate of growth of cars in Brazil and Colombia (Hidalgo and Huizenga, 2013), which poses a challenge for traffic safety issues.

Regarding cycling, tendencies in bicycle use are not the same across South America. For example, in Santiago the bicycle modal split doubled from 2% to 4% between 2001 and 2012 (SECTRA, 2014b), but in Lima it went down from 0.5% to 0.3% between 2004 and 2012 (MTC, 2013). Latent class models estimated in Santiago show that having dedicated cycling infrastructure is highly preferred by cyclists and that fully segregated cycleways are specially relevant for inexperienced users, older cyclists and women (Rossetti *et al.*, 2018). An interesting development in Colombia is a new law that entitles public servants to a half day free of work every 30 days that they cycle to work.[1] The future evaluation of the effect of cycling infrastructure alternatives and innovative demand management measures is relevant to increase the share of bicycle trips in South America, these matters forming important research opportunities for transport policy formulation.

## 14.3    Transport and social exclusion

The issue of sustainable transport in South America cannot be fully grasped if the high levels of urban spatial and income inequality, which are inherent in South American cities, are not analysed on a par with the study and development of new transport projects. Socioeconomic differentiation reflected in residential segregation is one of the most common forms of urban segregation in South America. Sabatini *et al.* (2001) describe a pattern of residential segregation in South American cities in countries like Argentina, Brazil and Chile, in which socioeconomic elites concentrate in a single area that usually grows like a cone from the city centre towards the periphery in one chosen direction. Other types of segregation include the unbalanced distribution of public space, parks, schools and employment centres, which coexist with residential segregation (Jirón, 2011) and contribute to the social isolation of the poorest neighbourhoods and suburbs (Jirón and Fadda, 2003).

People with lower income and education levels have lower mobility and take considerably more time to complete a trip as they rely on walking, cycling and public transport. On the other hand, car ownership is usually concentrated in high-income households. Low-income families limit their everyday destinations beyond walking

---

1  https://www.elespectador.com/noticias/actualidad/ley-daran-dias-compensatorios-quienes-lleguen-al-trabaj-artic ulo-662352. Accessed 10 October 2018.

distance as much as possible, and concentrate on trips related to work, education and the maintenance of the house (Ureta, 2008). The influence of the transport system on the quality of life of users is strongly influenced by personal factors, as, for example, a public-transport-dependent young mother who needs to drop her child to school before going to work, which forces her to use overcrowded morning-peak buses. Therefore, uneven mobility access is gendered (Jirón, 2011). In this context, public transport emerges as a key element that can alleviate or increase social exclusion.

Another relevant issue is that transport systems are unevenly distributed across most cities, worsening urban inequality (Jirón *et al.*, 2010). An example of this is an ambitious program to build 200 kilometres of tolled urban highways in Santiago, inaugurated between years 2004 and 2006, which benefit car drivers (the higher-income group) at the expense of segregating a number local of communities in lower-income suburbs (like the Vespucio Sur highway in the south of the city) and increasing walking distances of neighbours (Tirachini, 2015). Consequently, when analysing the value of mobility as an element to reduce the risk of social exclusion (Stanley *et al.*, 2011) in South America, it is necessary to go beyond estimating the relationship between mobility and income, to include elements such as gender, age and the quality of public transport services.

## 14.4    The modernisation of public transport

The design of efficient and sustainable public transport systems involves several decisions that have significant social and economic implications for citizens, the urban structure and the budget of local and national governments. These decisions include the design of networks, the choice of modal technology to provide a service (e.g., bus, tram, light rail, metro), the number of services per hour or per day, the fare structure and the location of stations and bus stops. The resulting choices usually have sizeable impacts on the cost of establishing, operating and improving a public transport system, and on the level of service provided to users. Factors such as accessibility, affordability, travel time, reliability, safety and crowding levels rank high amongst the attributes of importance to passengers, all of which depend on the decisions made when designing the system. Therefore, understanding the economic nature and social implications of urban public transport services is crucial to ensure the efficiency of a public transport network and, ultimately, the sustainability of the entire transport system. A synthesis of the historical evolution and current challenges of public transport systems in the cities of Buenos Aires, Montevideo, Curitiba, Bogotá and Pereira is presented in IDB (2017). A common factor in these cities is the replacement of trams by bus-based systems between the 1930s and 1960s (IDB, 2017).

A distinguishing contribution of South America to the world, in the field of urban mobility, is the development of Bus Rapid Transit (BRT) systems, with Curitiba and Bogotá usually crowned as pioneer cities. Bus Rapid Transit is commonly developed as a fast-forward way to replace old, polluting and inefficient (sometimes unregulated) buses, by modern, high-capacity vehicles in dedicated bus corridors, with high service frequency and off-board fare payment (Wright and Hook, 2007; Munoz and Paget-Seekins, 2016). The current quality problems of the once revolutionary Transmilenio system in Bogotá show that, without institutional stability, strong political support and financial sustainability, BRT systems can sharply deteriorate in a few years, jeopardising previous gains in quality-of-life for citizens. Notwithstanding, even with continuous financial and institutional support, it is worth noting that BRT has capacity limits that should be predicted in advance by policy-makers, in order to prevent future capacity and quality-of-service shortfalls and anticipate the need of higher-capacity transport technologies like Metro, that can coexist with BRT.

Another innovation in South America in the past 15 years is the use of cable cars for urban public transport in hilly landscapes with poor access by other public modes and low levels of urban development. The successful execution of the Metrocable in Medellín (2004) was followed by Caracas (2010), Rio de Janeiro (Complexo do Alemão, 2011) and La Paz-El Alto (2014), with implementation costs that range from 9 to 23.5 million USD/km (Garsous et al., 2019). The literature on South American cable cars is still scarce but growing. Garsous et al. (forthcoming) show that the La Paz-El Alto cable car reduced commuting times by 22% on average, whereas Bocarejo et al. (2014) estimate the benefits for the Medellín cable car users in terms of increased access to employment opportunities. Importantly, cable cars can be easily integrated with existing mass public transport options running through the main employment and services areas in cities.

## 14.5   Discussion: The way forward

Most South American cities appear to have a 'sustainable' transport system, in terms of modal shares of trips, as only a minority of the population have frequent access to motorised private transport. However, this is usually so not because of the quality of public transport, walking and cycling infrastructure, but rather due to a motorisation rate that is still lower than in Europe or North America. As population income levels rise, and more people have access to cars and motorcycles, this picture can change quickly. If public transport has lower quality and car driving is relatively cheap (there is no road charging and weak parking management and pricing), new cars will only mean more congestion and enlargement of the peak periods in large cities. Therefore, governments should be proactive and take, in advance, the necessary steps towards future sustainable transport systems. This implies the provision of comfortable, secure and safe facilities for walking and cycling, integrated high-quality public transport systems and disincentives on the use of private motorised transport, particularly at peak times. For example, to reduce congestion and transport emissions in Sao Paulo, Anas and Timilsina (2009) find that the ideal policy is to charge congestion and fuel consumption, and use the revenue to improve public transport, while Basso and Silva (2014) estimate that congestion pricing is not regressive in Santiago (because it increases bus speeds) and that introducing bus lanes is a highly desirable policy for the city. However, it is not obvious that countries in South America will be able to take this sustainable transport path (Hidalgo and Huizenga, 2013), due to institutional, political and financial bottlenecks. Those bottlenecks provide important transport policy research opportunities.

It is hard to agree on a South American city that has developed a fully integrated public transport system, that matches its Western European counterparts in terms of quality of service. Institutional weaknesses and lack of proper governance and funding may explain why the preferred approach to modernise public transport in South America is by means of packaged projects, usually BRT or Metro lines, that when developed significantly increase the quality of service. However, these are partial improvements that need to coexist with low-quality or even informal public transport providers, that still satisfy transport demand in most parts of large urban areas in countries like Bolivia, Peru, Colombia and Venezuela. Even a city that tried to change the whole public transport system at once – Santiago with the Transantiago system launched in 2007 – still suffers shortcomings of a poorly performing bus operation (with some vehicles, road infrastructure and bus stops that are in poor condition), which coexists with a high-performance Metro network.[2] It seems that authorities in South America have not fully grasped the idea that a public transport system is as strong as its weakest component, and, in order to have a system that serves a city well, it is necessary that all public transport components work well, not just a few links. More research on the transport governance at national, metropolitan and local scales is badly needed to support the institutional backbone of any major transport innovation in South America.

The joint planning of mass transport systems and urban development is still rare in South America, Curitiba being a notable exception due to its land use regulation in synchrony with the creation of a high-quality public transport network, based on BRT integrated with feeder and local bus routes (IDB, 2017). A strong integrated land use-transport governance framework is a vital step in seeking to replicate such experience in other cities where transport and land use are planned independently or in a poorly integrated way. Research studies are needed to support development of such frameworks.

The analysis of future transport trends in South America needs to consider present and future technological innovations, like ride-hailing and autonomous mobility. The eruption of ride-hailing applications, even without proper regulation, can seriously challenge urban public transport by decreasing its demand (Tirachini and Gómez-Lobo, 2019). On the other hand, the advantage of autonomous vehicles on reducing transport costs is expected to be relatively lower in South America, where labour costs (and, therefore, a potential saving of autonomous vehicles) are lower than in developed economies. The transition to autonomous mobility might be

---

2 For a detailed comparison of the developments of the Transantiago and Transmilenio systems, see Hidalgo *et al.* (2016).

longer and more hazardous in South America. These topics are unresearched today and in the coming years it is important that studies on the implications for mobility and public policy of new technologies emerge, especially on countries with weaker transport regulations and enforcement.

Finally, a word on freight transport. This topic is usually under-researched in South America due to the lack of reliable data, a problem that needs immediate attention from policy-makers because logistics competitiveness of South American countries is low and its improvement can have a significant effect on trade performance of South American countries (OECD/ITF, 2016). Freight transport is expected to become more relevant in the future due to the increase of e-commerce. On the other hand, around 50% of truck-kilometres are estimated to be empty hauls in Brazil, Argentina and Uruguay (IDB, 2015). The creation of national logistics observatories, strengthened supply chain collaborations and the introduction of state-of-the-art technologies on online load-matching software are central to boosting efficiency of the South American logistics (OECD/ITF, 2016).

## Acknowledgement

This work was supported by the Complex Engineering Systems Institute, Chile (CONICYT Grant FB0816).

## References

AMB (2016), 'Encuesta de Movilidad 2015', Alcaldía Mayor de Bogota D.C.

Anas, A. and G. R. Timilsina (2009), 'Impacts of policy instruments to reduce congestion and emissions from urban transportation: The case of Sao Paulo, Brazil', *World Bank Policy Research Working Paper Series*, Washington, DC: World Bank.

Basso, L. J. and H. E. Silva (2014), 'Efficiency and substitutability of transit subsidies and other urban transport policies', *American Economic Journal: Economic Policy* **6**(4), 1–33.

Bocarejo, J. P., I. J. Portilla, J. M. Velásquez, M. N. Cruz, A. Peña and D. R. Oviedo (2014), 'An innovative transit system and its impact on low income users: The case of the Metrocable in Medellín', *Journal of Transport Geography* **39**, 49–61.

Brennan, P. (2010), 'El Transporte Urbano de Pasajeros por ómnibus de Buenos Aires', Report Cámara Argentina de la Construcción. Accessed 3 October 2018 at http://biblioteca.camarco.org.ar/libro/el-transporte-urbano-de-pasajeros-por-omnibus-de-buenos-aires/.

CAF (2016), 'Observatorio de movilidad urbana, Informe 2015–2016', Resumen Ejecutivo. Banco de Desarrollo de América Latina (CAF).

EMTA (2016), 'EMTA Barometer 2016', European Metropolitan Transport Authorities. Report prepared by Consorcio Transportes Madrid.

GAMLP (2012), 'Plan de Movilidad Urbana Sostenible (PMUS)', Gobierno Autónomo Municipal de La Paz.

Garsous, G., A. Suárez-Alemán and T. Serebrisky (2019), 'Cable cars in urban transport: Travel time savings from La Paz-El Alto (Bolivia)', *Transport Policy* **75**, 171–182.

GESP (2013), 'Pesquisa de mobilidade da Regiao Metropolitana de Sao Paulo 2012, Principais resultados, pesquisa domiciliar', December 2013. Governo do Estado Sao Paulo.

Gwilliam, K. (2013), 'Cities on the move – Ten years after', *Research in Transportation Economics* **40**(1), 3–18.

Hidalgo, D. and C. Huizenga (2013), 'Implementation of sustainable urban transport in Latin America', *Research in Transportation Economics* **40**(1), 66–77.

Hidalgo, D., J. C. Munoz and J. M. Velásquez (2016), 'The path toward integrated systems'. In Muñoz, J. C. and Paget-Seekins, L. (Eds) *Restructuring Public Transport Through Bus Rapid Transit*, 31–50. Chicago: University of Chicago Press.

IDB (2015), *Freight Transport and Logistics Statistics Yearbook*, Inter-American Development Bank, Washington, DC.

IDB (2017), *Evolución de los Sistemas Transporte Urbano en América Latina*, Inter-American Development Bank, Washington, DC.

Jirón, P. (2011), 'Challenges for Latin American cities: Improving diagnosis or the need to shift the understanding urban inequality from fixed enclaves to mobile gradients', *Working Paper No. 2011/24*, UNU-WIDER project, World Institute for Development Economics Research, Helsinki.

Jirón, P. and G. Fadda (2003), 'A quality of life assessment to improve urban and housing policies in Chile', World Bank Urban Research Symposium 2003, Washington, DC.

Jirón, P., C. Lange and M. Bertrand (2010), 'Exclusión y desigualdad espacial: Retrato desde la movilidad cotidiana', *Revista INVI* **25**(68), 15–57.

MTC (2013), *Encuesta de recolección de información básica del transporte urbano en el área metro-politada de Lima y Callao. Informe Final*', Ministerio de Transportes y Comunicaciones (MTC), República del Perú, y Agencia de Cooperación Internacional del Japón (JICA).

Munoz, J. C. and L. Paget-Seekins (Eds) (2016), *Restructuring Public transport through Bus Rapid Transit*, Chicago: University of Chicago Press.

OECD/ITF (2016), *Logistics Observatory for Chile: Strengthening Policies for Competitiveness. International Transport Forum Report*, Paris: Author.

Rossetti, T., C. A. Guevara, P. Galilea and R. Hurtubia (2018), 'Modeling safety as a perceptual latent variable to assess cycling infrastructure', *Transportation Research Part A: Policy and Practice* **111**, 252–265.

Sabatini, F., G. Cáceres and J. Cerda (2001), 'Segregación residencial en las principales ciudades chilenas: Tendencias de las tres últimas décadas y posibles cursos de acción', *EURE* (Santiago) **27**(82), 21–42.

SECTRA (2014a), '*Actualización Plan de Transporte Valdivia y desarrollo de anteproyecto, I Etapa. Final report*'. Accessed 6 February 2019 at http://www.sectra.gob.cl/biblioteca/detalle1.asp?mfn=3290.

SECTRA (2014b), '*Encuesta de Origen y Destino de Viajes Santiago 2012* (in Spanish)'. Report and data-base. Accessed 6 February 2019 at www.sectra.gob.cl.

SGP (2015), Participación modal de viajes de transporte en el Distrito Metropolitado de Quito (proyección 2015). Open data website, Secretaría General de Planificación, Ecuador. Accessed May 2018 at http://gobiernoabierto.quito.gob.ec/?page_id=1779.

Stanley, J., D. A. Hensher, J. R. Stanley, G. Currie, W. Greene and D. Vella-Brodrick (2011), 'Social exclusion and the value of mobility', *Journal of Transport Economics and Policy* **45**(2), 197–222.

Tirachini, A. (2015), 'Probability distribution of walking trips and effects of restricting free pedestrian movement on walking distance', *Transport Policy* **37**, 101–110.

Tirachini, A. and A. Gómez-Lobo (2019), 'Does ride-hailing increase or decrease vehicle kilometers traveled (VKT)? A simulation approach for Santiago de Chile', *International Journal of Sustainable Transportation*. https://doi.org/10.1080/15568318.2018.1539146.

Ureta, S. (2008), 'To move or not to move? Social exclusion, accessibility and daily mobility among the low-income population in Santiago, Chile', *Mobilities* **3**(2), 269–289.

Wright, L. and W. Hook (2007), *Bus Rapid Transit Planning Guide*, 3rd edition, New York: Institute for Transportation and Development Policy.

# 15 European Union and United Kingdom: Research roadmap for transport policy

*Rosário Macário, Hilde Meersman and Eddy van de Voorde*

## 15.1 Introduction

The aim of this chapter is to address the main challenges faced by European Union (EU) and United Kingdom (UK) transport systems and identify the consequent research gaps to support the development of transport policy. Section 15.2 addresses the main societal changes observed in past decades that define the needs for mobility and accessibility. In Section 15.3 the role of transport in Europe and the UK is highlighted. Section 15.4 is focused on the gaps resulting from the evolution of past decades and the opportunity for innovation they represent. Section 15.5 identifies, in an aggregate way, the main objectives for transport policy to pursue that are common to the EU and UK. Section 15.6 identifies research needs as a consequence of what is discussed in preceding sections. Finally, Section 15.7 highlights some critical issues that support the need to change the research approach and to embrace challenging futures.

## 15.2 Societal changes and trends

Transport needs are a consequence of the territorial activities undertaken by societies, as well as being influenced by the degree of freedom in transactions between countries and/or regions. Movements of both freight and people are a direct consequence of the way societies operate. At the time of writing this chapter,[1] we are on the verge of the 4th industrial revolution, with technology helping a speed of change never observed before.

Looking to past decades, several societal changes can be observed. Their consequences have implications in the way transport can contribute to Sustainable Development Goals (SDGs) as defined by the United Nations (UN, 2016). This chapter cannot properly address all of them, so only the most relevant changes with impact on transport systems are identified in what follows.[2]

---

1 November 2018.

2 The reflections reproduced in this chapter benefited from the participation of the first author as member of the advisory boards of PTV Group: Traffic and Logistics Software & Technology and TAG – Transport Advisory Group program H2020 of the European Commission.

### 15.2.1   Urbanization

The world is becoming increasingly urbanized, IOM (2015) reporting that, by 2050, the world urban population is expected to represent 66 per cent of the total global population, with Africa and Asia making up nearly 90 per cent of the expected increase of urban population to 2050. Megacities increased from 29 in 2015 to 37 in 2017 and 41 are estimated by 2030, of which 10 will be in Asia and Africa (Demographia, 2018, p. 3). The development of these urban areas into megacities is almost always accompanied by a shift from a monocentric form of spatial organization towards a polycentric one. This brings new dimensions and complexity to urban transport planning in general, and specifically for modelling mobility patterns. This evolving spatial pattern highlights weaknesses in traditional radial mass transit and reveals gaps in mobility systems, which are usually bridged by informal innovative solutions. In South America, South Africa and Asia numerous examples of this phenomenon have been observed in recent decades and, paradoxically, the same or similar solutions are recently emerging in the EU and UK, despite the considerable cultural and environmental differences between these areas.

### 15.2.2   An ageing society vs a young society

Demographic evolution in different parts of the world is markedly different. The UK and most of the other countries in Europe have an ageing population, averaging above 40, while emerging countries have much younger averages (e.g., India and some parts of Asia have an average age just slightly above 25) (IOM, 2015). These differences are associated with different cultural attitudes that have great impact on transport.

For ageing societies, proximity and relaxed circulation by traditional mass transit is a preference, often slowing boarding and alighting times, with an associated impact on operational resource requirements. For a younger society, speed is an attraction and fast adoption of shared services/activities is a preference.

Moreover physical exercise is positively related to health, mainly the mental, social and physical aspects. This relation is also recognized by the SDGs and affects both ageing and younger clusters of society. Consequently, it becomes increasingly relevant to invest in understanding implications of soft mobility (or active mobility) and to create models that evaluate and study the 'physical activity' factor when related to health, both physical and mental, and the implications of a sedentary lifestyle (Caspersen et al., 1985), which often leads to the phenomenon of social exclusion.

The object of preference status has also changed from one generation to another. For older generations in the EU and UK, the car has been a central element connoted with status and quality of life, while for the younger generation, the smart phone is the key symbol both of status and of a cool life. Significant differences in behaviour can also be observed in countries of Northern Europe, which are more detached from car use, and other European countries, which are more attached to car use.

### 15.2.3    Large-scale migration flows

The migration crisis has led to EU member states restricting mobility between states and questioning the Schengen Agreement.[3] Transport operators and infrastructures are directly affected but the accessibility impact is uneven across members of the EU and UK. The most significant impacts can be detected in border management, increase of costs and enhancement of regional differences.

### 15.2.4    World growth is slowing, increasing uncertainty

The world economic outlook reports a slower growth path (IMF, 2018), associated with a declining ratio of international trade to GDP. Globalization seems to be in retreat in some sectors, with help from US trade decisions in 2018. This foresight has severe implications for trade and transport and creates an environment of increased uncertainty. After the last financial turmoil, developing countries achieved only low growth. Asian and emerging market slowdowns make them less able to drive economic growth, threatening European and UK exports. Pressure on European public budgets remains severe. This situation tends to delay maintenance of infrastructure and mass transit services, degrading quality and having direct negative impacts on accessibility, congestion, safety, costs and the overall efficiency of transport systems. The impact falls on mobility of both people and goods. Efficiency of supply chains is as dependent on last miles within the urban environment as on well-connected intermodal transport corridors. On the positive side, the constraint in public expenditures forces the opportunity to find innovative funding and financing solutions, with strong participation of private capital.

### 15.2.5    The positive impact of the COP 21 Agreement, and its implementation

The December 2015 adoption of the Conference of the Parties (COP) 21 Paris Agreement set the foundation for climate change mitigation and greenhouse gas reduction. From a European perspective, a most relevant aspect was the energizing of a slow moving context, through optimism and general commitment of European leaders. Moreover, the engagement of the private sector was a turning point in the process. COP 21 provided a clear obligation and agenda for the transport sector.

Emission scandals with the car industry subsequently exposed the controversy between the industry and the regulatory powers and processes, forcing a rethink of approaches and methods, and the introduction of innovation in regulation.

---

3  The Schengen Agreement, signed on 14 June 1985, is a treaty which led to the creation of Europe's Schengen Area (https://en.wikipedia.org/wiki/Schengen_Area), in which internal border checks have largely been abolished.

### 15.2.6    Oil price impacts many economic drivers and may hinder transport environmental target achievement

During the 2000s evidence revealed there is little prospect of global agreement on the opportunity cost of fossil fuels, their influence in the economic evaluation of investments, externalities and taxation, and such like, which complicates achievement of COP 21 goals.

Both air transport and the automotive industry can be seen as beneficiaries of low fuel costs, but in fact this has a double effect. There is relief to these industries, encouraging movement away from achieving environmental targets and, consequently, leading to delays in the transition towards a carbon-free economy. This price effect makes it harder to justify energy-/emission-saving measures, especially in the less developed countries. In Europe and the UK, no evidence exists, however, that consumers substantially benefit from lower oil prices (Martins, 2018), since taxes absorb most of the difference.

When oil prices rise, industry benefit reduces and stimulates the search for other energy options and strengthens support for a carbon-free economy, but when increases in oil prices are not reflected in final consumer prices, State revenues (taxes) are adversely affected and consequently there is less funding availability for infrastructure investments.

Also, oil-dependency has a strong impact on transport policy and decision-making processes regarding infrastructure investment.

### 15.2.7    Innovation and speed of technological evolution

The spread of information is one of the drivers of innovation and knowledge growth. There is a need to ensure that new concepts and theoretical developments are rapidly diffused. Outreach and diffusion of scientific achievements and knowledge is currently a major EU and UK weakness.

### 15.2.8    Digitalization, Information and Communications Technologies and their implications

The progress of communication and digitalization technologies has a very significant impact on transportation. Decision processes are affected, including in the freight sector, where decisions on transport have moved upstream in the production chain and are now discussed at the stage of product conception. Also, the efficiency of transport networks is positively affected by real-time information and automatic control systems. A good example lies with public transport, where real-time route control enables some vehicles to avoid and/or minimize delays and automatic vehicles are an alternative to human resources cost (driver costs currently representing 50–60 per cent of total operational cost). The performance of public transport is enhanced as well as the potential to manage and influence choice along the complete mobility chain, encompassing all modes and options (walking, cycling, mass transit). Resource optimization is a positive outcome but product delivery is also a benefit from the technological evolution, such as with MaaS (Mobility as a Service), as discussed in Chapter 21 of this book.

### 15.2.9   Security threats targeting Europe and its logistic and strategic centres

Terrorist attacks in recent years have confirmed the need for both strategic and tactical resilience planning, including contingency scenarios as a capacitation instrument. Similar planning approaches are also required for natural disasters, which are increasing in severity with climate change. This challenges the way large infrastructure and public transport systems need to be managed, and governance arrangements related thereto, adding a layer of complexity and cost to transportation. Urban transport services are particularly vulnerable to terrorist attacks, for the dimension of the impact caused.

### 15.2.10   Quality of governance and increasing political uncertainty

The main societal challenges for EU and UK transport systems relate to: demographic evolution; urbanization; rewinding of globalization; information technology; environmental preservation; and, last but not least, behavioural changes. Ultimately, responding well to this complex set depends on the quality of governance, and particularly the ability to take integrated decisions and step away from traditional silo-oriented perspectives. Since the late 1990s, questions have arisen about why some countries have less human capital, physical capital and technology than others and make poorer use of their available factors and opportunities. Acemoglu and Robinson (2008) argue that the answer lies in institutions and the quality of governance. This finding brings a different policy focus from previous decades, where answers were often seen to lie with deregulation, privatization and liberalization (Rodrik, 2008). More recent research (Spandou, 2010) reconfirms that institutional design and decision processes are at the root of underperformance of the mobility system. The multi-disciplinary character of transport demands closer links between transport research and research in related fields, such as economics and fiscal policy, land use management, health and social policies, systems management and climate change mitigation, as discussed in Chapter 5 of this book and in some other chapters.

## 15.3   The role of transport in EU and UK societies

Transport is a major contributor to the economy, accounting for 4.8 per cent of EU gross value added and 11 million jobs, UK included (Demographia, 2018, p. 3), and is also fundamental for development at all scales of human life – local, rural, urban, metropolitan, regional, national, continental and global. Mobility, which relates to the capacity to move around, is concerned with the performance of transport systems in their own right. Accessibility, which is concerned with the capacity to reach opportunities/activities, adds the interaction of transport systems and land use patterns as a further layer of analysis. Accessibility returns the feedback effects between transport infrastructure and services, territorial forms and the spatial distribution of activities. It is thus inevitable that accessibility is used as an aggregated concept and metric for quality of living and competitiveness of areas (urban, rural, national, etc.), due to its pervasive impact on business and personal activities.

Accessibility and mobility concepts have both taken specific roles and perspectives in the planning and policy universe. However the global view – the citizen holistic eye – has been lost in the discussion leading to technical simplifications that have distorted attitudes and decisions (i.e. behaviour and choices) of different players.[4]

To exemplify the problem, the conclusions of several studies suggest that growth in Gross Domestic Product is correlated to rises in average income and contributes to increased daily commuting travel distance, as citizens tend to search for a better quality/price ratio, buying houses further away from the city centre. Technology enables this achievement without increasing the travel time budget, through road and rail infrastructure improvements. This is a significant outcome in terms of impact on productivity and urban performance, since distance increases are often correlated with density decreases and density decreases, in turn, with lower productivity. The conclusions of some research studies question the idea that the traveller's strategy is travel cost minimization (Schaffer and Victor, 2000). This in turn weakens, or at least questions, the adequacy of the traditional modelling approach of minimization of generalized cost, and suggests that in the long term travel behaviour may not be about utility-maximization (Zheng and Hensher, 2005). In addition, there is widespread evidence in European culture that car ownership is often used as a second alternative to house acquisition. Together these reflections raise doubts over whether consumer behaviour should be assessed in relation to the aggregate available household budget for transport and housing which represent a substantial part of the household fixed costs in the short and medium term, rather than focusing more narrowly on just transport choices. This means looking at utility maximization through citizens' eyes, which is always a very integrated and holistic perspective. It is estimated that European households in 2017 spent 13.5–15 per cent of their budget on transport-related goods and services, which makes them the second most important budget item after house-related expenditures. Together these two items often exceed 50 per cent of the household budget (Eurostat, 2010). This high sensitiveness is also a reason why transport is often the object of popular decisions lacking sound supporting rationale. This is a growing trend, directly related to quality and accountability of governance.

Moreover, transport is a function of derived demand, driven by the evolution of society and evolution of territorial organization and forms. But cities, regions and

---

4 For a deeper analysis of this issue see Banister and Berechman (2003), Cervero et al. (1997), Macário (2014), Sclar et
   al. (2014), among others in the reference list.

countries differ substantially in their development strategies and outcomes. Even if we are dealing with similar problems, in any given moment each entity is conditioned by the choices made in the past that configure a different departure point. Consequently, decision-makers will have different perceptions on which are the main problems that need to be addressed and which are the best solutions to mitigate them. This means that transport policy is path-dependent and that in each moment of that path sustainability means meeting the needs of people without jeopardizing the capacity to answer needs of future generations. Path-dependency can indeed be a cause to miss opportunities to move to more sustainable transport futures.

The 2030 Agenda for Sustainable Development establishes a generic roadmap to that end through 17 Sustainable Development Goals. Some of these SDGs are directly and/or indirectly related to transport through targets and indicators. Worth highlighting is the role given to transport in the fight against exclusion, a problem much related with ageing and poverty (Target 11.2 SDGs). The United Nations Secretary-General's High Level Advisory Group on Sustainable Transport reinforces this idea:

> For all vulnerable groups, as well as for migrant communities and people living in remote and low density rural areas, safe, accessible and reliable transport services are a lifeline. (UN, 2016, p. 12)

These objectives, accessibility and equity are at the core of European transport policy, including in the UK. The development of information and other technologies provides momentum for transport policy and planning to adjust its tools and paradigms to the new rationales that support the behaviour of younger and future generations, both when they act as individual citizens and as professionals representing a corporate interest.

## 15.4    Innovation gaps and drivers of change

Transport policy should strive to create conditions to facilitate the development of innovation. This requires a long-term commitment, as the life cycle of innovation is long. The active participation of stakeholders can extend this life cycle, sometimes in support of vested interests, adding uncertainty in relation to closure.

Transport policy, both in technological domains (e.g., automation, electrical mobility, etc.) and in the socio-political and economic domains (e.g., procurement, regulatory and institutional environment), must be concerned with outreach. Much of the research and development (R&D) effort of the EU in transport is not properly commercialized, due to major gaps in the innovation and delivery chain.

In fact, transport policy must promote and ensure that the drivers of innovation are present in the sector, to minimize the time from an R&D output ('proven science') to full commercialization ('product intake in the market'). This path is by definition risky, long and expensive, and can only succeed if a system of innovation is in place. This is a weak point in Europe, where the outreach capacity is very low when compared with the amounts of funds applied to R&D, indicating weak articulation between policy, research and the innovation system. There is a need to change the orientation of research programs towards a more intense enrolment of industry along the research process, so that a more effective outreach can be achieved.

The structural drivers that support applied innovation are information, education, and entrepreneurship, all correlated with the capacity to define effective incentives to influence the behaviour of stakeholders regarding the speed of adoption of innovation.

## 15.5    Future objectives for EU and UK transport policy

Despite the potential tension created by the Brexit process, there are clear long-term macro objectives common to the EU and UK. Three main transport policy macro objectives are considered here.

### 15.5.1    Inclusive society

An inclusive society can be institutionally reflected in assumptions that see transport as a 'right' to accessibility to services and opportunities. Mobility is one of the instruments that provide accessibility but others also contribute, such as land use policy, and also energy, safety and security. An inclusive society can only be achieved through integrated and consistent policy action.

New knowledge is required to assess trade-offs between social benefits (e.g., increased security) and social costs (e.g., privacy) and to incorporate non-financial aspects like accessibility, comfort, security, and value capture.

### 15.5.2    A resilient transport system for sustainable cities and regions

This objective seeks to address the nexus of problems affecting urban transport, including congestion, pollution, accidents and inaccessibility, the latter much related to the inclusiveness objective. Procedures for urban mobility plans have been adopted in the EU and the UK and in many other countries, but there is a need to go further and also implement urban mobility audits. Urban transport challenges to achieving more sustainable European cities and regions include:

- achieving the required level of climate change mitigation in the sector;
- managing the impact of demographic trends and, in particular, the ageing population;
- effectively harnessing new transport and related ICT technology;
- making the transport system and, in particular infrastructure, capable of responding to new challenges;

- making quantum improvements in safety levels across the transport system;
- improving energy efficiency and reducing transport's dependence on fossil fuels; and
- redistributing passenger and freight traffic between transport modes on a large scale, primarily to ease environmental and congestion issues.

### 15.5.3    Europe-wide optimal connectivity

This is a complex objective and a necessary condition to achieve other EU objectives. It includes:

- concluding the Trans-European Transport Network (TEN-T) and building the smooth high-quality interconnections needed for the development of the internal market;
- promoting investment in transport by making sure that the national and European regulatory environments are appropriate and in place, and do not represent a barrier to the connectivity target;
- developing innovative financing instruments that can relieve pressure on public budgets and create a fair financial environment to conclude investments. Transport charging should be subjected to a review, to more properly reflect the 'polluter pays' principle;
- ensuring that the Brexit process will not jeopardize the achievements made in the past regarding connectivity and will not compromise the future potential for enhancement of connectivity as a main attribute of the European transport network.

## 15.6    Research opportunities: Implications for planning and decision-making

Meeting the objectives considered in the previous section faces some challenges. For example, demand for transport will increase, freight transport alone being expected to grow by 80 per cent by 2050, and the trend for urbanization will continue. Such growth will exacerbate existing problems of congestion, emissions and so on.

The EU is committed to reducing its greenhouse gas emissions by at least 80 per cent by 2050. The EU transport sector, particularly road transport, depends almost completely on oil as a fuel source. Research funds must concentrate on making alternative energy sources just as reliable and efficient, including the creation of infrastructure conditions to support the supply network. Transport has to make a very significant contribution to reducing emissions and this can only be achieved by both reducing mobility needs and adopting new sources of energy. Research is needed to identify the most effective transport policy pathways to combining such behavioural and technological contributions to lower emissions.

Congestion costs continue to proliferate despite the efforts at containment. In Europe it represents about 1 per cent of GDP every year. However, congestion pricing is still unpopular among citizens, and seen as unfair. Research must rethink the underlying paradigms that support this concept, and associated mechanisms, and identify opportunities for moving forward on pricing, to help drive behaviour change towards lower emissions futures.

Transport efficiency must be enhanced. This includes improving logistics and creating smarter 'travel behaviour' chains, by making the best use of modern ICT and satellite-based technology, thereby optimizing use and capacity of the various modes. Research must look into the economics of transport networks to identify policy opportunities for enhanced efficiency.

Lack of funding and financing is a critical issue, not only with regard to completing the TEN-T but also with regard to improving all modes and scales of transport. Research needs to identify new funding and financing mechanisms, including links to potential benefit flows, and identify policy requirements to support implementation.

Devising effective transport policy relies on the capability to evaluate, monitor, assess impact and return feedback, to adjust policy and/or measures. For many years, transport policy was largely based on the rationale of 'predict and provide'. Forecasting was at the core of this paradigm. Today it is largely understood that a change of paradigm towards 'aim and manage' is imperative, with more sustainable transport systems and services being the key for intended outcome. Transport policy cannot only be reactive: it must take a major role as a prospective driver of the evolution of mobility systems, towards greater sustainability. In the new paradigm, back casting is at the core, and it can be a game changer in the policy-making process. Research must invest in the development of methods and tools that enable improvement of these decision processes.

For this change of paradigm, robust and comprehensive sets of information are indispensable, as well as tools to simulate, assess and predict. Availability of open data is a crucial input. Research is required on how to best regulate the access and use of open data, while creating incentives to influence the right decision of the citizens when making their choices.

## 15.7   Conclusions

Many current transport-related databases and models and/or their input parameters are now largely obsolete. Essential inputs such as values of time, elasticity measures and monetary values of social and environmental externalities need to be updated to better reflect users' preferences and system performance and also be more closely aligned with the ultimate sustainability goals being pursued, under the 'aim and manage' approach. Innovative techniques for data collection impose changes in input integration in models. Models and simulation, in turn, need to reproduce the more holistic view of citizens' needs, instead of the more usual and fragmented 'ceteris paribus' perspective. Moreover, variables like comfort, security, and indicators that can measure the perceived acceptance of users are not, but should be, extensively studied.

Current risk assessment theories, methods and tools do not cope well with the increasing complexity of transport systems nor with the diversity of partners and interests associated with transport investments. Risks cannot be assessed from the exclusive perspective of the investor, as they are shared between investors, industry, citizens and society at large. Consequently, risk assessment must be done taking into consideration the exposure to risk of all those stakeholders.

The need to change should be understood as a milestone to set a future research agenda suited to the challenges that transport will face in the service of resilient societies and with a fast-changing technology as its main partner.

## References

Acemoglu, D. and Robinson, J. (2008), *The Role of Institutions in Growth and Development*, Washington, DC: World Bank.

Banister, D. and Berechman, J. (2003), *Transport Investment and Economic Development*, London: UCL Press, Taylor & Francis Group.

Caspersen, C. J., Powell, K. E. and Christenson, G. M. (1985), 'Physical activity, exercise and physical fitness. Definitions and distinctions for health-related research', *Public Health Reports* 100(2), 126–131.

Cervero, R., Rood, T. and Appleyard, B. (1997), 'Job accessibility as a performance indicator: An analysis of trends and their social policy implications in the San Francisco Bay Area', *Working paper 692*, Berkeley: University of California.

Demographia (2018), *Demographia World Urban Areas*. 14th Annual Edition: 201804.

Eurostat (2010), Household Budget Survey, European Commission, Brussels, Belgium.

IMF (International Monetary Fund) (2018), *World Economic Outlook*, April 2018: Cyclical Upswing, Structural Change. Washington, DC: IMF.

IOM (International Organization for Migration) (2015), *World Migration Report*, Geneva, Switzerland. https://www.iom.int/world-migration-report-2015. Accessed 16 October 2015.

Macário, R., (2014), 'Access as a social good and as an economic good: Is there a need of paradigm shift?' In Sclar, E., Lönnroth, M. and Wolmar, C. (Eds), *Urban Access for the 21st Century: Finance and Governance Models for Transport Infrastructure*, London: Routledge.

Martins, P. (2018), 'Modelação de politicas integradas para a redução do congestionamento rodoviário através do conceito de "responsabilidade partilhada"', PhD dissertation report, Instituto Superior Técnico, Universidade de Lisboa, Portugal.

Rodrik, D. (2008), 'Goodbye Washington Consensus, hello Washington Confusion? A review of the World Bank's *Economic Growth in the 1990s: Learning from a Decade of Reform*', *Panoeconomicus* 55(2), 135–156.

Schafer, A. and Victor, D. G. (2000), 'The future mobility of the world population', *Transportation Research Part A* 34(3), 171–205.

Sclar, E., Lönnroth, M. and Wolmar, C. (Eds) (2014), *Urban Access for the 21st Century: Finance and Governance Models for Transport Infrastructure*, London: Routledge.

Spandou, M. (2010), 'Institutional design as a performance factor in urban mobility systems', PhD dissertation report, Instituto Superior Técnico, Universidade de Lisboa, Portugal.

UN (United Nations) (2016), *Mobilizing Sustainable Transport for Development – Analysis and Policy Recommendations from the United Nations Secretary-General's High Level Advisory Group*, New York: Author.

Zheng, L. and Hensher, D. (2005), 'Prospect theoretic contributions in understanding traveller behaviour: A review and some comments', *Transport Reviews* **31**(1), 97–115.

# 16 Transport policies in Asia

*Junyi Zhang and Fuyo (Jenny) Yamamoto*

## 16.1 Introduction

Asia is a vast continent, accounting for roughly 30% of the world's landmass and 60% of its population. In recent years, the region has become a major driving force of global economic growth (IMF, 2017). To sustain this growth, many governments have started to address the critical gaps in their transportation systems as well as the negative externalities which come with rising private automobile ownership, such as congestion, air pollution and road traffic accidents. But while governments are increasing investments in more sustainable modes such as railways, inland waterways, coastal shipping, and urban transit systems, they are also steadily expanding their highways and road networks (UNESCAP, 2017). The region is thus at a critical crossroads, as the transport policies and investment decisions taken by Asia's governments today will shape their development paths into the future. Against this backdrop, this chapter aims to provide an overview of current transport policies in Asia and future research priorities. Due to space constraints, it is not possible to examine the policies for specific countries or modes in detail; instead, the chapter focuses on selected policy areas which the authors feel warrant greater research attention.

## 16.2 Infrastructure planning and development

In the past, Asia's high trade costs were often blamed on the quality of its physical infrastructure (Brooks and Hummels, 2009). Having seen the success of export-oriented growth strategies of the 'East Asian tigers', and more recently China, Thailand and Malaysia, many governments now plan infrastructure investments in conjunction with trade and development policies. One example is the resurgence of 'corridor-based' projects which integrate industrial development plans (Special Economic Zones, industrial clusters, technology parks) and modern transportation systems (dedicated freight corridors by rail, High Speed Rail, container terminals and logistics infrastructure, and highways). Both domestic initiatives, such as India's Delhi-Mumbai Industrial Corridor, and cross-border initiatives, such as the Nanning-Singapore Economic Corridor, Bangladesh-China-India-Myanmar Economic Corridor, and the Greater Mekong Subregion and Central Asia Regional

Economic Corridor (CAREC) programmes are gaining traction. Cooperation is also being strengthened between countries along major waterways, for example under the 2015 Lancang-Mekong Cooperation Framework.

Some authors question the assumption that infrastructure is always growth-enhancing (Ansar et al., 2016, for China), while others note that it is often difficult to attribute causality due to time lags between infrastructure construction and impacts (Straub et al., 2008). More case studies which reflect local contexts (Yoshino et al., 2018) would be useful, as would studies looking at dynamic network effects at the transnational or regional level (see Quium, 2018, for the Asian Highway network; ADB, 2014, and Fujimura, 2018, for economic corridors). More theoretical work on effects of large-scale projects is also needed (Ng et al., 2018).

Meanwhile, more research on different modal options is needed. Many authors, for example, have looked at the economic impacts of airports, but relatively few examine the effects of these investments on greenhouse gas emissions or from the perspective of life-cycle costs. Effects of better intermodal connectivity (intermodal facilities and dry ports) or removing non-physical barriers at border crossings have been poorly researched, too.

## 16.3   Changing role of government in transport infrastructure provision and management

The Asian Development Bank (ADB) recently estimated that the cost of meeting Asia's transport infrastructure 'gaps' for 2016–2030 is roughly US$7.8 trillion, and US$8.4 trillion if climate change adaptation measures are included (ADB, 2017a). In response to this deficit, there has been a tremendous push to diversify sources for financing infrastructure (sources of public finance: e.g., Rillo and Ali, 2017; public-private partnerships (PPP): e.g., ADB, 2017b; Gordon, 2012).

Early practices of using private funding to support infrastructure development can be found in Japan's *Ensen-Kaihatsu* (EK) and Transit Integrated Development (TID) in Hong Kong, Taipei, and Singapore (Taniguchi, 2018; Zhang, 2018). Now, such transit-oriented development (TOD) can also be found in many cities in mainland China (Doulet et al., 2017). There are many studies on funding mechanisms, including land value capture, user fees, and joint development (e.g., Zhao et al., 2012). However, there is still debate about the reasons for success or failure in privately financed projects; about the 'appropriate' level of risk which the public sector should shoulder; and how PPPs can help improve the efficiency of the transport network as a whole (Iwasaki, 2018). Chapter 19 of the current volume explores some of these issues.

Another relevant issue is the relationship between private sector involvement in infrastructure and the deregulation and liberalization of transport services. Globally, nearly 80% of global port terminal capacity is now managed by private sector companies, with some private terminal operators also expanding into rail and road infrastructure investment to improve access to ports (UNCTAD, 2017). The expanding role of air cargo in global value chains has also led major freight companies to establish regional hubs in an intra-Asian hub-and-spoke network, pushing up competition between airports (Bowen, 2012). Meanwhile the surge in tourism in Asia and the advent of low-cost carriers have led governments to solicit private sector financing to develop domestic airports, as well as enact legislation to liberalize air services. More research on the experiences of the aviation and maritime sectors could shed light on how the role of government changes under different financing models.

Research is also required on the influence of external agencies and governments. Bilateral agencies, for example, contribute funds and technical expertise as part of their official development assistance (ODA) programmes (see Kato, 2018, on Japanese ODA), but are increasingly leveraging private sector finance. Issues which require further exploration include: the political economy of foreign aid; debt burdens associated with ODA projects; extent of technology transfer through such projects; and technology 'lock-in', an issue which has come to the fore in the competition for High Speed Rail contracts in Asia. In this regard, more research is needed on China's Belt and Road Initiative (BRI), which comes with the promise of substantial financial backing (estimated to be around US$1 trillion), and whose impacts are expected to extend beyond infrastructure development (Djankov and Miner, 2016).

## 16.4   Policy challenges associated with rapid motorization

Municipal governments face many policy challenges associated with rapid motorization, including air pollution, noise pollution, greenhouse gas emissions, traffic congestion, road traffic safety, lack of integrated land-use and transport development, overloading of vehicles, poor quality of public transport services, and potential for social exclusion. To address these issues, many cities have been investing in all forms of mass transit. As of 2014, 53 cities in Asia and the Pacific had metro systems (UITP, 2015), while Light Rail Transit (LRT) and tramways are also being used. However, the fastest-growing mode has been Bus Rapid Transit (BRT), now operating in over 43 cities in Asia (Global BRTData).[1] However, because of their limited spatial coverage and concentration in commercial districts, connectivity will be an important issue, particularly the integration of new systems with existing formal and informal transit modes, and also connectivity between modern systems (e.g., operational connectivity through electronic ticketing systems). The relationships between these evolving transit systems and policies governing land-use, as well as policies to minimize negative social and environmental effects from their construction, need further research, particularly if they involve resettlement of habitations.

---

1 Global BRTData, https://brtdata.org/location/asia. Accessed 10 August 2018.

Meanwhile, policies to manage car use will continue to require attention. Though the number of two- and three-wheelers exceeds that of automobiles in several countries, the number of automobiles is expected to overtake as incomes rise. Reducing private vehicle use, including motorcycles, will continue to be a political issue in some countries. Several cities regulate car use through measures such as allocation of licences in China and parking regulations in Japan, but few utilize pricing policies to regulate cars, apart from Singapore's Electronic Road Pricing system and the Shanghai Car Plate Auction System in China. In terms of vehicle technologies, many countries employ taxes and/or subsidies to encourage the replacement of older vehicles and take-up of hybrid and electric vehicles (Bakker et al., 2017), but only China and Japan have introduced energy efficiency regulations for heavy-duty trucks and buses. China unilaterally introduced a zero emission vehicle mandate which requires automobile companies in China to publish 'New Energy Vehicle' scores by producing or importing battery electric and plug-in hybrid electric vehicles (GFEI, 2017). As countries tighten their environmental regulations on car emissions, the cascading effects on other automobile markets in the region need to be researched (e.g., the environmental and safety implications of imported second-hand cars).

## 16.5  Transport safety

There is an extensive body of research on safety issues for railways (Mao and Xu, 2018), the maritime sector (Luo and Shin, 2018), and aviation (Zhang and Feng, 2018). However, the lack of progress in domestic passenger ferry safety in Asia led the International Maritime Organization to issue a set of guidelines for the region in 2015. Meanwhile, road safety has moved onto the international development agenda as a global health issue:[2] four out of the ten worst performing countries (in terms of fatality rate per 100,000 inhabitants) are in South East Asia (Thailand, Vietnam, Malaysia, and Myanmar), while China and India have the highest number of fatalities in absolute terms (WHO, 2015). The highest proportion of road traffic deaths in the Asia and Pacific region in 2013 involved two-wheelers (30%), followed by four-wheelers (22%), pedestrians (20%), cyclists (5%) and others (23%) (UNESCAP, 2017).

There is already a large body of research on traffic safety in high-income countries/ regions such as Japan, Hong Kong, Korea, and Taiwan, where the rising average age of drivers has become a major topic. Recently more studies are being done on risk behaviours in middle-income countries, such as drink driving, safety belt use, helmet use, mobile phone use, and other factors contributing to accidents (e.g., Stephan et al., 2011; Truong et al., 2016 on motorcycle safety). Many countries already have road safety policies but these are often not enforced, pointing to problems of governance. Comparative studies could provide policymakers with a broader perspective on the relative effectiveness of existing policies.

---

2 The UN Sustainable Development Goals include an explicit target on road traffic accidents.

## 16.6    Adapting to climate change and disaster risk

Many cities and regions in Asia are vulnerable to natural disasters. The UN estimated that 10 cities with 1 million inhabitants or more in Asia, including three
megacities (Tokyo, Osaka and Manila), were at high risk of three or more types of
disaster (UN, 2015). At the same time, some areas are expected to be affected by
sea level rises caused by climate change. The vulnerability of transport systems to
natural disasters, and their critical role in responding to subsequent humanitarian
crises, was demonstrated by the 2011 Great East Japan Earthquake (Okumura and
Kim, 2018). Following the 2005 World Conference on Disaster Reduction, governments were expected to incorporate transport into their disaster response strategies, but whether and how they have done so are not well known. Meanwhile, the
cost implications of incorporating climate change effects into the design of transport infrastructure has been examined using the Infrastructure Planning Support
System (IPSS) (Schweikert et al., 2014, for Japan and the Philippines) and new
design parameters to 'climate proof' infrastructure (e.g., Regmi and Hanaoka, 2011)
have also been studied, but the practical implications of applying such parameters
are under-researched.

## 16.7    Socially inclusive transport policies

In both urban and rural areas, the mobility needs and patterns of groups at risk
of social exclusion (e.g., women, children, indigenous groups, differently abled,
low-caste groups, or the very poor) have been largely neglected by the research
community. Despite high rates of economic growth, a large proportion of the
population still live under the poverty line, with a significant proportion of the poor
living in rural areas (80% in South Asia and 75% in South East Asia) (IFAD, 2010).
Most governments have national rural road development programmes, often co-
financed by bilateral and multilateral funding agencies (e.g., Cambodia Rural Roads
Improvement Project; India's Pradhan Mantri Gram Sadak Yojana). Several studies
have examined the impact of new or rehabilitated roads on local development, such
as changes in or diversification of income sources (e.g., Mu and van de Walle, 2011,
for Vietnam), but few look at the equity effects over the medium to long term, such
as on households who do not have the means to own vehicles. Meanwhile, there
are relatively few studies on non-road transport modes, such as river transport in
Bangladesh and the Mekong River basin, or inter-island shipping in archipelagic
countries (such as Cao et al., 2017, for the Philippines), and even fewer on intermediate transport, such as tractors, animal-drawn carts, and human and animal
porterage, despite their importance in transporting people and goods in rural areas
(Starkey and Kaumbotho, 2000). As rural roads aim to increase access to social
services, there is a need for more research on cross-sectoral impacts of transport
infrastructure, including non-transport solutions to address accessibility in remote
areas, for example through tele-medicine and distance education.

## 16.8    New transport services and technologies

Asia has observed a rapid and massive deployment of various new technologies, but in a very flexible and adaptive way. In this regard, e-paratransit (e.g., e-jeepney in the Philippines, e-TukTuk in Thailand and Laos) is a good example of 'advanced low-tech' modes which have adapted to the local environment, while China has taken the lead in promoting e-bikes. Another good example is Ojol in Indonesia, an Uber-like motorcycle taxi service which has become very popular, partly because users no longer have to negotiate fares with drivers. Meanwhile, Mobility as a Service (MaaS) and shared vehicle systems, such as car-, motorcycle- and bike-sharing, are proving to be popular in China, Indonesia, the Philippines, Singapore, and Malaysia. In China and Vietnam, Uber was acquired by local transport service providers DiDi and Grab, respectively. Thus, Asian countries may play more and more important roles in deploying new mobility services in the global market. However, not all bike-sharing systems have been successful in China (Zhang et al., 2015). As new vehicle technologies and technology-driven mobility services evolve, research is needed to define government roles and design policies to manage their impact and diffusion.

## 16.9    Conclusions

Governments in Asia are employing a wide range of policy measures to address the challenges and opportunities arising from the transport sector. As such, it offers a treasure-chest of potential areas for further research. As much of the research generated by academia focuses on issues concerning high-income countries, there is an urgent need to direct more attention to Asia, particularly low- and middle-income countries which do not have well-established research traditions in transportation studies. Such efforts will draw attention to the poor quality of transport data in many Asian countries and put pressure on governments to improve data collection efforts. More transnational research collaboration would also facilitate cross-country learning of both policy successes and mistakes; such initiatives are likely to become more important as the transport systems in Asia become increasingly integrated.

## References

ADB (Asian Development Bank) (2014), *Economic Corridor Development for Inclusive Asian Regional Integration: Modelling Approach to Economic Corridors*, Manila: Author.

ADB (Asian Development Bank) (2017a), *Meeting Asia's Infrastructure Needs*, Manila: Author.

ADB (Asian Development Bank) (2017b), *Asian Development Outlook (ADO) 2017 Update: Sustaining Development through Public-Private Partnership*, Manila: Author.

Ansar, A., Flyvbjerg, B., Budzier, A. and Lunn, D. (2016), 'Does infrastructure investment lead to economic growth or economic fragility? Evidence from China', *Oxford Review of Economic Policy*, **32**(3), 360–390.

Bakker, S., Dematera Contreras, K., Kappiantari, M., Tuan, N.A., Guillen, M.D., Gunthawong, G., Zuidgeest, M., Liefferink, D. and van Maarseveen, M. (2017), 'Low-carbon transport policy in four ASEAN countries: Developments in Indonesia, the Philippines, Thailand and Vietnam', *Sustainability*, **9**, 1217.

Bowen, Jr., J.T. (2012), 'A spatial analysis of FedEx and UPS: hubs, spokes, and network structure', *Journal of Transport Geography*, **24**, 419–431.

Brooks, D.H. and Hummels, D. (Eds.) (2009), *Infrastructure's Role in Lowering Asia's Trade Costs – Building for Trade*, Cheltenham: Asian Development Bank Institute/Edward Elgar Publishing.

Cao, D., Stanley, J. and Stanley, J. (2017), 'Indicators of socio-spatial transport disadvantage for inter-island transport planning in rural Philippine communities', *Social Inclusion*, **5**(4), 116–131.

Djankov, S. and Miner, S. (Eds.) (2016), 'China's belt and road initiative: Motives, scope, and challenges', *Peterson Institute for International Economics, PIIE Briefing*, 16-2. https://piie.com/system/files/documents/piieb16-2_1.pdf. Accessed 1 September 2018.

Doulet, J-F., Delpirou, A. and Delaunay, T. (2017), 'Taking advantage of a historic opportunity? A critical review of the literature on TOD in China', *Journal of Transport and Land Use*, **10**(1), 77–92.

Fujimura, M. (2018), 'Evaluating impacts of cross-border transport infrastructure in the Greater Mekong Subregion: Three approaches'. In Yoshino, N., Helble, M. and Abidhadjaev, U. (Eds.) (2018), *Financing Infrastructure in Asia and the Pacific: Capturing Impacts and New Sources*, Tokyo: ADBI, Chapter 10.

GFEI (Global Fuel Efficiency Initiative) (2017), 'China publishes updated fuel economy standards with mandate for EVs'. https://www.globalfueleconomy.org/blog/2017/october/china-publishes-updated-fuel-economy-standards-with-mandate-for-evs, 11 October 2017. Accessed 1 September 2018.

Gordon, C. (2012), 'The challenges of transport PPP's in low-income developing countries: A case study of Bangladesh', *Transport Policy*, **24**, 296–301.

IFAD (International Fund for Agricultural Development) (2010), *Rural Poverty Report 2010*, Rome: Author.

IMF (International Monetary Fund) (2017), *Regional Economic Outlook: Asia and Pacific, 'Preparing for choppy seas'*, Washington, DC: International Monetary Fund.

Iwasaki, H. (2018), 'Financing mechanisms for transport infrastructure and services'. In Zhang, J. and Feng, C-M. (Eds.), *Routledge Handbook of Transport in Asia*, London: Routledge, Chapter 19.

Kato, H. (2018), 'Development assistance to transportation in Asian developing countries'. In Zhang, J. and Feng, C-M. (Eds.), *Routledge Handbook of Transport in Asia*, London: Routledge, Chapter 21.

Luo, M. and Shin, S-H. (2018), 'Maritime accidents'. In Zhang, J. and Feng, C-M. (Eds.), *Routledge Handbook of Transport in Asia*, London: Routledge, Chapter 6.

Mao, B. and Xu, Q. (2018), 'Railway accidents'. In Zhang, J. and Feng, C-M. (Eds.), *Routledge Handbook of Transport in Asia*, London: Routledge, Chapter 5.

Mu, R., van de Walle, D. (2011), 'Rural roads and local market development in Vietnam', *Journal of Development Studies*, **47**(5), 709–734.

Ng, A.K.Y., Jiang, C., Li, X., O'Connor, K. and Lee, P.T-W. (2018), 'A conceptual overview of government initiatives and the transformation of transport and regional systems', *Journal of Transport Geography*, **71**, 199–203.

Okumura, M. and Kim, J. (2018), 'Transportation in disasters: Lessons learned from GEJE 2011'. In Zhang, J. and Feng, C-M. (Eds.), *Routledge Handbook of Transport in Asia*, London: Routledge, Chapter 8.

Quium, A.S.M. (2018), 'The Asian Highway and Trans-Asian Railway networks: Origins, progress of development and prospects in the future'. In Zhang, J. and Feng, C-M. (Eds.), *Routledge Handbook of Transport in Asia*, London: Routledge, Chapter 3.

Regmi, M.B. and Hanaoka, S. (2011), 'A survey on impacts of climate change on road transport infrastructure and adaptation strategies in Asia', *Environmental Economics and Policy Studies*, **13**(1), 21–41.

Rillo, A.D. and Ali, Z. (2017), 'Public financing of infrastructure in Asia: In search of new solutions', *ADBI Policy Brief No. 2017-2* (April).

Schweikert, A., Chinowsky, P., Espinet, X. and Tarbert, M. (2014), 'Climate change and infrastructure impacts: Comparing the impact on roads in ten countries through 2100', *Procedia Engineering,* **78**, 306–316.

Starkey, P. and Kaumbotho, P. (2000), *Meeting the Challenges of Animal Traction: A Resource Book of the Animal Traction Network for Eastern and Southern Africa*, London: Practical Action.

Stephan, K., Kelly, M., McClure, R., Seubsman, S.A., Yiengprugsawan, V., Bain, C., Sleigh, A.; Thai Cohort Study Team (2011), 'Distribution of transport injury and related risk behaviours in a large national cohort of Thai adults', *Accident Analysis and Prevention,* **43**(3), 1062–1067.

Straub, S., Vellutini, C. and Warlters, M. (2008), 'Infrastructure and Economic Growth in East Asia', *World Bank Policy Research Working Paper No. 4589.*

Taniguchi, M. (2018), 'Ensen Kaihatsu (railway area developments) in Japan: A comparison with transit-oriented development (TOD)'. In Zhang, J. and Feng, C-M. (Eds.), *Routledge Handbook of Transport in Asia*, London: Routledge, Chapter 12.

Truong, L.T., Nguyen, H.T.T. and De Gruyter, C. (2016), 'Mobile phone use among motorcyclists and electric bike riders: A case study of Hanoi, Vietnam', *Accident Analysis and Prevention,* **91**, 208–215.

UITP (International Association of Public Transport) (2015), *World Metro Figures: Statistics Brief.* October 2015.

UN (United Nations) (2015), 'Risks of Exposure and Vulnerability to Natural Disasters at the City Level: A Global Overview'. *Department of Economic and Social Affairs, Population Division. Technical Paper No. 2015/2.*

UNCTAD (United Nations Conference on Trade and Development) (2017), 'Ports', in *Review of Maritime Transport 2017*, Geneva: Author, Chapter 4.

UNESCAP (United Nations Economic and Social Commission for Asia and the Pacific) (2017), *Review of Developments in Transport in Asia and the Pacific*, Bangkok: Author.

WHO (World Health Organization) (2015), *Global Status Report on Road Safety 2015*, Geneva: Author.

Yoshino, N., Helble, M. and Abidhadjaev, U. (Eds.) (2018), *Financing Infrastructure in Asia and the Pacific: Capturing Impacts and New Sources*, Tokyo: ADBI.

Zhang, J. and Feng, C-M. (2018), 'Introduction: Transport in Asia'. In Zhang, J. and Feng, C-M. (Eds.), *Routledge Handbook of Transport in Asia*, London: Routledge, Chapter 1.

Zhang, L., Zhang, J., Duan, Z-Y. and Bryde, D. (2015), 'Sustainable bike-sharing systems: Characteristics and commonalities across cases in urban China', *Journal of Cleaner Production,* **97**, 124–133.

Zhang, M. (2018), 'Urban development along rails in other Asian regions'. In Zhang, J. and Feng, C-M. (Eds.), *Routledge Handbook of Transport in Asia*, London: Routledge, Chapter 13.

Zhao, Z.J., Das, K.V. and Larson, K. (2012), 'Joint development as a value capture strategy for public transit finance', *Journal of Transport and Land Use,* **5**(1), 5–17.

# 17 Africa

*Jackie Walters*

## 17.1 Introduction

Transport policy formulation is a key responsibility of government and impacts multiple aspects of society. Transport policy, whether focused on the economics or social elements of the transportation system (entry to the market, ownership, competition, price setting, affordability, accessibility, etc.) or the technical dimensions of policy (often referred to as the safety aspects), is important in encouraging investments and employment in the transportation sector so that a country or region can trade effectively and efficiently. It is also important so that people can live fulfilled lives.

Transport and its related infrastructure play key roles in the economic well-being of a country and society. Policy sets the "rules of the game" for investors and trade and affects the costs of doing business. Poorly formulated and executed policies can hamper investments, lead to higher costs of trade for a country or region and diminish the well-being of citizens.

Formulating transportation policies depends on many role players: government, organized industry, users, organized labour, suppliers to the industry, financiers and the like. It also involves multiple government institutions such as departments of industrial development, foreign affairs, labour, energy, education, environment, finance, transportation, etc. These government institutions can manifest themselves at the national, regional/federal/state and local levels of government, resulting in complex inter-institutional arrangements.

One of the major challenges of policy making is the successful implementation, monitoring and review of policy goals and objectives. This requires high levels of skills, the management of stakeholders, careful planning and adequate resources (funding and data requirements). Institutional capabilities and the coordination of activities at various levels of government and implementing agencies are key to successful policy implementation, monitoring and evaluation. Other challenges may include over-ambitious time frames, inadequate resource provision – especially financial resources – inadequate data management and inadequate consultation with stakeholders across the policy domain.

The following sections provide regional policy perspectives on Africa: firstly, the role and complexities associated with large informal public transport operations in many cities in Africa; secondly, a general overview of major policy issues that have been experienced (mainly based on a number of World Bank studies to this effect in a number of African countries); and, thirdly, policy perspectives on the importance of institutional structures and the coordination of their activities in policy implementation.

## 17.2    The role of informal public operations in Africa

A key feature of many developing countries' public transit systems is the significant role that informal transport (called paratransit in some regions) plays in urban mobility. This is also the case in Africa. These services have different names depending on the country or city where they are present: for instance, Gbakas in the Ivory Coast; minibus taxis in South Africa; Matatus in Nairobi, Kenya; and Car Rapides in Dakar, Senegal. Informal transport, as opposed to formal commuter bus and rail services, is difficult to manage and control but has the advantage of flexibility in the offering of its services (as opposed to timetables and route networks in more formal public transport systems), thus leading to significant demand for these services. These services are generally seen as more demand-responsive than formal bus and rail services and often provide door-to-door services, even on relatively low-density routes. In many African cities informal transport dominates public transit modal shares and has contributed to lesser roles played by formal transit systems, due to their aggressive and uncontrolled growth and intense competition on existing public transit routes and networks.

In South Africa, after the legalization of the 16-seater minibus taxi in the mid-1980s, the market share of subsidized commuter bus services has reduced by an estimated 70% and the taxi industry's market share is still growing. For example, the industry's market share in public transport increased from 59% in 2003 to 68.8% in 2013 (NHTS, 2013). Negative aspects of informal public transport industries often include in-fighting amongst operators, disputes about route access and operations, poor maintenance and driving practices and their contribution to urban congestion. Due to the informal nature of these operations, authorities have difficulty in monitoring and controlling services and are often unable to provide accurate information about the number of informal operators, fare structures, routes over which operations take place and the financial characteristics of the industry. Authorities are also often, as in the case of South Africa, unable to enforce national labour legislation, such as hours of work and minimum wages, due to the informal nature of the industry. Data about these services is often scant and, in almost all instances, services operate on an unsubsidized basis and in competition with formal bus and rail services.

Despite the growth and popularity of informal public transport, many African cities have seen the introduction of new on-demand (app-based) taxi services, such as Uber and Lyft, in competition with traditional sedan car taxis. These services are hugely popular in, for instance, South Africa and, as is the case in many cities of the world, are causing major friction with traditional on-demand taxi services that accuse the new entrants of robbing them of their traditional markets. This has led to demands for the regulation of these services from traditional taxi operators. These new entrants are opening up an entirely new area of policy uncertainty, an area that the South African Department of Transport is currently grappling with.

The importance of informal transport in urban mobility in Africa is well understood by authorities and users alike and many efforts are being undertaken to assist in formalizing at least a section of these industries, so that they can progress to more formal transport. Initiatives include involving the operators in newly established BRT systems in South African cities such as Johannesburg, Pretoria, Cape Town, Port Elizabeth, Durban and elsewhere (Dar es Salaam, Tanzania, Nigerian cities, Morocco, Senegal and Uganda). In addition, it is the aim of the South African government to introduce set-asides in subsidized commuter bus contracts, which will force bus companies to include these operators in their bids for such contracts. These efforts are, however, fraught with difficulties and progress is notoriously slow due to the very nature of the informal industry and the way it is organized, a lack of skills to participate in formalized transport operations, its ability to attract finance and their (often) unwillingness to be formalized due to the challenges and uncertainties this would bring to their "traditional" way of operations.

The informal public transport industry has limitations in solving big city commuter transport issues. With African urbanization happening at an increasing pace, informal transit modes contribute significantly to externalities such as high levels of congestion, pollution and safety issues. The challenge this poses to the transport policy specialist is how to provide for these operations, and the social inclusion benefits they support, in transport policy formulation, transportation planning (including societal goals for public transport such as safety, regularity and reliability), policy implementation and policy monitoring.

## 17.3   Policy issues experienced in Africa

The World Bank, via its Sub Sahara Africa Transport Program (SSATP), has conducted a number of recent policy-related studies in African countries. These findings normally relate to the countries that are investigated and cannot always be generalized to the continent as a whole. Nevertheless, the insights gained in these studies are important, as many of the issues identified may be applicable to a lesser or greater extent to many other African countries.

In a major study on African transport policies in six African countries[1] the World Bank (2015a) found that transport policies were only implicitly linked to

---

1   Ethiopia, Benin, Burkina Faso, Gabon, Ghana and Zambia.

supranational commitments such as the Africa Millennium Development Goals (MDGs) or Regional Economic Community (REC) agreements. The study also found that transport strategies are beset by implementation challenges: there are inadequate human resources; the affordability of transport strategies is not well understood; there are inadequate information and information systems, as well as inadequate prioritization frameworks. The study also found monitoring and evaluation lacking substantially in many of the African countries studied, with one of the reasons being insufficient data.

Good quality, reliable data is critical to assist in monitoring and evaluating the impact of transportation investments as well as for evidence-based policy decisions and planning (World Bank, 2015b). The World Bank lists key challenges with monitoring and policy evaluation (ex post) as:

- the ownership of monitoring and evaluation systems – the nature and primary objectives of monitoring and evaluation are often not well understood and incentives to establish them are inadequate;
- assessments of monitoring and evaluation systems – very few countries carry out assessments of their monitoring and evaluation systems and, if they do, the assessments are not comprehensive.

The study also found that many of the existing information systems are not coordinated and do not complement each other. There is also duplication of efforts in monitoring and evaluation systems, with consequential inefficient allocation of scarce resources. The study also found that the balance that ought to exist between monitoring and evaluation is more strongly focused on monitoring, with an inadequate attempt to measure the impact of transport policies. Where information systems exist, the available data is often limited and generally of poor quality, generated on an irregular basis and improperly collected (World Bank, 2015b). The data is also often biased towards transport infrastructure, with limited information available on transport services.

Issues related to the monitoring and evaluation of transport policies, available data, skills and affordability issues, as well as well-structured and capacitated institutional structures and management are found in a number of transport areas in South Africa. This has led to a lack of policy implementation and progress over many years, especially in public transport, despite excellent White Papers on national transport policy, national and provincial transport legislation, numerous strategy documents and large amounts of funding for public transport. At the core of the lack of implementation, especially related to public transport, appears to be insufficient planning around the coordination of implementing agencies (governance failure) and funding constraints to implement policy goals effectively.

There are many reasons why implementation is often a challenge – all over the world. CIPE (2012) refers to the policy implementation gap as the difference that is envisaged in laws and what is achieved in practice. It attributes this to: political factors (including state bureaucracy, legitimacy of the laws, quality of the laws and divergent political agendas); economic factors (including resources to implement laws, barriers to economic activity, vested interests); and social and cultural factors (including influence of the local elites, social structures, cultural legacy, institutions and incentives).

According to McLaughlin (1987, p.172), Pressman and Wildavsky were the first analysts who showed that

> ... *implementation dominates outcomes – that the consequences of even the best planned, best supported, and most promising policy initiatives depend finally on what happens as individuals throughout the policy system interpret and act on them.*

Their analyses, together with those of other authors, showed how *local factors such as size, intra-organizational relations, commitment, capacity, and institutional complexity molded responses to policy.* McLaughlin (1987, p.172) also postulates that it is *incredibly hard to make something happen, most especially across layers of government and institutions.* These factors are still present in current-day policy implementation.

## 17.4   Institutional structuring for effective policy administration and implementation

Institutional fragmentation and a lack of coordination is often found, due to several agencies/departments, at multiple levels of government (national, provincial/state level and local levels), with overlapping responsibilities (land use, transportation, infrastructure, housing, safety and security to name a few) and jurisdictions (municipal boundaries, provincial/state boundaries) responsible for transportation policies and implementation. This often leads to a lack of a coordinated approach to, for instance, urban transport planning and operations, with the resultant lack of policy progress, sub-optimal funding of transport projects and programmes and sub-optimal urban transport arrangements (e.g., a lack of integrated land use transport plans). The uncoordinated structures then lead to silo planning, funding and management, implementation challenges, a lack of data gathering (who is responsible?), gaps in policy monitoring and adjustment and eventually a sub-optimal transportation system. In assessing institutional responsibilities, it is important to identify arrangements and responsibilities as well as strengths and weaknesses in such arrangements (World Bank, 2015b). Institutional design for effective horizontal and vertical integration, or at least co-ordination, is thus central for good policy making (also see Chapter 5 of the current book).

In an evaluation of the World Bank Group's support (projects and interventions) for urban transport (World Bank, 2017), it found that inadequate attention has been paid to institutional developments and that monitoring and evaluation of institutional developments is still weak. The report points to major issues with institutional structures in the more than 100 cities supported by the World Bank.

More time ought to be spent on designing effective, coordinated and capacitated institutional structures, such as authorities that undertake integrated transport and land use planning in, for instance, the urban environment. These institutions are developed based on city/urban contexts such as the size, scope and the makeup of the city region. For instance, a single local authority is to be found in cities such as Stockholm and Malmö in Sweden and Freiburg in Germany. Then there are authorities structured to serve multiple local authority areas, such as London, Leeds and Vancouver, Canada (Stanley, Stanley and Hansen, 2017). Similar institutions exist in most European countries and elsewhere in the world, such as in Australia (Melbourne, Sydney, etc.) and the USA.

The Australian National Audit Office (2014) found that, on occasion, policy implementation involves several entities and that it is imperative to establish clear governance and accountability arrangements to clarify responsibilities, underpinned by a commitment to work together in a cooperative manner. This requires senior leadership to lead by example, to promote cooperation and avoid territoriality. Policy implementation challenges also ought to be considered in the policy design. Where these challenges are not considered, problems such as sub-optimal delivery methods, overambitious time frames, resources not being available when required, inappropriate skills or capacity for the policy initiative and insufficient consultation and contingency planning may arise (Australian National Audit Office, 2014).

CIPE (2012) points to the fact that the policy implementation gap is a universal problem throughout the world and that it occurs in all countries and at all levels of government but that its negative effects are *particularly visible and most painfully felt in developing countries where poor governance and weak implementation of laws have the greatest impact on daily lives of ordinary citizens* (CIPE, 2012, p.4).

The World Bank (2017) found that institutional structuring is critical to policy implementation, monitoring and evaluation. It has also acknowledged that it (the World Bank in its respective projects) has not done enough, over a period of time, in terms of the redesign of urban institutional structures. This would require continuous engagements through dedicated transport projects but many of its projects were "one-off" projects. In developing countries, many local governments lack administrative and fiscal capacity to deliver adequate services (World Bank, 2017).

In South Africa, urban transport faces the same issues, with fragmented funding and management streams at the metropolitan and provincial levels of government. Funding streams are mostly earmarked for specific public transport systems. Similarly, the transport agencies and departments mostly work in silos, with insufficient regard for overall systems efficiency and effectiveness. This arrangement leads to sub-optimal planning and funding of urban transport operations and a lack of effective policy implementation – especially in regard to integrated public transportation systems, a major objective of the South African government.

Proposals have been made in South Africa to establish transport authorities in an effort to better coordinate funding and planning at the metropolitan levels of government. Progress is, however, excruciatingly slow due to, amongst other things, the protection of political domains and consequent potential loss of political influence, dedicated modal funding streams and the concern for loss of authority over transportation decisions should such authorities be established. There have also been issues with Constitutional requirements in the way proposals for the establishment of transport authorities were drafted in legislation for the management of public transport (in South Africa public transport is a concurrent function between national, provincial and local government).

## 17.5   Emerging research areas

Issues related to policy making, implementation and monitoring are complex and multi-faceted and have occupied the minds of many researchers in the policy domain over the years. Research into the areas below should help to improve decision-making and implementation and could take the form of case studies, where learning could be taken from real world situations.

- **Accommodating the informal public transport operators in more "formal" public transport systems.** This is important for integrated system and service development but is complicated and time consuming. There is a need to conduct more research on approaches to formalization, identification of the difficulties, the solutions adopted as well as the general outcomes of such initiatives, to shape better policy responses.
- **Institutional structuring** is critical to ensuring effective policy implementation, monitoring and adjustment. Although a structure in itself cannot guarantee policy success, the absence of a well-considered and coordinated institutional setup contributes to policy failures. Research is needed on the impact of poorly conceptualized and structured institutions that are responsible for policy implementation, monitoring, evaluation and adjustments. The way institutional structures could be conceptualized, their responsibilities and structures in themselves, under various circumstances, such as a single entity serving a municipal area compared to metropolitan authorities servicing multiple local authorities, is an area for research in the African context and elsewhere.
- **Resources** are critical to successful policy implementation. These include human resource skills to develop, implement, monitor and adjust policies and funding resources to implement policies, programmes and projects. Research is needed on the impact these impediments have on policy implementation, monitoring and adjustments and on developing solutions that recognize the constraints that will be experienced in developing countries.
- **Monitoring and evaluation** of policy effectiveness is dependent on data gathering and appropriate information systems. This points to the need to link policies to measurable key performance areas and indicators and to

measure outcomes to these objectives. It is also important to link policies to supranational commitments such as the MDGs and Regional Economic Community agreements. Other measures could be linkages to environmental goals, road traffic accident reductions, congestion, etc. In addition, local realities and capacity constraints have to be considered in monitoring and evaluation of policies, as these will impact on the ability of institutions to carry out these functions effectively. This may require more simplified transport indicators that could contribute to the intended policy outcomes. Key areas for research include the potential of data gathering techniques such as smart cards, the potential contribution of big data, vehicle tracking via GPS systems and advanced ticketing systems in a developing nation/city context.

- **Data gathering** is necessary for policy and strategy development, transportation sector programme and project investments and the monitoring and evaluation of policy outcomes. Data is often limited, of poor quality, duplicated and uncoordinated, generated on an irregular basis and often improperly collected. Research ought to be considered regarding the import link between data gathering and information systems and successful policy development and design, implementation, monitoring and adjustment.
- **Policy implementation challenges** need to be identified in the policy development process and need to be considered in the policy design phase. These challenges could relate to available skills, institutional structures and their capabilities to implement, monitor and adjust policies, technology, adequate funding, data availability, etc. Researching the typical challenges to be expected in policy implementation, monitoring and adjustment (in a developing country context) will assist the policy maker in having a more comprehensive overview of aspects to consider in these critical phases of policy making.
- **Policy complexity** needs to be considered in the policy development phase. Complexity could be found (for example) in the ability to implement policies at the different levels of government involvement (national, provincial/state, and local government) in policy development and implementation and funding arrangements. Research into the issues to be expected in policy design will assist the policy maker in having a more realistic view of what to expect and how to plan for these complexities.
- **Leadership** is important in policy development and implementation. Effective leadership ought to consider the promotion of cooperation and avoidance of territoriality. Leadership is important in effective institutional structuring and intra- and inter-institutional coordination. Research into the importance and impact of effective leadership throughout the entire policy process will assist the policy maker in identifying critical institutions, people, structures and functions in the policy development and implementation phases and in development of good leadership.

## References

Australian National Audit Office (2014), *Successful Implementation of Policy Initiatives. Better Practice Guide* (October 2014), Canberra: Author. http://nla.gov.au/nla.obj-494733031/view. Accessed 12 February 2019.

CIPE (Centre for International Private Enterprise and Global Integrity) (2012), *Improving Public Governance. Closing the Implementation Gap between Law and Practice*. Contributors: Nadgrodkiewicz, A., Nakagaki, M. and Tomicic, M. https://www.cipe.org/sites/. . ./GI%20CIPE_Implementation%20Gap_for%20web.pdf. Accessed 18 May 2018.

McLaughlin, M.W. (1987), 'Learning from experience: Lessons from policy implementation', *Educational Evaluation and Policy Analysis*, **9**, 171–178.

NHTS (National Household Travel Survey) (2013), *Statistical Release P0320*. http://www.statssa.gov.za/publications/P0320/P03202013.pdf. Accessed 27 July 2018.

Stanley, J., Stanley, J. and Hansen, R. (2017), *How Great Cities Happen. Integrating People, Land Use and Transport*. Cheltenham: Edward Elgar Publishing.

World Bank Group (2015a), 'Africa Transport Policies Performance Review. The Need for More Robust Transport Policies (2015). SSATP Africa Transport Program', *Working Paper No. 103*, January.

World Bank Group (2015b), 'In Search of Evidence to Define Transport Policies. SSATP Africa Policy Program', *Working Paper No. 114*, January.

World Bank Group (2017), *Mobile Metropolises: Urban Transport Matters. An IEG Evaluation of the World Bank Group's Support for Urban Transport*, Washington, DC: International Bank for Reconstruction and Development/The World Bank.

# 18 Australia

*John Stanley*

## 18.1  Introduction

As a vast country settled at low density, with most people living in a small number of low-density cities, transport policy has long been a central concern of Australia's federal and state governments. The focus has traditionally been on urban transport, transport connections between the state capital cities (typically over 600km air distance between adjacent capitals) and transport of bulk exports (resources, energy and agricultural products).

The country has had a high rate of population growth over the past decade, with 3.7 million people being added (+1.65% per annum, on average), growth rates tending to decrease with increased regional remoteness (RAI 2015; ABS 2017). Over the 2011–16 period, for example, Melbourne population growth averaged 2.4% p.a., the city adding 100,000 people annually. Some 57% of this population growth occurred at low densities in outer suburbs. Thus, while Australian city land use plans typically talk about achieving more compact urban settlement patterns, experience suggests that the reality of growth is different, often continuing as urban sprawl at low density. This chapter focuses on transport policy concerns as they relate to growth in Australian cities.

One reason why the populations of Australian cities are growing strongly is likely to be their generally high ratings in international liveability scales, which seems likely to encourage the current strong levels of international migration. For example, Melbourne has been rated as the world's most liveable city by The Economist Intelligence Unit every year from 2011 to 2017. Sydney (10) and Melbourne (16) continue to rank highly in the Mercer 2018 Quality of Living Ranking,[1] and Melbourne (5), Sydney (7) and Brisbane (23) all rank within the top 25 cities in the Monocle 2017 Quality of Life Survey.[2]

While Australia's major cities may be well regarded for the quality of life they offer residents and visitors, their rapid growth rates are raising a number of transport-related policy concerns. These concerns range from shaping these cities to capture

1  https://www.mercer.com/newsroom/2018-quality-of-living-survey.html. Accessed 10 October 2018.

2  https://hypebeast.com/2017/6/monocle-magazine-most-liveable-city-2017. Accessed 10 October 2018.

productivity benefits from increasing scale and ensuring these benefits are widely shared among residents, to coping with high and increasing levels of traffic congestion, a lack of accessible affordable housing, dealing with social exclusion associated with low mobility options in fast-growing outer suburban areas, finding efficient means of moving freight in increasingly congested cities and developing sustainable ways to fund transport system and service development.

This range of policy issues is common in developed, low-density cities that are experiencing high population growth rates – arguably an indicator of both *urban success* and *urban excess*. Section 18.2 elaborates briefly on the context within which these challenges and opportunities arise, identifying a number of associated research priorities for transport policy.

The breadth of these issues underpins perhaps the most significant transport policy challenge facing Australian cities: establishing high-quality, integrated planning and policy-making processes to develop and then implement priorities that effectively tackle the opportunities and challenges of growth. Melbourne illustrates the scale of this challenge, being in the unique position of paying out $A1 billion to *not go ahead* with a major inner-middle urban toll-way. This example suggests that governance arrangements should be very high up the transport policy research agenda for Australia, if not at the top. Section 18.3 discusses this matter. Section 18.4 presents the chapter's conclusions.

## 18.2    Transport challenges and opportunities in Australian cities

### 18.2.1    What kind of city do we want?

If media coverage is any guide, road traffic congestion is the most pressing transport policy problem facing Australian cities, partly driven by high population growth rates and years of underinvestment in transport systems, encompassing road, public and active transport. A dominant Australian political response is to build more 'congestion-busting' roads, suggesting that Australia's planners and policy makers are not familiar with the work of Duranton and Taylor (2011, p. 2646), who conclude that 'road capacity expansions . . . are not appropriate policies with which to combat traffic congestion', because of the way such additional capacity generates larger traffic flows over time. Instead, they conclude that congestion pricing 'is the main candidate tool to curb traffic congestion' (Duranton and Taylor 2011, p. 2646).

Cities like Vancouver, which have a better grasp of the importance of land use transport interaction, take a quite different approach to Australian cities, responding to traffic congestion concerns by asking the question: What kind of city do we want? Answering this question requires understanding of societal values, as the starting point. Cities such as Vancouver (Canada), Portland (USA) and Freiburg (Germany) are leaders in this area. Stanley et al. (2017) have noted the commonality of goals set in many land use strategies, around the following goal areas:

- Increase economic productivity
- Reduce environmental footprint
- Increase social inclusion and reduce inequality
- Improve health and safety outcomes
- Promote intergenerational equity – this goal is likely to be achieved if the preceding goals are met
- Engage communities widely
- Implement integrated land use transport plans.

There are many transport policy research opportunities involved in exploring ways in which societal values can be better identified and understood, recognizing their foundational role in land use transport policy.

## 18.2.2    Land use transport integration

Answering the question, 'What kind of city do we want?', from a delivery viewpoint, requires a deep understanding of connections between travel and the built environment, from which transport and related policy measures can be developed. A meta-analysis of research in this area has been provided by Ewing and Cervero (2010). They emphasize the five 'Ds' of built form in terms of how they impact on car travel distances, public transport use and walking: **density**, **diversity** (of land uses, mixed use), **design** (particularly street network characteristics), **destination accessibility** (ease of access to trip destinations) and **distance to transit**. Particularly interesting are their reported impact elasticities, which show the relative sensitivity of various response variables (particularly motor vehicle kilometres of travel or VKT) to changes in a range of potential causal influences. Most elasticities are quite small, those with respect to neighbourhood land use variables (e.g. population density, land use mix, street network connectivity) being typically between −0.02 and −0.12 and those with respect to regional access to employment between −0.05 and −0.2 (Boarnet 2011). Even with small individual impacts, the combined effect of a number of measures can be significantly large, implying that policy packages are important in the land use/transport space. These policy packages need to encompass both regional- and neighbourhood-level considerations, underlining the vital importance of including both in an integrated approach to land use and transport planning and associated policy making.

Most of the elasticities cited above have been estimated in US studies. It is arguable that higher values might be found in countries/cities where fuel prices are higher, slow modes (walking, cycling) are more significant and public transport plays a bigger role (Van Wee and Handy 2014). These considerations suggest that built form may have a higher impact in Australian cities than is suggested by the elasticities identified by largely US research. Transport policy formulation for Australian cities will benefit from a stronger local research base on these elasticities, shaped in terms of developing packages of complementary and supporting measures.

Land use development directions espoused by most Australian cities are framed around achieving more compact settlement patterns, in line with the thinking behind the Ewing and Cervero (2010) work, anchored by:

- the central business district (CBD) and close surrounds, to support urban agglomeration economies
- a small number of high-tech/knowledge-based clusters, as focal points for inner-middle urban area growth to increase productivity and provide accessible, well-paid employment opportunities for outer urban residents
- major transit corridors, which should form a focus for population and jobs growth, building on Vancouver's successful experience
- infill/urban renewal opportunity areas, drawing on the London development concept
- a series of constituent (20 minute) neighbourhoods, including higher densities in growth suburbs.

This is a *polycentric + (transit) corridors + neighbourhoods* development model. Sydney, Melbourne and Perth, for example, embody a polycentric and transit corridors approach, with Sydney and Melbourne, especially the latter, also recognizing the strategic importance of neighbourhoods.

Spatially oriented transport directions to support this land use development direction include:

- ensuring strong radial public transport to the centre
- improving circumferential arterial roads. Road-based public transport, cycling and freight should be prioritized in use of these roads
- providing fast and frequent trunk public transport services supporting inner-middle urban nodes and development corridors, including for circumferential movement (including better public transport connections from outer suburbs to areas of employment/activity concentration)
- upgraded trunk arterial roads in outer growth areas (to deal with current backlogs but seeking to avoid encouraging further sprawl)
- increased local public transport opportunities in outer neighbourhoods, to support delivery of 20 minute neighbourhoods (an idea embedded in Melbourne's land use plan) and
- improved walking and cycling opportunities throughout the whole city, with a particular focus on clusters/nodes and facilitating the city of 20 minute cities.

A significant theme through these development directions is what is sometimes called *transit oriented development* (TOD). Experience in many cities, including London, Melbourne and Vancouver, is that TOD is often associated with gentrification, accessible locations attracting higher property prices and sometimes displacing those who can no longer afford those high prices (Stanley et al. 2017). The connections between land use, transport and housing affordability must form a key area for future transport policy research in Australian cities, to help ensure that

TOD and similar developments do not accentuate inequities in urban opportunities. This demonstrates the importance of taking a broad view of land use transport integration, because of the pervasive influence of transport systems on activity patterns and lifestyles. The Western Australia State Government understands these connections, supporting some affordable housing developments in Perth, linked to public transport hubs, with associated community facilities.

While most Australian cities *talk* about land use transport integration, the *practice* is mixed. Greater Sydney is a good performer, its strategic land use plan (Greater Sydney Commission 2018) and transport strategy (New South Wales Government 2018) generally showing requisite elements of mutual support. Sydney has adopted a three cities land use focus, based around a Western Parkland City, Central River City (centred on Greater Parramatta) and Eastern Harbour City (based around the CBD and Harbour) and the transport strategy has generally been structured to support delivery of this land use development direction, aiming (for example) to improve public transport so that by 2056, 70% of people will live within 30 minutes of work, study and entertainment. Sydney's 30 minutes, however, excludes public transport access/egress time, which is limiting in terms of encouraging more compact settlement patterns.

Pricing policy does not form an integral part of future land use transport development directions for Sydney (or for other Australian cities). Pricing can be used to directly tackle congestion, other external costs of transport, and to help shape future development, taking care to ensure that the consequences associated therewith are not regressive. The potential contribution which pricing reform can make to sustainable transport funding arrangements is also important. Transport pricing reform should be a rich area for Australian transport policy research in coming years, as governments seek alternative revenue streams to replace what will be dwindling fuel tax revenues (as electrification of the vehicle fleet accelerates).

Melbourne also has a well-developed land use plan, *Plan Melbourne 2017–2050* (Victorian Government 2017), which has a poly-centric focus like the Sydney Plan. However, there is no complementary transport strategy for Melbourne, a series of major road and rail projects seemingly being mistaken for a transport strategy. This project-level focus means that the opportunity to use transport planning and policy making to help deliver on the societal goals laid out in the city's land use plan is substantially reduced and unintended consequences are more likely over the long term (e.g. accelerated urban sprawl). Understanding how this gap in the strategic planning armoury has come about, and how to achieve better land use transport integration, is a research opportunity in Melbourne.

Better understanding the dynamic connections between land use and transport development is an important input to better transport policy formulation. In this regard, further development of the Institute of Transport and Logistics Studies (University of Sydney) MetroScan model (as discussed in Chapter 2 of this volume), and similar models, should be a research focus. This model, for example, incorporates feedback from transport system improvements to location decisions and shows how the long-term behavioural impacts of transport policy measures may be bigger than has been predicted in the past, once this dynamic element is incorporated. It is early days in this work, which holds out the promise of a substantial advance on traditional four-step land use transport modelling.

### 18.2.3   Neighbourhoods

The Sydney and Melbourne approaches outlined above suggest that another important area for Australian transport policy research is how neighbourhoods fit within the planning and policy framework. A particular focus concerns delivering 20 minute neighbourhoods or 30 minute cities.

Melbourne approaches the idea of 20 minute neighbourhoods from the bottom up, seeking to provide people with 20 minute, or better, access by active or public transport to most of the things needed for a good life. However, transport planning and policy measures in Melbourne, in implementation, largely neglect this level in the spatial hierarchy. For example, there is little attention to prioritization of local public transport service provision that supports 20 minute neighbourhoods, the city's public transport focus being primarily on major projects in trunk corridors. Sydney's 30 minute city focus is inherently more regional and includes access to employment, which is not part of the Melbourne 20 minute conception. It needs a stronger local- or neighbourhood-level orientation. Perth's land use transport planning, which has long recognized the importance of land use transport integration, talks about the importance of vibrant communities and such like but has no focus on how integrated land use transport planning will encourage their emergence at the neighbourhood/local level. The focus in *Perth and Peel at 5 million* (Western Australian Planning Commission 2018), the city's new land use strategy, is strategically focused at regional level, without a strong integrating local perspective.

The role of neighbourhood development in meeting societal goals for cities goes to questions such as what children, youth, older people and others need for a good life and the role of local service provision, mobility and transport policy measures in supporting better neighbourhood outcomes. Identifying policy packages to support walking, cycling and local public transport is central. The increasing policy focus on trade-offs between movement and place, in cities such as London, is an encouraging development, in terms of increasing the focus on neighbourhood.

## 18.3   Governance

Introducing neighbourhoods as one focus for transport policy research draws attention to questions of urban governance, since neighbourhoods rarely have a formal (or even informal) voice in transport policy-making processes. Governance is the subject of a separate chapter in this book, so the discussion here only draws attention to some particular Australian areas for research, incorporating the neighbourhood level into policy-making processes being one such area.

Australian cities are relatively unusual in land use transport governance terms, in that planning and decision-making powers sit at state government level, rather than at city level. The more usual arrangement is to have city-wide planning and policy powers vested in local government, which may align with a single authority, particularly in smaller cities (e.g. Malmö in Sweden; Freiburg in Germany), or may involve an aggregation of individual local authorities into a regional decision-making authority, as in Vancouver.

Institutional arrangements for planning and delivering land use and transport systems have historically been based on functional specialization, linked with the expectation that this would deliver effective organizational performance. It is increasingly recognized, however, that such administratively based functional separation often leads to concerns about agencies operating in 'silos', with diminished overall effectiveness in the face of increasing urban complexity. The effects of cross-cutting issues on the performance of cities are increasing the importance of thinking in more integrated ways about the best policy and programme directions to support pursuit of multiple outcome goals. A broad integrated approach needs to encompass a wide span of interests and a deep level of stakeholder engagement, across a wider and more diverse range of stakeholders. These components essentially define the scope of integrated governance. Finding the most effective and enduring way of achieving such integration is a major challenge, involving questions of both horizontal and vertical integration. Bringing neighbourhoods into the land use transport planning and policy-making framework is a challenge for vertical integration. Small-scale issues, such as place-based neighbourhood improvement, may be best suited to devolved local solutions, with local empowerment (and some devolution of funding). Even then, however, this may require cooperation or some coordination and may be more effective, at scale, if framed within a broader coordinated or integrated governance framework, which is clear about interfaces between neighbourhood and regional matters but allows the maximum flexibility for the neighbourhood to forge its own future.

The longevity of land use transport plans for Australian cities tends to be short, particularly relative to the planning horizons embedded in those plans (e.g. 25 or so years). This is likely to be because long-term plans have not been firmly grounded in societal values, as elaborated in extensive community engagement programmes. Land use transport planning and policy then becomes a short-term contest over particular major initiatives, rather than a concerted attempt to deliver widely agreed long-term outcomes. If local government, acting at regional level (through some representation process), was to be a partner with the state government responsible for strategic land use transport planning and its implementation, increased longevity of such plans might be expected. This should be a fruitful area for transport policy research, going to questions such as balancing power and revenue-raising capacities (which is likely to require shifts in local government revenue-raising powers), the most appropriate scale of individual local authorities and how they can best be aggregated to think, plan and contribute to regional decisions, skill requirements and mechanisms for engaging with the federal government. Inter-governmental funding agreements linked to integration arrangements then need to support delivery (e.g. the Stockholm Agreement).

In a multi-local authority setting, London has chosen a mayoral model as a way to achieve more integrated land use transport planning and policy making (including closely related matters such as economic development and access to affordable housing). This has been an effective way of developing a voice for the city, which has survived changes in the occupant of the mayoral position. Whether Australian cities might achieve more effective long-term integrated land use transport planning and policy making under a mayoral model, such as in London, is a question that would benefit from the illumination provided by good research. London's experience also reinforces the value of a strong evidence base sitting behind transport policy development, the city being a leader in this space.

## 18.4  Conclusions

Many of Australia's cities are currently experiencing high population growth rates. This, combined with structural economic changes that are leading to increasing centralization of high productivity knowledge-based jobs but continued rapid population growth on the fringe and lags in infrastructure and service provision, is producing problems of congestion on road and radial public transport networks, high housing costs, social exclusion problems in outer growth areas, growing obesity concerns and very high per capita greenhouse gas emissions from transport. Tackling such connected problems requires integrated land use transport planning of a quality that few global cities have demonstrated, London being a good example for a city of size. Improving this integrated planning, and governance arrangements within which it is located, are central to whether Australian cities will continue to remain among the most liveable. Evidence-based transport policy will be foundational for such progress.

## References

ABS (Australian Bureau of Statistics) (2017), Regional population growth Australia 2015–16, *Cat 3218.0.* Released 30 March 2017.

Boarnet, M.G. (2011), 'A broader context for land use, and travel behaviour and a research agenda', *Journal of the American Planning Association,* **77**(3), 197–201.

Duranton, G. and Taylor, M. (2010), 'The fundamental law of traffic congestion: Evidence from US cities', *American Economic Review,* **101** (October), 2616–2652.

Ewing, R. and Cervero, R. (2011), 'Travel and the built environment', *Journal of the American Planning Association,* **76**(3), 265–294.

Greater Sydney Commission (2018), *Greater Sydney Region Plan: A Metropolis of Three Cities* –

*Connecting People*, Sydney, Author, https://gsc-public-1.s3.amazonaws.com/s3fs-public/greater-syd ney-region-plan-0318.pdf. Accessed 11 May 2018.

New South Wales Government (2018), *Future Transport Strategy 2056*, Author, https://future.trans port.nsw.gov.au/sites/default/files/media/documents/2018/Future_Transport_2056_Strategy.pdf. Accessed 11 May 2018.

RAI (Regional Australia Institute) (2015), *Population Dynamics in Regional Australia*, January, Regional Australia Institute, Canberra.

Stanley, J., Stanley, J. and Hansen, R. (2017), *How Great Cities Happen: Integrating People, Land Use and Transport*, Cheltenham: Edward Elgar Publishing.

Van Wee, B. and Handy, S. (2014), 'Do future land use policies increase sustainable travel?' In Garling, T., Ettema, D. and Friman, M. (Eds), *Handbook of Sustainable Travel*, Dordrecht: Springer.

Victorian Government (2017), *Plan Melbourne 2017–2050*, Author, 11 March 2017.

Western Australian Planning Commission (2018), *Perth and Peel at 3.5 Million*, Perth: Author. https://www.planning.wa.gov.au/dop_pub_pdf/Perth_and_Peel_Sub_Region_March2018_v2.pdf. Accessed 11 May 2018.

# PART V

Policy perspectives on future transport

# 19 The future of big projects: Lessons from Australia

*Martin Locke*

## 19.1 Introduction

The procurement and financing of transport projects has changed markedly since the impact of the Global Financial Crisis over the period 2008–2010. The scale of major projects in the road and rail sectors, such as Sydney Metro and WestConnex, has increased substantially. New and innovative ways have been explored around procurement and financing to deal with this challenge of increasing scale. The manner in which the responsibilities for constructing and operating the infrastructure have been shared has required further evolution in the Public Private Partnership (PPP) model for big projects but alternative contracting solutions, including Design and Construct (D&C) contracts, alliances and operating franchises are widely used. Project scale has increased debate about splitting projects into several smaller discrete packages, in turn raising concerns around management of interface risk. Increasing cost has triggered the call for more sharing of the financing burden between the public and private sectors.

Using Australian examples, this chapter reviews how the procurement of major transport projects is evolving, given the expectation of further increases in scale. The conclusion is that there will be further intensification of pressure for Government to play an anchor-sponsoring role, with marginalization of the role of PPPs, politicians favouring populist projects with public finance, taxpayers being more exposed to high risk and super funds being forced to look for other ways to invest in infrastructure. The onset of road pricing presents massive challenges to the traditional PPP model and could result in termination and buyout of all current toll road contracts, as road funding transitions to a regulated asset base model.

## 19.2 Use of the PPP model

The rationale for using the PPP model in transport is based on the fundamental premise that outsourcing the provision of transport infrastructure enables the private sector to deliver cost efficiencies, improved risk management, innovation and ultimately better service outcomes for travellers.

Reviewing recent procurement decisions on major projects provides evidence supporting this premise. In the Capital Metro Business Case the Capital Metro Agency concluded that PPPs offer advantages in relation to certainty over cost and time outcomes, optimal risk transfer and scope for innovation. Financiers are stated to be *the 'glue' that holds the risk transfer and interface management together* and to act as *a significant driver of cost minimization within PPP consortia, and exercise significant risk management activities within bid teams* (Capital Metro Agency 2016, p. 119).

Similar themes are referred to in the Brisbane *Cross River Rail Business Case* with the statement that

> *PPPs are typically used where government is seeking the whole-of-life, innovation and efficiencies that the private sector can deliver in the design, construction and operating phases of the project. PPPs also have the potential to provide a greater degree of time and cost certainty than traditional delivery approaches through the discipline of private finance. PPPs also provide an opportunity for the transfer of project risk to the PPP consortium.* (Building Queensland 2017, p. 212)

These theoretical arguments encourage the use of the PPP model. It makes commercial sense for Government to outsource delivery of major transport projects but applying the PPP model in practice on big transport projects is problematic, given challenges around contract value, risk management, market capacity and appetite and contract inflexibility.

## 19.3   Impact of scale

The most significant factor constraining the application of PPPs for big projects is sheer scale. Put simply, how does the level of capital compare to market capacity and appetite from both a financing and a contracting perspective? There has been a huge escalation in the cost of big transport projects. In 1992 the Sydney Harbour Tunnel opened at a cost of $A685m, which now looks exceptionally small compared to the current cost of big projects. Brisbane's Airportlink toll road cost $A4.8b completed in July 2012 but current cost budgets have soared, with Sydney's WestConnex currently standing at $A16.8b. And increasing scale and complexity have been very evident in the rail sector with Sydney Metro Northwest estimated to cost $A8.3b and Sydney Metro City and Southwest estimated to cost $A11.5–12.5b.

The increasing scale of projects has presented a challenge in terms of market capacity and appetite. How much risk is a contractor willing to accept in delivering a project in terms of exposure and balance sheet impact? Key metrics compare contract value to historic turnover or net assets and the objective to retain a diversified workload. Financiers focus on contractor creditworthiness and ability to pay liquidated damages and other potential liabilities under the contract. Banks themselves manage risk by imposing limits on credit exposures to specific deals, counterparties and sectors and final holds may be restricted to $A200–300m. Appetite has been explored in market soundings designed to test the acceptable limits of credit and risk and market convention suggests that as soon as project size exceeds $A5–6b, the threshold of financial and risk tolerance is reached.

Increasing scale has also had impact on tendering, access to resources and pricing. Diversifying competition has been helped by the growing list of foreign entrants bidding for large projects (the foreign bidders shortlisted on Brisbane's Cross River Rail include the likes of Ghella, Bouygues, Salini, and Acciona) but the number of large projects coming to market means demand for skilled resources exceeds supply.

So if the capital cost of big projects is set to exceed $A10b moving forward, but the preferred deal size should not exceed $A5–6b, projects have needed to be disaggregated into smaller packages to meet with contractor appetite. In relation to management of financial market capacity Government has needed to provide support. These matters are discussed in the next two sections.

## 19.4   Approach to packaging

Whilst it makes sense to split big projects into smaller package elements to make them more deliverable from a financial risk perspective, this approach introduces difficulties, particularly regarding the management of interface risk.

The *Cross River Rail Business Case* identifies several benefits of procuring and delivering large, integrated packages: (i) reducing interface risk, (ii) reducing cost through integrated design outcomes and economies of scale and scope, (iii) creating a single point of accountability, (iv) creating a more efficient and streamlined process, (v) creating greater capacity for the private sector to drive innovation and assume risk, (vi) attracting major industry players (Building Queensland 2017).

On the other hand, splitting major projects into multiple packages has the advantage of potentially creating a larger pool of bidders with the capability and capacity to bid for different packages. So to determine the optimal approach to packaging, the technical characteristics of each project component – and their relationship to each other – need to be considered, along with the implications for cost, risk, market capacity and appetite.

Similar themes are contained in the ACT Capital Metro Business Case, which concluded that a single vertically integrated package was the preferred option on the basis that this

> . . . provides optimal risk transfer . . . mitigates interface risks . . . integration is also seen to best drive outcomes in relation to cost, time and management of community impacts, and allows the market to identify and attract the best suppliers. (Capital Metro Agency 2016, pp. 115–116)

Delivery of Capital Metro as a single integrated package was feasible, given the smaller size of that project with a construction cost of $A707m. However, when the procurement strategy for Sydney Metro Northwest was assessed, market capacity constraints indicated that the project cost at $A8.3b was too big to be delivered as a single contract and should be split into smaller works packages. Consequently it was determined that the project be delivered in three packages: tunnels/stations and surface/viaduct civil works, to be delivered as two separate D&C contracts, and an operations, trains and systems (OTS) package, to be delivered as a PPP with a cost of $A3.7b. The rationale for selecting the OTS package, as a PPP, compared to the other two civil works packages, reflects improved scope for innovation, whole-of-life cost efficiencies and risk transfer, when considering the delivery of train services, rather than the construction and maintenance of tunnels and bridges.

When the procurement strategy for the next stage of Sydney Metro, City and Southwest, was progressed, the packaging structure was updated to better match market capacity, improve risk allocation and achieve better value for money. Key elements were now broken up into six package elements covering trains, systems, operations and maintenance (TSOM), to be delivered as an augmentation to the Northwest PPP, but the other five contract packages, covering such works as tunnel ventilation, stabling, power supply and traction supply, tunnels and stations, are to be largely D&C, so private finance would potentially only be required for the TSOM package and over-station property developments (Sydney Metro 2018b).

This approach to packaging is further evolving with the delivery strategy for Sydney Metro West, the next phase of the project. It is expected that the cost of this project could be in excess of $A15b. In the April 2018 Industry Briefing a summary of market feedback indicated that the project was considered too large for a single turnkey contract, with preference for separate packages that align with market sectors. Design, build, maintain (DBM) contracts have been suggested for rail/line-wide systems and rolling stock (with potential for PPP). D&C contracts for tunnels are suggested with use of collaborative models for higher-risk elements. Performance-based contracts for operations are suggested with terms of 5–10 years (Sydney Metro 2018b).

The final delivery strategy will be updated to reflect the outcome of the sounding process, with Government specifically exploring with industry the opportunities and risks of including or excluding vertical integration of operations and maintenance. It is clear that a broader trend is emerging whereby the commitment to retain a PPP component and adopt an integrated solution combining operations, trains, systems and maintenance is being questioned. Moreover, operations are potentially being split out as a completely separate stand-alone shorter-term operating contract. There is the prospect of further disaggregation in project delivery and potential discounting of the benefits of integrated delivery under the PPP model. This suggests potential marginalization of PPPs and losing benefits of risk transfer and cost efficiency.

Pressures in the market place have triggered calls for collaborative contracting, where contractors may be more willing to bid for work, as Government retains more risk. But any absence of fixed price contracting presents a challenge to private financiers. The typical response of project financiers is to seek completion guarantees and standby equity. The only party capable and potentially willing to stand behind delivery of the integrated project is Government.

Government is also under pressure to be more intelligent in de-risking a project to create a more competitive bidding environment. Government needs to better manage such risks as site contamination, construction access and utility connections rather than expecting the private sector to step up into the void. Maintaining healthy bidding competition is key to innovation and value for money.

## 19.5    Sharing the financing burden

As a result of future project financing requirements potentially exceeding $A10b, the question becomes how best to share the financing burden between the public and private sectors. If the underlying benefits around risk transfer, innovation and efficiency justify PPP procurement for a $A10b project but there is only sufficient private financing in the market for $A5b, the State capital contribution has been used. This mechanism involves the public sector contributing funds to reduce the private financing required. Government has adopted this mechanism commonly on social infrastructure projects with availability payments, with the critical structuring issues being the timing and quantum of the contribution. Early payment during construction exposes the public sector to project completion risk. The capital contribution is structured as a non-repayable grant and not categorized as debt or equity.

In the case of the $A6b Melbourne Metro project, the Victorian Government agreed to provide a contribution of up to $A2.5b during construction and a further $A1.5b contribution upon provisional acceptance, thereby potentially reducing the private financing required to $3.5b during construction and $2b during operations. The critical issue is that there remains sufficient private financing to retain the value drivers around risk transfer. The Government concluded in the Melbourne Metro Project Summary that there was *no material impact on the risk allocation . . . as (the private sector) may still incur significant payment reductions if the services are not delivered to the required standard* (Melbourne Metro Rail Authority 2018, p.18).

The conclusion is that private financing still can be effective.

Sharing the financing burden on economic infrastructure, where private financiers are expected to take a risk on the uncertain revenue streams, such as tolls, is more challenging. The NSW Government addressed this problem on WestConnex by establishing its own special purpose vehicle, Sydney Motorway Corporation (SMC), which is initially wholly financed by Government. As the toll revenue stream is initially uncertain, reflecting patronage risk, private financiers prefer to take revenue risk later, when traffic has ramped up and stabilized. Consequently, it was originally intended to sell equity later (this sale process was brought forward with financiers being able to attach some reliance on the proven M4 toll revenues). The financing burden between the public and private sectors can be shared, with the private sector acting as a take-out financier.

The Australian Federal Government has similarly intervened in the financing of transport projects through the provision of equity investment for Western Sydney Airport and Inland Rail. The commitment of public finance has enabled these projects to proceed in the absence of private finance appetite. In the case of Western Sydney Airport, Sydney Airport Corporation Limited (SACL) elected not to exercise its first right of refusal to take up the development right; the prospective revenues were too distant and failed to meet shareholders' risk/return requirements. This has led to some criticism that the provision of public finance is either crowding out private finance or investing in projects that are unduly risky.

A further way in which the public sector can promote the development of transport projects, such as toll roads, is to proceed initially with the private sector developing the project but with the public sector making an availability payment to provide the revenue stream in exchange for ownership of the toll revenue stream. The Victorian Government is adopting this structure on the North East Link with the State retaining patronage risk until such time as traffic has ramped up and reached a steady state. The Government can later sell the proven toll revenue stream to private financiers through a securitization. The benefit of this approach compared to the SMC structure is that all of the project development risks are transferred to the private sector other than patronage risk. The downside is that private financiers will require a risk premium and reflect this in the pricing of debt and equity.

Finally, there have been recent suggestions that public finance should be focused on health and education with private finance exclusively used for transport infrastructure. This approach is not feasible as public transport projects are not financially viable, given that fares only recover around 25% of operating costs.

## 19.6    Management of risk

If the increasing scale of projects and market appetite leads to greater disaggregation, with work being split into smaller packages, there will be greater exposure of Government to interface risk. If work is undertaken in separate packages, interface risk can occur in two main ways. Firstly, the quality of the work in one package may be dependent upon another package. Secondly, the ability to complete work on schedule in one package may be dependent upon another. So in the example of Sydney Metro Northwest, Government was required to retain the risks relating to both (i) time overruns on the tunneling and viaduct civil works delaying the

OTS works under the PPP and (ii) defects in the tunneling and viaduct civil works adversely affecting the OTS PPP project company. The main concern is potential misalignment between the contractual incentives, such as liquidated damages, under a small contract compared to the potential liability to provide compensation under an interdependent but much larger contract. So in the case of Sydney Metro Northwest, the delay in completion of the viaduct works would have triggered a potential claim for liquidated damages of a significantly lesser quantum than Government's potential liability to the OTS PPP contractor, given that the viaduct contract was valued at $A340m compared to the $A3.7b OTS PPP contract. Government is left exposed as the middleman or contract aggregator.

A further example is the potential separation of the operator role on Sydney Metro West. Effectively, the operator is being asked to accept risk on delivering train services, when the trains, systems and track have been delivered by other parties. The operator is likely to seek to limit potential liability under adverse outcomes. This contrasts with potential exposures under an integrated contract structured as a PPP with abatement of availability payments, reflecting the full private capital at risk. Government again needs potentially to step up and intervene.

Management of interface risk is complex and potential shortcomings in Government processes around planning and scoping of work with strain on governance were reflected in the Auditor-General comments on the Sydney Light Rail PPP (Audit Office of NSW 2016).

The approach to contract disaggregation leaves Government inevitably retaining interface risk with potential exposure to costly failures due to misalignment of contract outcomes and incentives.

## 19.7    Accommodating future change

One of the major criticisms leveled against the use of PPPs for major transport projects is potential difficulty in dealing with future changes. These contracts are typically long-term, with contract periods of up to 30–40 years. Contracts set out detailed terms as to technical requirements for the facility and how the private sector will be paid. In the case of recent rail contracts, such as Sydney Metro, attention has focused on the provisions dealing with potential expansion of the system, called the augmentation regime. The concern is, if Government is negotiating an expansion with an incumbent provider, how can competitive tension be preserved in order to obtain value for money? As a result these contracts have been set with a shorter term than a typical PPP contract. So, in the case of Sydney Metro, the operating term has been reduced to 15 years to coincide with mid-life refurbishment.

Secondly, provisions have been incorporated into the contract, such as on Sydney Metro, requiring the incumbent to competitively tender future work, and commit to fixed prices for the supply of additional trains/systems and a target price for the operation and maintenance for the augmentation. The intention is that these provisions help Government achieve value for money. The ultimate fall-back is for Government to exercise its right to terminate the PPP contract for convenience, but this requires Government to make a termination payment that enables the project company to prepay its debt (including hedge break costs), fully compensate its operator for early termination of the operations and maintenance contract (including profits foregone), and give its equity investors the return they expected to receive on their equity investment when the PPP contract was signed.

Clearly, the difficulty with this fall-back is the substantial financial cost in paying out debt and equity investors and breaking contracts at full value.

The lack of flexibility is an even bigger concern in the case of toll roads, given that the contracts are typically long term; for example, in the case of SMC/WestConnex the contract extends for 40 years to 2060. This raises the prospect of needing to deal with change and renegotiate with SMC in the future. At some stage there will be a need to alter the tolling regime as more efficient road pricing is introduced, such as time of day tolling, other forms of congestion pricing or amendment to the registration charge rebate currently proposed to improve the affordability of tolls. The standard approach in PPP contracts is for investors to be kept financially harmless and to be provided with the same return originally forecast. This opens up possible claims for compensation and preservation of the status quo, with demand for toll revenue support similar to the scheme in place on the Sydney Harbour Tunnel. This triggers concerns of inequity, as SMC should arguably only be entitled to a lower return if the risk of insufficient toll revenue has some recourse to Government. Again the ultimate protection is an early termination of the contract but at the cost of fair market value, reflecting private financiers' original return requirements.

A better approach might be to shift to a regulated asset base model (similar to that used in the energy sector), rather than regulation by contract to provide much greater flexibility and fairness. The regulator would then need to determine the quantum of the regulated asset base and the appropriate return but existing methodologies are readily available.

## 19.8  A vision of the future

Speculating about the future of big transport projects based on an extrapolation of the above trends might result in the following scenario:

- increasing scale of overall transport projects results in Government being forced to disaggregate projects into smaller packages to fit with market capacity and appetite
- it is no longer feasible for Government to structure an integrated PPP for the whole works, resulting in loss of benefits around risk transfer

- Government is forced to step up as major sponsor and risk taker and address the challenge of managing interface risk
- despite the abundance of private finance from both debt and equity, Government opts to use public finance and contract models based on D&C, DBM and collaborative contracting, leading to a decline in the use of PPPs
- concerns over the need for flexibility in a dynamic environment of emerging technologies and avoiding being locked into long-term contracts results in public transport largely being delivered as short-term rail operating franchises
- roads are now delivered through new road fund utilities structured using regulated asset base principles and hypothecated road pricing revenue streams with all historic toll road contracts having been terminated and assets transferred to the new utilities, financed by super funds, and
- in the face of critical challenges around risk management in delivering big transport infrastructure, there is a greater chance of Government policy failures around project governance.

### 19.8.1   Priority areas for research

Selection of the right contract model by Government requires significant expertise to assess the potential value of future benefits associated with risk transfer, innovation and improved service outcomes against the specific characteristics of each project. Tightness in the contractor market is pushing Government away from PPP towards collaborative contracting. Is this justified? Procurement decisions are taken prior to commencement but whether they are correct depends upon outcomes. There have been widespread calls for more evidence to support procurement strategy decisions and retrospective post-completion reviews to measure actual performance and realization of benefits against forecasts. With the prospect of increased Government intervention and risk retention, access to data on actual project performance and detailed evidence-based research will play a vital role in testing the validity of current procurement approaches. Realization of cost outcomes and anticipated benefits needs to be subject to rigorous quantitative evidence-based research comparing the cost outturn performance of past projects. The University of Melbourne undertook a cost benchmarking study for the National PPP Forum in 2008 (University of Melbourne 2008). Now is the time to refresh the findings of that study based on empirical analysis of current projects to validate the shift from PPP to collaborative contracting.

Delivery of large complex projects through disaggregated contracts is common to big resource projects, where the project sponsor is a multinational heavyweight such as BP, Shell or BHP Billiton. What are the project governance processes that have been used to manage the interface risks that provide some learnings for Government? What are the approaches that Government could be taking to upskill its own workforce, given the need for greater intelligence around risk management?

What are the impediments to the transition of road funding to the regulated asset base model away from the traditional toll road contracts? What has been the experience of other jurisdictions, such as New Zealand and the UK, that have already engaged in roads reform and made the interim step by creating commercialized entities? How should externalities be reflected in this new model?

## References

Audit Office of NSW (2016), *Performance Audit, CBD and South East Light Rail Project*, Sydney: NSW Government.    https://www.audit.nsw.gov.au/publications/latest-reports/cbd-and-south-east-light-rail-project. Accessed 28 August 2018.

Building Queensland (2017), *Cross River Rail Business Case*, Brisbane: Queensland Government. http://buildingqueensland.qld.gov.au/business-case/cross-river-rail/. Accessed 28 August 2018.

Capital Metro Agency (2016), *Full Business Case*, Canberra: ACT Government. https://www.tccs.act.gov.au/__data/assets/pdf_file/0010/887680/Light-rail-Capital-Metro-Business-Case-In-Full.pdf. Accessed 24 August 2018.

Melbourne Metro Rail Authority (2018), *Metro Tunnel Project Summary*. Melbourne: Victorian Government.    https://www.dtf.vic.gov.au/sites/default/files/2018-02/Metro%20Tunnel%20PPP%20Project%20Summary%20-%2021%20February%202018.pdf. Accessed 28 August 2018.

Sydney Metro (2018), *Project Overview*, Sydney: NSW Government. https://www.sydneymetro.info/west/project-overview. Accessed 28 August 2018.

Sydney Metro (2018), *Industry Briefing*, Sydney: NSW Government. https://www.sydneymetro.info/sites/default/files/document-library/Sydney_Metro_Industry_Briefing_April_2018.pdf. Accessed 28 August 2018.

University of Melbourne (2008), *National PPP Forum – Benchmarking Study*, http://infrastructureaustralia.gov.au/policy-publications/publications/files/PC_Submission_Attachment_K.pdf. Accessed 28 August 2018.

# 20 Transport technology

*Brian Collins*

## 20.1 Introduction

The purpose of this chapter is to highlight where technology over the centuries has contributed to the effectiveness and safety of transport systems and services, where the market and where governments have played a role, and to outline where research and new technologies may contribute and how policies for their exploitation might be governed.

## 20.2 Transport and technology – a history

This section gives a brief outline of where technology innovation has supported transport; some of the governance of such innovation is the same now as it was centuries ago, with resulting advantages and disadvantages.

### 20.2.1 Sea

Some of the earliest transport technology initiatives occurred in the maritime sector. Trade was the major driver for this, followed closely by support for defence or the prosecution of warfare. Early initiatives included navigation aids using stars and the sun, chronometers, coded flags for communications, materials for hulls and rigging, charts and maps, devices for assessing weather and lighthouse systems to avoid danger. All of the needs that these original techniques addressed are still being met by the integration of a mixture of old and new technologies. Global standards are governed via the International Maritime Organization (IMO), created by the UN in 1948, although it did not convene until 1959. The IMO currently has 174 member states.

### 20.2.2 Roads and canals

Following the period of Roman developments in Europe and other regimes across Asia and South America, little development of roads or canals occurred until non-horse-drawn surface transport was developed, which in turn was contingent on the widespread availability of new propulsion systems, based on internal combustion engines. The mass production of such engines, accelerated by the First World War (WWI), gave rise to the need for better roads and new routes to support the increased urbanisation of manufacturing and trade. Canals made a passing contribution in smaller nations such as the UK but, at a continental scale, canal and large river traffic was, and still is, ideal for bulk movement of goods and materials. Better fuels, innovative safety features, advanced powertrain and road holding technologies have been developed over the decades since the explosion of private car ownership after the Second World War (WWII), but the vehicle of today would be recognised by the driver of 1925. The bus, in its various forms (urban bus, coach, mini bus, tram, guided bus) has also been developed over the same period, but again little has fundamentally changed over the last 80 years. Heavy goods vehicles, now on roads in much greater numbers than 50 years ago when the apparent cost saving of moving from rail freight occurred, have been significantly improved by better high power engine technology and power train management. Business support for both light and heavy freight for just-in-time delivery has been transformed by real-time location information, derived from satellite systems.

Congestion on roads is now one of the major factors for the day-to-day experience of travellers or fleet operators. Technology is looked to to improve the situation, but with little analysis to date of exactly how any solution might be other than a short-term fix. The International Road Transport Union (IRU), the international body governing road user standards, was founded in Geneva to help war-torn Europe rebuild devastated trade and commercial links. It now has global reach and is addressing digital interoperability and environmental impact issues connected with private car ownership.

### 20.2.3    Rail

The rail traveller and indeed rail service operator of 1930 would recognise most of a modern railway system. Speeds are greater due to better propulsion systems and more accurate track configurations. Signalling is still based on fixed block signalling in the UK but moving to dynamic allocation, in accord with the European Rail Traffic Management System or ERTMTS, already in use in Europe and elsewhere. Better information systems are helping both traveller and operator have a better experience but congestion and overcrowding are now an increasing issue, much as for roads. Global governance arrangements for long haul rail systems, since they predate the creation of the UN, are many. All represent various factions, which are either service type or geographic region oriented. They all seek to stimulate innovation for improved service quality, safety and legal frameworks.

### 20.2.4    Air

Civil aviation is described as one the greatest global engineering achievements of the last half century. From a low base following the end of WWII, the rate of development of aircraft for civilian airlines was explosive. The invention of the jet engine still further accelerated the take-up of the opportunity of air travel anywhere on the planet. Materials technologies to enable the manufacture of strong lightweight aircraft structures, advanced fuels and engine design to deliver overall aircraft efficiency, combined with global agreement on navigation and air traffic control systems, facilitated the development of global civil aviation in a matter of four decades. The creation of the International Civil Aviation Organization (ICAO) by the UN in 1944 initiated this global reach and the current 192 member states push forward innovation and technology to further improve the safety and acceptability of the traveller's experience.

### 20.2.5   Space

Information derived from space-based systems is vital for all forms of modern transportation but has only been available in the last 20 years; location, navigation, timing, weather services and incident management are now totally dependent upon sophisticated space-based technologies. Old techniques are now inadequate for meeting the modern requirements for air traffic control, docking of large ships, incident management on motorways and railways and support for global high-speed data communications systems, which are now used by all modes.

### 20.2.6   Data

The data revolution is the newest technological opportunity to impact transportation; whilst all modes have used spatial or temporal data at a local level, the growing availability of ubiquitous data sets, that are readily shared and analysed by high-power cloud-based computing platforms, allows predictions and responses on a scale and at a speed that would have only been dreamed of 10 years ago. Sensors of a wide range of types, including personal smartphones, are the source of such data and, particularly in urban areas, are fuelling the so-called smart cities revolution.

## 20.3   Technology perspectives: Technology for the vehicle

### 20.3.1   Propulsion, fuel and energy

For the last century the almost exclusive motive power for surface road and maritime transport has been the internal combustion engine. Some rail systems run on electricity. Aviation, since the invention of the jet engine, uses kerosene. The pressure to reduce carbon emissions is causing a major shift away from these petrochemical sources to electricity for all forms of transport, except aviation, where biofuels show promise of delivering a much lower carbon emission fuel that can be used in jet engines. This shift places the onus for carbon emission reduction on the electricity generation industry, which itself is switching out of coal, gas and oil to other 'clean' forms of electricity generation, such as nuclear, solar, wind and geothermal. A critical technology that is vital to support this switch is energy storage, which can deliver electricity with no emissions. It has been assumed that the market will find solutions to these problems, with some incentives, but recently governments have realised that the pace of investment has been insufficient to meet their climate change obligations. As a result, initiatives in some countries have been put in place to directly invest in energy storage technologies (see, for example, UKRI 2018).

The other critical technology is high-performance, lightweight, highly efficient electric motors, for which magnets are the key component. The underlying design of, and materials for, such components are also areas of government intervention, although market forces have kept pace with need.

### 20.3.2    Navigation

At the beginning of the last century travel was an adventure for most; for most of their lives, most people never travelled more than 50 kilometres from where they were born. Navigation aids were the almost exclusive domain of mariners, explorers and the military. Maps of cities and towns were only for local use. As travel became cheaper and more ubiquitous, the need for navigation aids grew and accuracy and topicality became vital. The use of electronic methods grew out of WWII bombing aids and radar, evolving to, and resulting in, modern satellite-based systems that give extremely accurate timing and positioning information to the mobile user. This information can, in turn, be shared across a number of other information platforms, for use by many types of operators. The availability of satellite systems is critical to the operation of almost all terrestrial navigation systems currently in use, so redundant systems are being put in place to improve their resilience and performance (RAE 2018). The sharing of time and place information at a density and tempo to allow real-time management of congestion on roads is probably the next research breakthrough and will be coupled to autonomous vehicles and dynamic reconfiguration of road space usage.

Enhanced digital-enabled railway signalling and inter-train communication should allow greater density of trains to be achieved on already crowded rail infrastructure, and accurate timing information shared across modal platforms should permit modal shift in journeys to be enabled with greater predictability. Air movements near airports are already close to fundamental limits, with aircraft already 'talking' to each other, but the use of shorter runways may allow more air traffic movement in localised areas; but unless this is combined with better feeder transport to and from airport, further congestion will occur. Research into integrated, multi-modal system design is essential. Similar arguments apply to shipping and ports; smaller ships and more ports but land transport infrastructure must be researched, planned and built to cope.

### 20.3.3    Safety

All modes of transport now use technology to achieve greater safety levels: the design of the vehicles to survive collisions without incurring serious harm to passengers, collision avoidance and vehicle stability in every mode are part of the design and certification for use rubric. National and international standards are mandated and a whole industry has grown up around transport safety but still accidents happen. This occurs because the operator takes the transport platform outside the expected envelope of operational parameters, driving too fast, or too close to the vehicle in front, taking trains round bends too fast, docking in port too fast or inaccurately.

Aircraft are fitted with numerous systems to avoid pilot error and these are still being improved. Similar approaches are now appearing in the systems in cars, to override the driver's wishes and limit speed or vehicle proximity, which has cultural issues for some parts of the world. The reliability of the safety system itself is, of course, of paramount importance and is the subject of further research, especially when it is enabled by software and is network enabled. The security of the safety system (and privacy) is then also important.

### 20.3.4    Data

The integration of the Internet of Things (IoT) with transport systems of all sorts is just commencing. Different modes are at different stages of maturity and there is little or no intermodal sharing of real-time data. The big data revolution, as discussed in Chapter 22 of this volume, could transform transport experiences using the same or similar travelling vehicles to those of today, by making intermodal transfers more predictable and convenient: predictable for passengers and convenient and efficient for operators. There will be issues in some cultures on privacy and protection of identity but, within those ethical and legal constraints, considerable gains could be achieved for all concerned by using what we know in real time to better effect the availability and use of transport systems.

## 20.4    Technology for the traveller

### 20.4.1    Finance

The use of technology over the last century has radically reduced the cost of travel, but how that reduction will carry forward is partly dependent upon the financing model of transport systems, both investment and operation, in the context of wider public and private investment in infrastructure and building development. Value sharing, scale of ambition, risk management are phrases that are now being used to research new financing models for transport systems. Their viability is predicated on accurate and timely data and very good estimation techniques, neither of which is yet ubiquitously available. But without reliable long-term funding and finance, the potential advantages of new technologies in all modes of transport will be less than optimum and unlikely to be realised. Research in this area is on-going, at institutes such as the International Centre for Infrastructure at University College London, but, as yet, has made little impact on business practice. Few countries have any policies on such matters, yet they are central to the success of transport mega projects. Each one is typically treated as a special case. The area provides important research opportunities for transport policy development.

### 20.4.2   Navigation

Maps and timetables have been the mainstay of navigation and journey planning for a century. The quality varies from one part of the world to another, with very mature centuries-old maps in countries such as the UK and France but very limited mapping in parts of Africa and South America. This is not to say that the people who lived in those countries did not know where features useful for navigation were; the knowledge was not codified or stored on some shareable form. Charts for mariners and timetables for railway operators also developed as a result of need; sometimes the need was military and sometime trade, or both, and sometimes systems efficiency.

This situation has been transformed in the last 20 years, due to the availability to everybody with a smartphone of very high resolution imaging and positioning information from satellites. It is predicted that the number of smartphone users in the world will exceed 2.5 billion by 2019 (Tech 2 2018). The exploitation of information to aid people and operators in achieving better journeys is probably one of the most rapidly growing technologically supported transformations in the transport sector and is largely market driven.

### 20.4.3   Communication

Thirty years ago when a person was travelling they were unable to communicate with anybody not in close proximity. Operators had primitive radio systems: on roads, citizens band radios, and on trains, proprietary systems, mainly for emergencies. Air transport was always more advanced, and communications was extensively used for air traffic control, which grew from maritime use for collision avoidance and ship docking.

The use of mobile telephony and data communication based on GSM, 4G and 5G will transform how information of a wide range of types is shared between transportation platforms and other assets involved in the transport system. The combination of navigation and timing information and modern communications is the biggest revolution in transport. Research is needed into how it will affordably improve the predictability of journeys, improve their resilience against unforeseen events and allow real-time adaptation to changing demand.

### 20.4.4   Safety

Accident rates on rail systems reached unacceptable proportions in Britain in the mid-19th century and safety systems started to be of paramount importance; indeed the current UK board overseeing systems is called the Rail Systems and Safety Board, RSSB, part of the Office for Rail and Road (ORR). Once traffic densities on roads increased, with associated increases in collisions and injuries, a similar statutory body was created, now the Vehicle Certification Agency (VCA). The air system regulator in the UK, the Civil Aviation Authority (CAA), is part of a global network of regulators supervised by the ICAO, responsible in part for air systems safety. The IMO achieves similar goals for the maritime sector. All these bodies sponsor research and development into safety systems and safety policies, and accredit products and services as being suitable for use.

### 20.4.5   Comfort and health

The major technological advance to improve health has been in emissions control for fuels in road vehicles (ICCT 2016). The removal of toxic additives in fuel, better use of catalysis for removing dangerous gases, the filtering out of particulates and better engine design have all improved the situation for both motorists and the general public who breathe the air close to vehicle movements. All of these improvements have come about as a result of government and industry working together, sometimes in response to community concerns. Safety belts, whilst seen as safety technology, also improve the wellbeing of passengers and drivers. Comfort has been improved by the use of better materials in seating, better design for visibility and air conditioning to improve local climate inside the vehicle, in both hot and cold ambient conditions. These initiatives have partly been driven by vehicle certification and safety requirements but also by market forces to achieve product differentiation. The further development of in-car infotainment services (audio, video, online access) is being driven by product differentiation and, in some cases, safety regulation (use of mobile phone handsets is the prime example). Further research in the context of autonomous vehicles is essential, however, to ensure that potential pollution problems are managed (see, for example, Fox-Penner et al. 2018).

### 20.4.6   Accessibility

Increasing awareness of the demographic shifts that have occurred in the last 30 years, particularly increased numbers in older age groups and greater societal acceptance of the need to provide mobility services for all, have changed attitudes to accessibility. Wheelchair access, reserved seating, and support for the visually or auditory impaired are now mandated in most countries, with consequent design and integration challenges. Subtler needs are now being examined to do with mental health, dementia, and cultural barriers where technology may be able to provide partial solutions.

### 20.4.7   Data

All of these services are critically dependent upon the availability of personal and ambient data in real time and consistently over long periods for service design and delivery. Spatial accuracy and granularity increasingly are issues but, with satellite systems, both are feasible. The computing power to carry out the analysis of such complex data sets is available now in a way that was not the case 10 years ago. This is a revolution in service delivery that will have profound impact on the concept of travel, the need for travel and how people feel about the experience (see, for example, Gov.UK 2016).

## 20.5    Technology for the transportation infrastructure

### 20.5.1    Surface (rail and road), sea and air

There are two major technological impact domains: materials for travel surfaces and information. There is little that can be done to change the nature of the air we fly through or the sea on which we sail, except to predict its state, but road and rail surfaces are man-made and can be improved with respect to (for example) durability, pollution and noise. All are parameters that research into material science and engineering will address to improve the infrastructure of surface transport.

Information about the infrastructure is the other major advance. The health of every jet engine is now routinely monitored in real time, while flying. Similar techniques are beginning to be used in other moving platforms but, at present, the monitoring of the fixed infrastructure in real time is in its infancy. Internet of Things (IoT) initiatives around the world will deliver platforms to do this in a widespread and transformative manner (University of Wollongong 2018; University College London 2018).

### 20.5.2    Traffic management

Congestion and overcrowding comes from too many transport platforms (cars, buses trains, aircraft and ships) trying to use the same spatial and temporal asset: a road, port, runway or length of track. Information-based management of the asset and the competing platforms will allow much greater efficiency in use of the asset and throughput of platforms. Air traffic management is the most advanced and port management is close behind. The perceived need for autonomy of the private car owner is inhibiting the take-up of such techniques in dense urban road transport areas, to (for example) tackle problems such as traffic congestion through pricing, although the feasibility has been proven for some time. The take-up by railway infrastructure system operators has been even slower. Few national governments have been prepared to act on this issue at a system of systems scale and, without such intervention, fragmentation and less than optimum performance will continue to be the result. Some research activity at European Union level is, however, visible (e.g., ERTICO ITS Europe 2018).

### 20.5.3    Capacity

The capacity of all infrastructure systems in support of transport is inadequate for future needs, if the projections for future journeys per person per annum growth are as predicted. Building more roads, railways, airports and ports seems to be the only solution, tempered by much more efficient use of existing assets by the use of information-based services, as above, together with improved land use transport planning to (among other things) reduce the need to travel, and measures to encourage travel by the most sustainable modes. Accelerating the take-up of information-based services would be a useful government policy initiative, as markets will not see the return on that investment for a long time.

### 20.5.4    Resilience

Urban densities are increasing and the impact on transport of extreme events, whether manmade (e.g., climate change) or natural, is increasing in severity, as noted in Chapter 3 of this book. Better meteorology is helping limit the impact of extreme weather events on people but infrastructure that was not built to withstand such events is being badly damaged, with consequential loss of capacity and cost of replacement. Resilience of cities is now a major thread of governance activity and technological solutions are being used in a number of ways to improve matters, illustrated (for example) through the work of groups such as 100 Resilient Cities.[1]

### 20.5.5    Data

Data sources that can be used for infrastructure design, management and operation are critical. The use of sensors of all sorts will allow much more useful data sets to be created. The concept and development of urban labs or observatories is accelerating the availability of such data sets, with consequent understanding of what is actually going on in cities, not only about transport but all other flows which transport either depends on or contributes to.

## 20.6    Policy frameworks and issues

### 20.6.1    International, national, local, community

The drivers for change in transport services – such as low carbon, demographics, cost, environmental protection, resilience – are all shifting the balance of governance supremacy at different spatial scales. Cities and city leaders are gaining in visibility, product and service interest groups are circling around areas of common interest, mainly information and data related, with little or no government intervention, whilst governments are still supporting mega projects, such as high speed rail systems and major road improvements. The concept of sectors is weakening, as multimodal, and indeed social value capture, ideas take off. This is causing instability and uncertainty in the political and policy landscape, which inhibits investments. And yet some of the investments, particularly those to do with climate change, are urgent. Bodies such as the National Infrastructure Commission in the UK are helping apply pressure for more rapid change.

---

1  https://www.100resilientcities.org/

### 20.6.2    Human rights, permission to use, licence to operate – in a space and place

As transport service offerings become more varied and accessible to all, the legal issues that surround those able to, and wishing to, deliver services have become more complicated. The rights of the passenger, the obligations of the service operators and the role of government in giving permission to operate have become intertwined in complex ways, at a range of spatial scales: city, nation and international. These complexities are compounded by the demand of transport systems for the disclosure of identity or other personal information, directly or via ownership of a vehicle, to optimise the transport service offering. This issue is likely to get worse as information becomes the means by which better transport services are constructed and operated. In some cases, international agreements are needed and, where personal data protection services are not aligned, issues will arise; the development of General Data Protection Regulation (GDPR) may aid the situation.

### 20.6.3    Taxation and pay at point of use

A mechanism for optimising the use of infrastructure is that payment is made at the point of use: tolls on bridges and motorways are examples. This may be to limit use, so can be dynamically changed as is the case in Singapore, or used as a levy to retrospectively fund the asset's development. How these payment systems interact with taxation is a vexatious subject, when tax is collected at local, regional, city and national levels and, in some cases, is not hypothecated to the level at which it is collected. This results in difficulties incentivising local funding for maintenance and modernisation. The use of automatic revenue collection techniques could alleviate these issues but the politics and policies of hypothecation need to be resolved as well, within the context of evolving governance arrangements.

### 20.6.4    Community obligations

Such measures extend to the delivery of community obligations, where devolution from central government has been granted. Unless there is alignment of authority responsibility and accountability, together with financial capacity, the capability for local government or city government to deliver innovative, technologically based solutions to enhance local transport will be limited. An overall systems model, including the political framework, is an essential component of delivering a governance framework for such cases, as is also argued in a number of the chapters in this volume.

### 20.6.5    Resource security and low carbon

It is now widely recognised that natural resources of all sorts are becoming limited. It could be argued that governments have an obligation to ensure the supplies of strategic resources for low carbon transport. Such obligations may only be met through global trade agreements, which are not always easy to achieve. The delivery of low carbon transport may therefore be harder, and take longer to achieve, than the ideal, slowing down the delivery of electric and autonomous cars and other advanced clean transport systems, while adding to planetary pressures from climate change.

## 20.7   Reflections

Transport systems have become much more complex in the last 40 years as a result of much greater ownership of cars across the world, greater expectations of low-cost air travel, massive increase in global trade, mainly maritime, and recognition that resources are not unlimited, that transport has to reduce its carbon emissions and that data and information, whilst producing increased quality of transport service offerings, delivers vulnerabilities, from a standpoint of both cyber security and protection of privacy.

In order to achieve good outcomes in the face of these challenges, some governments are seeking packages of policies that deal with the issues in a combined manner, so that the overall mission of better transport for all can be achieved, within environmental and resource constraints. Such packages, and similar means of improving integrated policy approaches, are ripe for research to improve transport policy outcomes. The use of technology road maps has been particularly influential in some cases. Packages of policies do not easily align with a lot of government departmental structures for public spending but, unless an holistic approach is taken, the promises of governments to deliver green transport within resource limitations are unlikely to occur. The role of independent bodies, such as National Infrastructure Councils or such like, that can apply pressure in an apolitical sense should not be underestimated.

## References

ERTICO ITS Europe (2018), *ERTICO-ITS Europe: Shaping intelligent mobility for Europe together*, https://ertico.com/. Accessed 7 November 2018.

Fox-Penner, P., Hatch, J. and Gorman, W. (2018), 'Spread of self-driving cars could cause more pollution – unless the electric grid changes radically', *The Conversation*, October 25, https://theconversation.com/spread-of-self-driving-cars-could-cause-more-pollution-unless-the-electric-grid-transforms-radically-101508. Accessed 7 November 2018.

Gov.UK (2016), Future of Cities, 22 August, https://www.gov.uk/government/collections/future-of-cities. Accessed 7 November 2018.

ICCT (The International Council on Clean Transportation) (2016), *A technical summary of Euro6/VI vehicle emission standards*, https://www.theicct.org/sites/default/files/publications/ICCT_Euro6-VI_briefing_jun2016.pdf. Accessed 7 November 2018.

RAE (Royal Academy of Engineering) (2018), *Cyber safety and resilience: Strengthening the digital systems that support the modern economy*, London: Author. https://www.raeng.org.uk/publications/reports/cyber-safety-and-resilience. Accessed 7 November 2018.

Tech 2 (2018), *Growth of unique smartphone users globally to grow by a single digit for the first time*, https://www.firstpost.com/tech/news-analysis/growth-of-unique-smartphone-users-globally-to-grow-by-a-single-digit-for-the-first-time-4389341.html. Accessed 7 November 2018.

UKRI (United Kingdom Research and Innovation) (2018), *Faraday battery challenge*, https://www.ukri.org/innovation/industrial-strategy-challenge-fund/faraday-battery-challenge/. Accessed 7 November 2018.

University College London (2018), PETRAS Internet of Things Research Hub, http://www.ucl.ac.uk/steapp/research/projects/petras-iot-hub. Accessed 7 November 2018.

University of Wollongong (2018), Smart IoT Hub, https://smart.uow.edu.au/laboratories/smart-iot-hub/index.html. Accessed 7 November 2018.

# 21 Intelligent Mobility and Mobility as a Service

*Corinne Mulley, John Nelson and David A. Hensher*

## 21.1 Introduction

This chapter sets the scene with the background and definition of Intelligent Mobility (IM). IM links technology in the broadest sense to different aspects of mobility. The chapter presents a number of applications of IM in the passenger and freight domains. The penultimate section on Mobility as a Service (MaaS) is perhaps the most important contemporary application of IM: this section highlights the policy and research agenda for this application. The chapter concludes by drawing attention to the research agenda in the broad IM sphere.

## 21.2 What is Intelligent Mobility?

The emergence of the term Intelligent Mobility (IM) is closely associated with the rise of digital technologies and their application within the transport sector. IM *per se* is not a new concept and is seen by many as a natural progression from the earlier focus on Intelligent Transport Systems (ITS) which has been variously defined. ITS UK, for example, refers to ITS as representing '*a combination of Information Technology and telecommunications, allowing the provision of on-line information in all areas of public and private administration*' (ITS UK, n.d., italics added). A notable feature of this definition is a focus on the enabling role of technology and in particular Information and Communication Technologies (ICTs), which itself can be defined as an umbrella term that includes all devices, networking components, applications and systems that combined allow people and organizations to interact in the digital world (TechTarget, 2017).

A key characteristic of IM is the appropriate use of new and emerging technologies linked to the wider societal objective of enabling the smarter, greener and more efficient movement of people and goods. From a technology perspective IM application areas can be argued to encompass everything from connected and autonomous vehicles (see Chapter 20), to the provision of systems to support the planning and execution of seamless multi-modal journeys and the supporting intelligent infrastructure and services required to achieve this. Applications are applicable to both passenger and freight contexts.

There is no shortage of available 'roadmaps' to facilitate the implementation of IM. An early and comprehensive example was the EC-ITS Roadmap (European Commission, 2007), which was set within a policy framework of "Efficient", "Safe" and "Clean" mobility systems supported by a set of core ITS applications, including traffic and travel information, electronic payment, public transport operations, freight and advanced safety systems.

The IM agenda is also of strong interest to many governments. In Germany, the national High-Tech Strategy (The Federal Government, 2014) aims to move the country forward as a worldwide innovation leader. Intelligent Mobility is identified as one of the six priority tasks important to future prosperity and quality of life. Similar ambition can be found in the *Strategy for American Innovation* (National Economic Council and Office of Science and Technology Policy, 2015). It has been estimated that IM will have a global market value of £900 billion by 2025 (Transport Systems Catapult, 2016) but, if this is to be realised, it is necessary to appreciate the skills gap, particularly the need for high-value digital skills.

It is the strong policy context of the IM agenda that is of wider interest. IM can be posited as representing a more integrated approach to addressing the challenges of the transport sector (e.g., congestion, pollution, and lack of 'joined up' thinking between different means of transport), whilst also addressing the wider societal challenges of a growing and ageing global population, urbanisation, fossil fuel depletion and the digital divide. IM offers the possibility of mobility solutions that are more user-focused, integrated, efficient and sustainable of which Mobility as a Service (MaaS) is prominent in contemporary discussions, including those relating to social inclusion.

## 21.3   Application areas

### 21.3.1   Journey planning

The importance of accurate, good-quality information for journey planning has been acknowledged for many years, and providing travellers with journey planning information in real-time is now common place. A well-documented example is the Transport Direct UK-wide multi-modal journey planner (covering road, rail, walking, cycling and ferry options), which was launched in 2004 (see Lyons et al., 2007, for a full description). Transport Direct recorded over 10 million user sessions in the first two years and, although widely considered to be a successful initiative, it closed in September 2014 when the Government identified sufficient journey planning services being provided by the private sector.

Apps for journey planning have been steadily entering the market, particularly for urban areas, with options such as OneBusAway (USA), Citymapper (UK), Transit App (Canada), NextThere (Australia) and Moovit (Israel) providing real-time platforms. Evidence from the OneBusAway system implemented in Seattle, USA, found that 91% of users reported spending less time waiting, while 8% reported no change (Ferris et al., 2010); of course the actual wait time savings will vary according to the frequency of the bus services in place. More recently, the use of social media platforms has been emerging as a medium to allow for real-time sharing of information between transport operators and their passengers, as well as other key information providers. Current research agendas relate to how social media may be linked with journey planners to provide dynamic transport information, which can incorporate multiple sources of information, including user (i.e., traveller) generated content.

## 21.3.2   Automatic Vehicle Locationing

Automatic Vehicle Locationing (AVL) systems allow fleet managers to track and monitor the location of their vehicles, for example comparing the positions of buses against the timetable or scheduled headway. Bus AVL equipment commonly comprises a GPS receiver fitted to each bus, together with a radio transmitter and a central server (Figure 21.1). The bus communicates its position either

### Key

| | |
|---|---|
| **A** Bus priority fault detection and performance monitoring reports | **G** Bus door sensor |
| **B** System databases | **J** GPS receiver |
| **C K** Bus priority radio link | **K** Central system server (located remotely) |
| **H** Bus processor (contained within traffic signal controller) | **L** iBIS plus unit |
| **C** Traffic signal controller | **M** GPS satellites |
| **F N** Bus detection points | **O** Bus garage (when bus is in garage, it is linked to the central system server to send and receive bus priority data) |

**Source:**   Transport for London Group Archive (2002).

**Figure 21.1**   Technologies commonly applied in a bus management system

on a regular (e.g., every 30 seconds) basis, or by exception (when it reaches a certain point or does not reach a certain point within a time-limited period). The central server then interprets the information from the bus and communicates the information using another radio transmitter, to (for example) bus stop signs or to websites and mobile devices. AVL forms the foundation of bus management systems, which in addition to tracking and monitoring buses can record and analyse demand profiles via smartcard payment systems. Such sophisticated systems provide opportunities for better services to the travelling public, through provision of real-time information and bus priority. Today the use of some form of AVL amongst bus operators has become almost ubiquitous and as at December 2016, 97% of the 34,900 buses in England were fitted with AVL compared to 35% in 2006/7 (DfT, 2017).

AVL is also a core application within the freight and logistics sector and highly relevant to the emerging concept of the Physical Internet. 'Motes' – often called 'smart dust' – are enabling self-connecting networks which provide information available over the internet and are a possible development to make AVL systems less dependent on hardwired infrastructure.

Figure 21.1 illustrates the technologies commonly applied in a bus management system.

### 21.3.3   Bus priority systems

Bus priority systems have several benefits: reducing passengers' travel times, operational savings for the operator due to quicker bus journeys, or increased service frequencies with the same number of vehicles. Although methods of providing priority to buses at traffic signals have been available at isolated junctions since the late 1970s, these often required pre-signals and bus advance areas to enable the bus to get to the front of other traffic at junctions, requiring physical use of road space. 'Virtual' bus priority measures use various methods of communication to detect the presence of buses and activate traffic lights to give priority to buses at junctions. Technologies range from those which detect when a bus arrives at the traffic lights, and then seek to turn the lights green for the bus as soon as possible (with limited benefits), through to technologies which can detect the location of a bus as it passes along its route and seek to set the lights ahead to provide priority to the bus – the level of this priority can be variable depending on whether the bus is running late or not.

Bus priority in SCOOT, a control strategy for traffic signals in urban areas, has provided reductions in delay as high as 50% when the degree of saturation is low. At high degrees of saturation, the reduction in delay is of the order of 5–10%. In extensive trials in London reductions of delay of around 4 seconds per bus per junction are typical. In terms of journey time savings this also varies widely according to traffic conditions but an average value of 0–20% can be expected (Gardner et al., 2009).

Some urban areas, where there is not sufficient bus traffic to make a bus lane an efficient use of road space, have introduced no car lanes rather than bus lanes. Freight as well as passenger services, such as taxis, are permitted in no car lanes; this is a concept which should be explored further. For more details see Mulley (2010).

### 21.3.4   Smart parking

Whilst most cars spend more than 90% of their time parked outside the home, the pressure on parking at destinations has led to technology-enabled solutions to provide more efficient parking outcomes.

Smart parking is a typical Internet of Things application (IoT), since it uses the opportunities provided by the internet to enable computing devices that exist in commonplace objects to send and receive data. In parking, this can range from sensors in the car park floor to link to a light identifying when a space is filled, thus reducing search costs, to the delivery of billing for a specific parking event, remote parking reservation, billing by radio frequency identification (RFID) tags rather than paper etc.

In 2011, San Francisco led parking reform to introduce a smart parking pilot that dynamically adjusts the pricing for parking in real-time to achieve one or two empty spaces per block. Sensors report the occupancy of the parking spaces and parking charges vary by time of day, in response to observed occupancy, to achieve between 60% and 80% occupancy, so prices might rise on a crowded block and fall on a less populated block, thus increasing the efficiency of both (Pierce and Shoup, 2013). Other benefits such as an increase in economic activity were noted in the pilot areas, suggesting that there may be benefits beyond parking efficiency. The pilot was extended in December 2017 to a city-wide system without sensors but with dynamic pricing, whereby each day is broken into three time bands with the prices on each block and band being based on usage data collected by wirelessly connected parking meters. A similar sensor-based system exists in a small part of Los Angeles.

Future systems could integrate information about pricing to provide advance information for motorists as to where there are spaces, thereby providing an integrated system including billing. A future research area is understanding how user behaviour changes as a result of smart parking.

### 21.3.5   Smart ticketing

Smart ticketing for public transport use is a ticketing system that uses technology to electronically store travel ticket information on a microchip, which is then usually embedded in what has become known as a 'smartcard'. Smart ticketing relies on a secure data interchange system being in place with point of sale terminals, usually placed on the public transport vehicle or at the public transport station, which can communicate with the smartcard.

Use of smartcards is rapidly spreading, typically in cities, in both developed and developing countries. Despite appearances of modernity, the technology is not new, with a plastic card containing a microchip having been first patented by Dethloff and Grotrupp in Germany in 1968 (Shelfer and Procaccino, 2002, as cited by Pelletier et al., 2011).

With increasing numbers of operators being involved in the provision of public transport in a spatial area, the interoperability of smartcards between operators can be an issue. In the UK interoperability is ensured by use of common specifications of the non-profit membership organisation ITSO (Integrated Transport Smartcard Organisation). There is a move in some cities to tap on and off with contactless credit/debit cards (e.g., AMEX, Visa, Mastercard) on public transport such as the ferries in Sydney. In time we expect this to provide wider opportunity for cashless payment and replace mode-specific smartcards.

Smart ticketing is typically motivated by the ability to provide more robust and more secure revenue collection as well as providing an opportunity to have more diverse and flexible fare structures. Card payments reduce dwell times as well as reducing the potential for fraud. But probably the greatest benefit from smart ticketing comes from the robustness of the data and the wealth of information that can be provided for planning purposes. Interrogating smartcard data has provided a wealth of research outcomes, with studies providing input into strategic, tactical and operational decisions (Pelletier et al., 2011, provide a review of this). One of the greatest challenges is in governance of data and ownership, with much of it being obtained by private organisations such as Google, Amazon and Telcos. Research on data access is a high agenda topic.

The future of smart ticketing will be no longer needing to carry a public transport specific card and to use other payment cards for fares, such as in London where any contactless card can be used. This is already achieved in some countries: in the UK in 2016/17 91% of buses outside London were ITSO smartcard enabled and therefore able to provide cashless ticketing, with 97% of the bus fleet being AVL enabled (DfT, 2017). The research agenda is now more about how to benefit from this new source of data, what different statistical methods will be required and problems associated with legal and privacy concerns which will need to be addressed. Research methods will also need to address the loss of origin and destination data as the industry moves more towards using contactless cards which are not dedicated to public transport.

## 21.4   Mobility as a Service (MaaS)

The MaaS alliance[1] defines Mobility as a Service (MaaS) as *the integration of various forms of transport services into a single mobility service accessible on demand* (see

---

[1] https://maas-alliance.eu/

Wong et al., 2017, for a review). Key to this is the recent step change in technology as illustrated by the applications of IM discussed above which is enabling change to provide a customer interface with an integrated back office. So the traveller wanting to consume at the destination (whether it is a commute or a more recreational activity) can benefit from journey planning options, supported by ticketing options to seamlessly move from an origin to a destination. Typically MaaS will be provided in the form of mobility packages (akin to the packages available for mobile phone use). Mobility packages offering a mix of public transport, car club access, bike hire and taxis are predicated on mobility being accepted as a *service* rather than on mobility needing to be an output of a purchased investment such as a car. This ties into the evidence of peak car (where young people in particular are showing less inclination to purchase their own car, or are at least deferring purchase) and the way in which economies are changing. Consumer behaviour towards ownership is changing, and digitisation, increasing automation and new business models are revolutionising industries which will necessarily impact on the way in which cars are used (Gao et al., 2016).

MaaS is becoming a reality in many places: from a policy point of view it can help to fulfil the desire to create greater sustainability through reducing private car ownership and use. On the supply side, the critical issue is who or what organisation will be the 'integrator' (or 'aggregator') providing the link between the customer and the provider. Jittrapirom et al. (2017, pp.17–18) provide a review of a number of MaaS operational and pilot schemes, including the following as operational: TransitApp (USA, UK, Canada, Europe, Australia), Optymod (Lyon, France), Mobility Shop (Hannover, Germany), Tuup (Turku Region, Finland), My Cicero (Italy), Moovel (Germany) and Whim (Helsinki, Finland). Mobility 2.0 services (Palma, Spain), Ubigo (Gothenburg, Sweden), Smile and Wien Mobil Lab (Vienna, Austria) are described as pilot schemes and SHIFT – Project 100 (Las Vegas, USA) as planned. But the field is moving so quickly that there are now more new schemes in place (e.g., Whim in Birmingham and Navigogo in Dundee, UK) and many schemes planned (e.g., Whim in Amsterdam). Significant policy issues surround the implementation of MaaS, including the governance arrangements (e.g., pricing deals from operators on government (subsidised) service contracts), and the ownership and use of the data arising from MaaS implementation. All these issues are made more complicated by the institutional framework having an impact on how these issues can be resolved. Hensher (2018) discusses these issues in more detail.

The research agenda for MaaS is actively investigating the requirements of users, as the MaaS models already implemented show considerable variations in their offerings. State-of-the-art choice experiments are being used to determine the willingness to pay for different mobility bundles under different business models on the demand side. On the supply side, the research agenda includes understanding governance issues and how MaaS might be integrated into contractual agreements between governments and operators, the future roles of authorities and operators, as well as improvements in algorithms for route optimisation.

## 21.5    Research agenda and conclusions

This chapter has traced the development of the term IM and illustrated its reach with reference to a selection of application areas. These application areas demonstrate the important role of technology as an enabler but, as shown by the example of MaaS, a clear appreciation of issues such as user requirements, business models, governance and the wider policy context is required if transformational change in the organisation and delivery of mobility services for passenger and freight is to be achieved.

Each of the application areas described above was accompanied by suggestions for future research. This section concludes with some overarching suggestions for a research agenda in Intelligent Mobility:

- Ensure that the IM agenda incorporates the best of the latest advances in big data/data science, IoT, digital economy;
- Continue to understand the necessary regulatory requirements and legal implications of data management and the implications for IM application areas across the passenger and freight sectors, as well as the associated implications for transport policy;
- Explore the respective roles of both the public and private sectors in the development and delivery of IM application areas considering how this may change over time (e.g., transport authorities, and/or public transport operators, might morph into MaaS providers, to survive/grow), how this relates to different segments of the population (to achieve the efficiency and social agendas of a multi-dimensional transport policy); and
- Maximise the cross-sectoral opportunities for IM in debates relating to connected cities, smart rural mobility and the information economy.

## References

DfT (Department for Transport) (2017), *Annual Bus Statistics: England 2016/17*, London: Department for Transport. https://assets.publishing.service.gov.uk/government/uploads/system/uploads/attach-ment_data/file/666759/annual-bus-statistics-year-ending-march-2017.pdf. Accessed 3 October 2018.

European Commission (2007), *ITS Roadmap Outline – Intelligent Transport Systems (ITS) for more efficient, safer and cleaner road transport*. http://ec.europa.eu/transport/sites/transport/files/modes/road/consultations/doc/2008_03_26_its_roadmap_outline.pdf. Accessed 3 October 2018.

Ferris, B., Watkins, K. and Borning, A. (2010), *OneBusAway: Results from Providing Real-Time Arrival Information for Public Transit*, CHI 2010, April 10–15, 2010, Atlanta, Georgia, USA. http://dl.acm.org/citation.cfm?id=1753597. Accessed 4 March 2016.

Gao, P, Kaas, H-W., Mohr. D. and Wee, D. (2016), 'Disruptive trends that will transform the auto industry', *McKinsey Report*, January 2016.

Gardner, G., D'Souza, C., Hounsell, N., Shrestha, B. and Bretherton, D. (2009), *Review of Bus Priority at Traffic Signals around the World*, UITP Working Group on the Interaction of buses and signals at road crossings. http://content.tfl.gov.uk/interaction-of-buses-and-signals-at-road-crossings.pdf. Accessed 3 October 2018.

Hensher, D.A. (2018), 'Tackling road congestion – what might it look like in the future under a collaborative and connected mobility model?', *Transport Policy*, **66**, A1–A8.

ITS UK (n.d.), 'What is ITS?' http://its-uk.org.uk/about-its-uk/. Accessed 3 October 2018.

Jittrapirom, P., Caiati, V., Feneri, A., Ebrahimigharehbaghi, S., Alonso-Gonzalez, M.J. and Narayan, J. (2017), 'Mobility as a Service: A critical review of definitions, assessments of schemes and key challenges', *Urban Planning*, **2**(2), 13–25.

Lyons, G., Avineri, E., Farag, S. and Harman, R. (2007), *Strategic Review of Travel Information Research, Final Report to the DfT*. http://webarchive.nationalarchives.gov.uk/+/http:/www.dft.gov.uk/adobe-pdf/245385/249577/Strategic_Review_of_Travel_1.pdf. Accessed 3 October 2018.

Mulley, C. (2010), 'No car lanes or bus lanes – which is best?', *Traffic Engineering and Control*, **51**(11), 433–439.

National Economic Council and Office of Science and Technology Policy (2015), *A Strategy for American Innovation*, The White House. https://obamawhitehouse.archives.gov/sites/default/files/strategy_for_american_innovation_october_2015.pdf. Accessed 3 October 2018.

Pelletier, M.-P., Trépanier, M. and Morency, C. (2011), 'Smart card data use in public transit: A literature review', *Transportation Research Part C*, **19**, 557–568.

Pierce, G. and Shoup, D. (2013), 'Getting the prices right', *Journal of the American Planning Association*, **79**(1), 67–68.

TechTarget (2017), 'Definition of ICT'. http://searchcio.techtarget.com/definition/ICT-information-and-communications-technology-or-technologies. Accessed 3 October 2018.

The Federal Government (2014), *The New High-Tech Strategy – Innovations for Germany (2014)*, German Government. https://www.bmbf.de/pub/HTS_Broschuere_eng.pdf. Accessed 3 October 2018.

Transport for London Group Archive (2002), LT000083/010/001/001, 'Bus priority at traffic signals keeps London buses moving – Selective Vehicle detection'. http://content.tfl.gov.uk/svd-brochure.pdf. Accessed 20 February 2019.

Transport Systems Catapult (2016), *Intelligent Mobility Skills Strategy: Growing New Markets in Smarter Transport*. https://tics.shef.ac.uk/wp-content/uploads/2016/10/IM-Skills-Strategy-2016-1.compressed.pdf. Accessed 3 October 2018.

Wong, Y., Hensher, D.A. and Mulley, C.M. (2017), 'Emerging transport technologies and the modal efficiency framework: A case for mobility as a service (MaaS)', Paper presented at the *15th International Conference on Competition and Ownership of Land Passenger Transport* (Thredbo 15), Stockholm, Sweden, 13–17 August 2017.

# 22 Big data and transport

*Marcela A. Munizaga*

## 22.1 Introduction

In the last 30 years, our world has changed. Population and incomes have increased and cities have become bigger, but our transport systems are basically the same. Cities still have a combination of private car and public transport (usually buses and Metro), and big cities still have congestion and pollution problems. Currently, the most important change in transportation systems has been the availability of information. In terms of user experience, the big difference between the 1980s and now is that now we have online information about the levels of congestion, so we may be able to avoid the most congested zones/times, we have online information about the position of buses and trains, so we can plan our trips better and, if something fails, we can instantly communicate with those we are going to meet and let them know we are going to be late.

From the transport planner's point of view, the big change also comes from the information side. In the 1980s, the most popular data collection methods were paper and pencil face-to-face surveys to observe travel behavior, and direct observation with chronometer to measure travel speeds. A significant source of cost and error was the transcription of handwriting to computer files, a process called "digitation", which is now probably extinct. The survey methods have gradually adopted the new technologies, incorporating computers for direct input of data, GPS trackers to measure position, and more recently using apps as survey platforms. Also, the availability of data generated automatically by technological devices constitutes a new source that has been explored by researchers. Some of these new data sources are mobile phone traces, public transport fare collection and vehicle location data, different types of payment data (credit card, tickets, toll roads) and information voluntarily provided by users through social media (Twitter, Facebook, TripAdvisor, among others). The possibilities of these new data sources are infinite, but so are the challenges.

## 22.2    Data access

One of the first challenges that needs to be faced is to obtain access to the data. Some of the above-mentioned sources of data come from technologies operated by public entities, but the majority of them come from technology owned and operated by private companies. An interesting question is "Who owns the data?" Regulations usually aim at protecting user privacy: for example the European regulation that went into effect in May 2018 (EU 2016). However, there is not much regulation regarding potential uses of the aggregate information, which may have significant social benefits. One example is that of the telecommunications companies, which, as a side product of their business, are able to observe mobility; other examples are toll roads and different types of ticketing (airlines, bus companies, train companies, ferries). In the case of a regulated market, which is not unusual in a natural monopoly context, access to the data by the regulator can be included as part of the negotiation of the contracts. In some cases, the contract establishes that the regulator is the owner of the data. This is the case of smartcard data from the public transport system in Santiago, Chile (Gschwender et al. 2016), where a private company operates the technological system, but it is established in their contract that the data belong to the transport authority, which is a public entity. This is the ideal case, as the regulator can use the data for planning and management of the system. Pelletier et al. (2011) discuss the uses of smartcard data at different levels of management. There are some other cases where access to the data is not guaranteed to the regulator, and only limited data are obtained through negotiation. This is the case, for example, of toll roads in Santiago, Chile. In the case of private companies operating in non-regulated markets, the access to the data is even more elusive.

## 22.3    Methodological challenges

Once data are available, and the privacy issues well accounted for, the next question is how we use these new data sources for modeling. The first stage usually consists of descriptive statistics and visualization, which can actually be very valuable, as we are able to observe in high definition a phenomenon that is difficult to observe with traditional data, due to the time and space disaggregation. As an example, Figure 22.1 shows the time distribution of public transport trips obtained from one week of smartcard data from Santiago, Chile (Gschwender et al. 2016), and the time distribution of the public transport trips observed in the last origin-destination survey (Muñoz et al. 2016). Both graphs show the same tendency, but the amount of information available in the smartcard database provides a more accurate visualization, while the survey data produces some alternating jumps from low to high values. This is due to the fact that survey data contains declared time of travel, and people tend to declare round numbers such as eight o'clock, eight thirty, nine o'clock, rather than a very specific time which is what is obtained from payment transactions (e.g., 8:23:56). Also, the information density and continuity allows the capturing of infrequent trips, such as a weekend recreation trip made by public transport, and the effects of infrequent events, such as sports events or festivities.

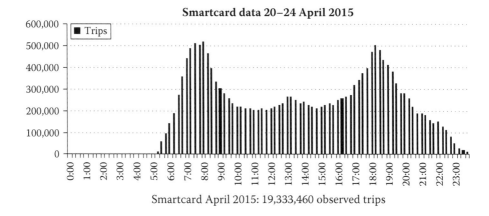

Smartcard April 2015: 19,333,460 observed trips

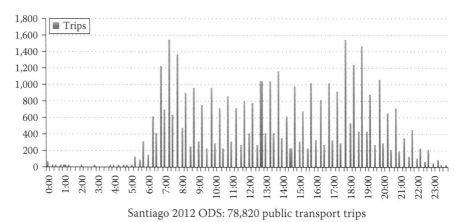

Santiago 2012 ODS: 78,820 public transport trips

*Note:* 15 minute time intervals.

**Figure 22.1**    Visualization of time distribution of public transport trips in Santiago, Chile

The amount of information provided by passive data allows more detailed descriptive analysis, using more disaggregate time and space units, and analyzing longer periods of time. Some examples are the analysis of the performance of the transit system considering network supply and passenger service (Trépanier at al. 2009) and the analysis of stability in time and space trajectories observed from mobile phone data (González et al. 2008). Carrel et al. (2015) combine high-resolution smartphone data with vehicle location data to analyze level of service of the public transport system. This detailed information also enables the development of visualization tools that can help planners to better understand travel behavior and transit operation (see, for example, Poonawala et al. 2016).

The next stage is pattern analysis and the application of clustering methods. This has been done by Morency et al. (2007) using data from Gatineau (Canada), and applying a k-means clustering algorithm to observe regularity of behavior over time. González et al. (2008) also analyze regularity of behavior over time but using data from mobile phone usage. Ma et al. (2017) analyze travel behavior of the massive Beijing public transport system, identifying commuting patterns and home and work location. Most of these studies show that, in the aggregate, users follow simple predictable routines, but interesting differences can be found when observing in more detail. For example, the aggregate daily pattern is very consistent with the behavior of commuters, with notorious morning peak and afternoon peak. However, the majority of users are non-frequent users who cannot be classified as commuters (Ma et al. 2017).

And finally, there is the stage of developing predictive models, which is the challenge that is currently being addressed. The question here is whether we need new models, or whether we need to adapt the traditional models to the new data. Can artificial intelligence models replace traditional linear regression and discrete choice models? Another question is: Given that the data is now more massive, does it mean that we need more sophisticated or more simple models? There is a research opportunity here, which is to test different modeling approaches, and to compare the results. Also, a relevant consequence of the availability of passive data is that it allows validation and ex-post analysis. The validity of predictive models can be easily evaluated when demand can be observed on a daily basis at negligible cost.

The first attempts to develop predictive models from passive data have been devoted to predicting behavior within the public transport system. Kusakabe et al. (2010) and Asakura et al. (2012) use ticketing information from a train service to model train preferences. Nassir et al. (2018) propose a method to calibrate stochastic route choice models using smartcard data from Queensland (Australia). Jánošíková et al. (2014) develop a logit model of route choice that considers on board travel time, transfer walk time, number of transfers and line headway among the independent variables, all observed from smartcard data, street map and timetable. The importance of this study is that massive revealed preference data are obtained from smartcard records.

Furthermore, it has been stated (see, for example, Kuhnimhof et al. 2018) that traditional data collection methods still have an important role to play, because of the continuation of time series and because they provide information that is not available with the new data sources, such as sociodemographic information and individual preferences. Also, they might be necessary to reach users who are not observed with passive data: for example those who don't use a mobile phone or those who are reluctant to be tracked, and refuse to use technology that allows tracking. Therefore, there is an additional challenge, which is how to merge different data sources, and how to define sampling methods that ensure an efficient use of the resources, considering the data already available from other sources. We are facing a situation in which standard statistical methods are no longer applicable. The research opportunity here is to develop new sampling methods, looking at the sampling problem from a wider perspective.

Some researchers are more radical. Willumsen (2016) says that recent events have shown us that the future is less forecastable than we assumed. Some of the examples he mentions are Brexit, Trump, autonomous vehicles, virtual reality, etc. Willumsen states that we need to review our whole modeling approach, questioning basic aspects such as: Are we asking the right questions? Are we still constrained to the old assumptions made many years ago? Liu (2018) explores the possibility of designing tailored transport services to satisfy individuals' demand, taking advantage of "the increased observability". In a similar line, in one of the plenaries of the last Transport Survey Methods Conference, the traditional approach for selecting a representative sample was questioned. The traditional approach for transport surveys sampling is based on household address. This might be correct for home-based studies, with a limited sample size. However, if we have the possibility of observing mobility in a much denser way, both in terms of space and time, does it still make sense to do sampling based on home address?

The availability of massive/passive data also allows the exploration of certain aspects of travel behavior that were difficult to study with traditional data. One example is to analyze the effect of variability. It has been largely known that the variance of travel time is a very important variable that affects perceptions and level of use of public transport systems (Bates et al. 2001). However, variance is difficult to measure with traditional survey methods. Some authors have proposed methods to measure and predict variability taking advantage of massive data (see, for example, Mazloumi et al. 2011).

Another interesting aspect of travel behavior that can be explored with the new data is group travel behavior. There have been some attempts to collect data that incorporate the social dimension of activities and travel. Carrasco et al. (2008) propose a data collection method that explicitly incorporates social networks. However, this type of survey is very complex to make, and usually only small sample sizes can be achieved with this method. Sun et al. (2013) use smartcard data to observe the social encounter network in a public transport system. Stopczynsk et al. (2014) explore the possibilities of what has been called Computational Social Science (CSS), using information from multiple data sources, including questionnaires, wi-fi, and mobile phone data, to build networks and study the social phenomena among a population of students. Among the findings, they mention the ability to study the diffusion of behavior (happiness, academic performance, among others), and that a single stream of data rarely supplies a comprehensive picture of human interactions, behavior, or mobility. The study they present is based on the above-mentioned sources of data and an anthropological field. It is the combination of different data sources that opens the gates to new research possibilities.

These are the opportunities we foresee with the data available now, but new opportunities will arise with the spread of autonomous vehicles, and vehicle-to-vehicle and vehicle-to-infrastructure protocols. The operation of these new systems will generate enormous amounts of data, which at the first stage should be used to improve the systems themselves. However, once the technology becomes more common, it could be used for other purposes also, such as travel pattern analysis.

## 22.4   Policy challenges

Even though a number of studies have been devoted to public transport data, practical big data applications are relatively limited. This indicates that big data has not been used to its full potential in practice yet, meaning that public transport passengers currently do not fully benefit from the opportunities big data offers in terms of public transport quality and attractiveness (Yap and Munizaga 2018). There was a workshop at the Thredbo 16 conference, held in August 2017 in Stockholm (Sweden), devoted to discussing why this is moving so slowly, and what can be done to accelerate the process. The conclusion is that the most difficult challenges are institutional rather than technical. The technical challenges can be addressed using new methods and more powerful computers. The institutional challenges require something more difficult: coordination between different entities whose purposes are not always aligned. Public agencies should actively identify priorities and opportunities, and develop standards, as well as common definitions and data formats. Information has to be consolidated, integrating data from different sources. Hard work is required to promote cooperation and coordination, and to build trust. Private companies willing to participate in this revolution have to be open to collaborate and share data and methods. In order to learn from previous experiences, we need to look at successful and unsuccessful cases. Another interesting perspective would be to look at other sectors; different sectors are facing similar challenges (e.g., health, telecommunications, marketing). Yap and Munizaga (2018) propose a framework to stimulate a further and faster adoption of big data in practice, directing to different stakeholders or relations between stakeholders. The framework is illustrated with case studies from Chile, the Netherlands and Sweden.

Another aspect that has to be considered is the implications of these new data sources on sample bias. It has been identified that some population segments are "hard to reach" or "survey shy" (Lucas and Madre 2018). Some examples are young people, non-travelers, and residents of informal settings. There is the possibility that technology could help us to overcome these difficulties, but there is also the risk that it could make them even more disadvantaged, for example if we rely on data coming from a technological device that does not reach certain population segments. There is an equity challenge here, which is to use technology to reduce the biases of previous survey methods. One possibility is that, given that information from most advantaged population groups can be obtained from the technological devices they use, traditional surveys can be focused in the population segments that are more difficult to reach.

The questions for the future are: How do we enter and navigate this new era of big data? Do we need to adapt our manuals and standards? How do we build trust? How do we ensure accountability, transparency, privacy and social equity?

## 22.5    Conclusions

The new availability of large amounts of data, coming from the operation of technological devices, presents us with significant opportunities and important challenges. Some authors have stated that we need to re-think our whole modeling scheme. This new data availability provides us with the ability to observe highly dynamic processes at a microscopic level. We are experiencing a quantum leap in information availability and cost. Many tools can be developed to improve the planning, operation and control of transport systems. For researchers, this is an ideal situation to advance on understanding behavior and test hypotheses. For policy makers, this opportunity presents solid grounds to formulate new (better focused) policies.

The research and political challenges are multiple. The research challenges include data fusion, developing models to study the effects of uncertainty and variability, group behavior, and time/space disaggregation. The political challenges are identification of priorities and opportunities, definition of standards, consolidation and integration of different data sources, promotion of cooperation and coordination, and social equity. For both researchers and policy makers, we make a call to report both successful and unsuccessful cases, to contribute to development of a future based on solid ground.

### Acknowledgement

This work was supported by the Complex Engineering Systems Institute, Chile (CONICYT Grant FB0816).

### References

Asakura, Y., Iryo, T., Nakajima, Y. and Kusakabe, T. (2012), 'Estimation of behavioural change of railway passengers using smart card data', *Public Transport* **4**(1),1–16.

Bates, J., Polak, J., Jones, P. and Cook, A. (2001), 'The valuation of reliability for personal travel', *Transportation Research Part E: Logistics and Transportation Review* **37**(2–3), 191–229.

Carrasco, J. A., Hogan, B., Wellman, B. and Miller, E. J. (2008), 'Collecting social network data to study social activity-travel behavior: An egocentric approach', *Environment and Planning B: Planning and Design* **35**(6), 961–980.

Carrel, A., Lau, P. S. C., Mishalani, R. G., Sengupta, R. and Walker, J. L. (2015), 'Quantifying transit travel experiences from the users' perspective with high-resolution smartphone and vehicle location data: Methodologies, validation, and example analyses', *Transportation Research Part C: Emerging Technologies, Part B* **58**, 224–239.

EU (European Union) (2016), Regulation 679 of the European Parliament and of the Council: On the protection of natural persons with regard to the processing of personal data and on the free movement of such data, and repealing Directive 95/46/EC (General Data Protection Regulation).

González, M. C., Hidalgo, C. A. and Barabasi, A. L. (2008), 'Understanding individual human mobility patterns', *Nature* **453**(7196), 779–782.

Gschwender, A., Munizaga, M. A. and Simonetti, C. (2016), 'Using Smartcard and GPS data for policy and planning: the case of Transantiago', *Research in Transport Economics* **59**, 242–249.

Jánošíková, Ľ., Slavík, J. and Koháni, M. (2014), 'Estimation of a route choice model for urban public transport using smart card data', *Transportation Planning and Technology* **37**(7), 638–648.

Kuhnimhof, T., Bradley, M. and Straub-Anderson, R. (2018), 'Workshop Synthesis: Making the transition to new methods for travel survey sampling and data retrieval', *Transportation Research Procedia* **32**, 301–308.

Kusakabe, T., Iryo, T. and Asakura, Y. (2010), 'Estimation method for railway passengers' train choice behavior with smart card transaction data', *Transportation* **37**(5), 731–749.

Liu, J. (2018), Passenger-focused Scheduled Transportation Systems: From Increased Observability to Shared Mobility, PhD Dissertation, Arizona State University.

Lucas, K. and Madre, J.-L. (2018), 'Workshop Synthesis: Dealing with immobility and survey non-response', *Transportation Research Procedia* **32**, 260–267.

Ma, X., Liu, C., Wen, H., Wang, Y. and Wu, Y. J. (2017), 'Understanding commuting patterns using transit smart card data', *Journal of Transport Geography* **58**, 135–145.

Mazloumi, E., Rose, G., Currie, G. and Sarvi, M. (2011), 'An integrated framework to predict bus travel time and its variability using traffic flow data', *Journal of Intelligent Transportation Systems* **15**(2), 75–90.

Morency, C., Trépanier, M. and Agard, B. (2007), 'Measuring transit use variability with smart-card data', *Transport Policy* **14**(3), 193–203.

Muñoz, V., Thomas, A., Navarrete, C. and Contreras, R. (2016), 'Encuesta origen-destino de Santiago 2012: Resultados y validaciones', *Ingeniería de Transporte* **19**(1), 21–36.

Nassir, N., Hickman, M. and Ma, Z. L. (2018), 'A strategy-based recursive path choice model for public transit smart card data', *Transportation Research Part B: Methodological.* https://doi.org/10.1016/j.trb.2018.01.002

Pelletier, M.-P., Trepanier, M. and Morency, C. (2011), 'Smart card data use in public transit: A literature review', *Transportation Research Part C: Emerging Technologies* **19**, 557–568.

Poonawala, H., Kolar, V., Blandin, S., Wynter, L. and Sahu, S. (2016), 'Singapore in motion: Insights on public transport service level through farecard and mobile data analytics'. In *Proceedings of the 22nd ACM SIGKDD International Conference on Knowledge Discovery and Data Mining* (pp. 589–598). ACM.

Stopczynski, A., Sekara, V., Sapiezynski, P., Cuttone, A., Madsen, M. M., Larsen, J. E. et al. (2014), 'Measuring large-scale social networks with high resolution', *PLoS ONE* **9**(4), e95978. https://doi.org/10.1371/journal.pone.0095978

Sun, L., Axhausen, K. W., Lee, D. H. and Huang, X. (2013), 'Understanding metropolitan patterns of daily encounters', *Proceedings of the National Academy of Sciences* **110**(34), 13774–13779.

Trépanier, M., Morency, C. and Agard, B. (2009), 'Calculation of transit performance measures using smartcard data', *Journal of Public Transportation* **12**(1), 79–96.

Willumsen, L. G. (2016), 'Modelación de transporte e incertidumbre', *Ingeniería de Transporte* **20**(2), 83–90.

Yap, M. and Munizaga, M. (2018), 'Workshop 8 report: Big data in the digital age and how it can benefit public transport users', *Research in Transport Economics* **69**(C), 615–620.

# Index

Note: many main entries can also be found under chapter headings pertaining to specific modes of transport and particular countries/continents.